K

DATE DUE

Speaking from Elsewhere

Speaking from Elsewhere

A New Contextualist Perspective on Meaning, Identity, and Discursive Agency

José Medina

State University of New York Press

Published by
STATE UNIVERSITY OF NEW YORK PRESS
ALBANY

© 2006 State University of New York

For information, address
State University of New York Press
194 Washington Avenue, Suite 305, Albany, NY 12210-2384

Production by Ryan Hacker
Marketing by Michael Campochiaro

Library of Congress Cataloging-in-Publication Data

Medina, José, 1968–
  Speaking from elsewhere : a new contextualist perspective on meaning, identity, and discursive agency / José Medina.
    p. cm.
  Includes bibliographical references and index.
  ISBN-13: 978-0-7914-6915-6 (hardcover : alk. paper)
  ISBN-10: 0-7914-6915-8 (hardcover : alk. paper)
  1. Contextualism (Philosophy)   I. Title.
  B809.14.M43 2006
  149—dc22   200503459

10   9   8   7   6   5   4   3   2   1

To my siblings, Inma and Joaquín,

for all those times we have spoken to each other from elsewhere.

Contents

Acknowledgments

I WANT TO THANK ALL my colleagues and friends who have given me unconditional support and have helped me with their exciting discussions of the topics and ideas of this book. I am especially grateful to two philosophers whose work has been a source of inspiration for my recent research and whose generous support and encouragement have contributed enormously to the writing of this book. They are Linda Alcoff and Naomi Scheman. My philosophical conversations with them on philosophical issues concerning meaning, identity, and agency have been pivotal for the development of this book. In addition, Scheman was also generous enough to give me detailed comments on an earlier version of this manuscript. Her provocative comments, sharp questions, and helpful suggestions have enriched and deepened my views and arguments tremendously. Although sometimes I give credit to Scheman explicitly, I am sure there are many more ideas that have been inspired by her comments and echo her work. The reader should feel free to assume that any fruitful idea contained in this book (if there is any) comes from my philosophical engagements with Scheman or with Alcoff.

Earlier versions of sections 1.3, 2.1.b, and 4.1–4.2 have previously appeared in the following publications: "In Defense of Pragmatic Contextualism: Dewey and Wittgenstein on Meaning and Agreement," *Philosophical Forum* 35 (2004), 341–69; "Identity Trouble: Disidentification and the *Problem* of Difference," *Philosophy and Social Criticism* 29 (2003), 655–80; and "The Meanings of Silence: Wittgensteinian Contextualism and the *View from Elsewhere*," *Inquiry* 47 (2004), 1–18. I would like to thank the journals that published these articles for granting permission for the partial reproduction of those texts. I would also like to thank Josh Houston for helping me to compile the index of this book.

Introduction

Language is a labyrinth of paths. You approach from *one side* and you know your way about; you approach the same place from *another side* and no longer know your way about.

—Wittgenstein, *Philosophical Investigations* §203; my emphasis.

THE AIM OF THIS BOOK is to articulate and defend a new kind of contextualism that brings together converging trends in post-analytic and neo-pragmatist philosophy as well as in theories of identity across disciplines (Philosophy, Women's Studies, Sociology, and Political Science). The book discusses influential contextualist perspectives in philosophy of language (esp. Wittgenstein's, Dewey's, and Austin's), in feminist theory (esp. Butler's), and in social and political theory (esp. Bourdieu's). What the book offers is a critical elucidation of our situated perspective as speakers, agents, and community members. Many philosophical accounts of the positionality of our perspective have been offered. Among the most influential ones are Thomas Nagel's *The View from Nowhere* and Claude Lévi-Strauss's *The View from Afar*. Reacting against these accounts, many contextualists have characterized our positionality as *The View from Here*: a good example in the Wittgenstein literature is Peter Winch; a good example in the pragmatist literature is Richard Rorty. These spatial conceptualizations of our positionality as speakers, thinkers, and agents offer different views of how we shape our meanings, develop a sense of self, and form a voice. In this book I argue that these conceptualizations rest on problematic assumptions about what constitutes the inside and the outside of our linguistic practices, assumptions that become distorting for our elucidations of meaning, identity, and agency. I propose and defend an *eccentric* kind of contextualism that calls into question the traditional dichotomies between the inside and the outside of language and the false dilemma between internalism and externalism in the philosophy of language. This eccentric contextualism is what I call *a View from Elsewhere*.

xi

My *view from elsewhere* is a contextualist account of discursive practices that exhibits two crucial features: a thoroughgoing pluralism, which is elaborated throughout the book with the *polyphony thesis* that applies in different ways to meaning, identity, and agency; and a *normative perspective* that emphasizes the responsibility of speakers and the critical power of their agency. The central theses of this contextualist view are developed through an argument about the instability and eccentricity of linguistic perspectives, and through an argument about the critical and transformative power of marginal discourses for questioning and challenging the limits erected in language, that is, for interrogating and contesting the normative boundaries of our discursive practices. The continuous emphasis on the margins of our language games that you will notice throughout the book conveys what is most distinctive about my philosophical perspective, underscoring the pluralism and the normative-critical standpoint of my eccentric contextualism.

I develop my own contextualist account of meaning, identity, and discursive agency by engaging critically with some of the most influential views in the literature and by drawing on Wittgenstein, pragmatism, and Speech Act Theory. My interpretation of Wittgenstein figures prominently in my discussions of meaning, identity, agency, normativity, and community in the four chapters of the book. In these discussions I have also relied heavily on my interpretation of pragmatist figures and particular aspects of their philosophical views: Dewey's view of meaning for chapter 1; Mead's view of identity for chapter 2; and Bourdieu's theory of *the habitus* for chapter 2. I also make ample use of Speech Act Theory, especially in chapter 3, in which I develop my own interpretation of Austin's view, which I term "the New Austin." This interpretation contrasts sharply with the traditional reading of Austin that has been so influential both in Anglo-American and in French philosophy of language. I use this interpretation to save Austin's view of the performative from his critics (esp. Derrida). I also put Austin's view in dialogue with contemporary feminist theory—in particular, with Butler's performativity theory—and I draw the political implications of performative accounts of speech such as Butler's and mine. But, besides Austin's and Butler's views of the performative, a Wittgensteinian elucidation of speech acts animates my argument from the beginning.

In chapter 1, I develop an argument against semantic skepticism and I articulate an account of the *contextual determinacy* of meaning through my interpretation of Wittgenstein's and Dewey's philosophy of language. According to my contextualist perspective, semantic determinacy is the always fragile and relative accomplishment of communicative interactions and is always undergoing transformation. What distinguishes my view from traditional contextualist perspectives is the thesis that meanings are not susceptible of localization: they cannot be confined to *anywhere in particular* and always remain constitutively elusive. There is always more to meaning than what a single context by itself can offer. And this is not a claim made from *nowhere*, a claim that requires that we abandon the situated perspective of language users and adopt an impossible acontextual view. Rather, it is a claim made from *elsewhere*, that is, a claim about particular contexts made from the perspective of other contexts. Thus my view underscores the crucial importance of *intercontextual relations*. Paralleling this argument about meaning, I will then argue in chapter 2 that the identity of a speaker is abstract and empty (radically indeterminate) when considered outside particular contexts of action and interaction, but it becomes *contextually determinate* in relation to particular communities and practices. My central thesis here is that identity involves a social bond, a constitutive relation to others, which is at the same time a constitutive relation to differences: one's identity is bound up with the identity of others and, therefore, with differences. Drawing on Mead, Bourdieu, and Butler (among others), I develop an account of the performative and unconscious formation of identity through the address of the other. This account involves an examination of the way in which speakers' identities are interwoven and dialectically entangled with each other's in discursive practices. The most fundamental notion of my contextualist view of identity is the notion of a *voice*. By calling attention to our voices, my contextualist view tries to underscore that the identity of a speaker is embodied, situated, relational, and multifaceted.

Building on this view of speakers' voices, chapter 3 offers a contextualist account of discursive agency or performativity that challenges some of the central presuppositions of classical Speech Act Theories. As an alternative to the standard one-factor accounts of performativity that focus exclusively either on intentional or on social aspects of communication, I defend a hybrid notion of agency that defies both determinism and voluntarism. What is at the core of this hybrid notion is the dialectical relation between contextual constraints and discursive freedom. With this hybrid notion of agency my contextualist view of performativity reformulates the notion of *discursive responsibility* (i.e. the responsibility of particular speakers and particular linguistic communities for the words they use and how they use them). I argue that although a speaker is not the free and autonomous source of her own agency, she is an active participant in the production of speech, contributing to the chains of performances through which linguistic practices are maintained and reproduced. Therefore, speakers must assume responsibility for their contributions to the maintenance and perpetuation of discursive practices. This is what I call "echoing responsibility."

Intercontextual relations are forged performatively through the echoing of our speech acts, which signify by invoking, implicitly or explicitly, other contexts—past, future, and contemporaneous contexts, both actual and possible or imaginary ones. The notion of *intercontextuality* captures well how past, present, and future contexts interpenetrate each other and become tied together in a nondeterministic way through our performances and ongoing negotiations. On my view, discursive agency involves a process of constant recontextualization or *echoing*, in which our discursive acts are constantly being oriented by histories of use and at the same time they are constantly reorienting these histories as well. We have to take responsibility for continuing or discontinuing available discursive contexts in particular ways through our agency, but also for opening up *new contexts*, contexts that by definition have not yet been legitimated by any normative framework. Thus my contextualist view of agency emphasizes the crucial importance of opening up discursive spaces for critique and transformation, for radical resignification or *echoing*.

Using my contextualist account of discursive agency and responsibility, I conclude the book with a discussion of the space for *critique and subversion* in our discursive practices. The goal of my eccentric contextualism is precisely to show how we can critically exploit discursive limitations, how we can make limits productive. My contextualist view underscores *the critical productivity of discursive limits* and gives center stage to those who speak at the limits or on the margins of our discursive practices. It is for this reason that I conclude with a discussion of *marginal discourses* in the final chapter. My *view from elsewhere* calls attention to the critical and transformative potential of the eccentric speech of those who have a frontier identity and speak on the border of what is deemed unsayable and nonsensical, troubling the always contingent boundary historically erected between the sayable and the unsayable. These marginal discourses that speak on the borders or at the limits constitute a risky speech that has a dangerous and precarious life. For trying to speak at the limits or on the margins of discursive practices is always perceived as a menace, as a threat to the very normative identity of what counts as legitimate speech. Through a discussion of imposed silences and marginalized standpoints, my polyphonic contextualism tries to show that our linguistic practices always exhibit an irreducible diversity and heterogeneity of points of view that cannot be subsumed under a unified perspective. I will argue that silences can always be broken, but they cannot be altogether avoided, that is, we cannot break all silences once and for all: breaking linguistic barriers and dismantling censorship mechanisms (whether explicit or implicit) is a never ending task. I will conclude this discussion and the book with the critical challenge that my polyphonic contextualism raises for the study of discursive practices, namely, to elucidate how silences can be broken, how linguistic communities can be disrupted, and how new communities can be created. It is our responsibility as speakers and community members to open up discursive spaces for new voices and to facilitate new discourses that can break up silences and empower marginalized voices.

Chapter 1

Contextualizing Meaning

1. 1. The Indeterminacy of Meaning:
"Unnatural Doubts" and "Theoretical Diagnosis"

In *Unnatural Doubts* Michael Williams argues that skeptical problems won't be resolved until they receive the proper diagnostic treatment. According to Williams, traditional skeptical doubts concerning the external world are foolproof traps that don't admit a direct solution; but they won't be resolved by any kind of philosophical diagnosis either. Williams argues against the kind of diagnostic treatment that tries to show that skepticism is self-undermining in such a way that, when examined in its own terms, it falls into incoherence. This kind of diagnosis—quite popular in the twentieth century among Wittgensteinians—is what Williams terms "therapeutic diagnosis." Its aim is to unmask skeptical doubts as unintelligible, as producing only the *appearance* of intelligibility. Williams proposes a very different kind of diagnostic treatment, one that tries to make sense of skeptical claims and questions by placing them in a broader theoretical context. This alternative diagnostic treatment is what Williams terms "theoretical diagnosis." Its central strategy is to challenge the *naturalness* of the skeptic's doubts and to shift the burden of proof to the skeptic's shoulders, "not necessarily to shift it entirely [. . .] but, at least initially, to get him to acknowledge his share" (p. 41). The theoretical diagnostician proceeds by making explicit the theoretical assumptions and claims that the skeptic relies on, thus showing that "the skeptic is less of a plain man than he likes to appear" (p. 39). The theoretical diagnostician tries to show that the starting point of the skeptic is not uncontroversial, that it is more

1

than an unproblematic intuition we all share or a set of "platitudes we would all accept." At the very least the skeptic has to acknowledge that his starting point is the theoretical reconstruction of our epistemic intuitions or of the tacit presuppositions of our epistemic practices. As Williams puts it, even if we grant that the skeptic exploits only the demands of our ordinary epistemic concepts, "we have not conceded that it is obvious what the demands of these concepts are" (p. 34). The goal of theoretical diagnosis is to show that the skeptic is committed to a theory: "a theory of our ordinary concept of knowledge," "a theory of the systematic demands on knowledge that ordinary practice implicitly imposes" (p. 34).

But what is accomplished by theoretical diagnosis? This kind of diagnosis does not aim at a definitive refutation of skepticism. Its goal is far more modest, namely, to show that skeptical claims and conclusions are *not inescapable*, that there is room for an alternative theoretical reconstruction of ordinary epistemic concepts and the epistemic presuppositions of ordinary practice. Starting from ordinary concepts and practices as we must, "we are under no compulsion to add what the skeptic adds" (p. 40). Far from stemming directly and inescapably from our ordinary concepts and practices, skeptical doubts require quite a bit of theoretical work to arise. And in this way their alleged naturalness is challenged: if not unnatural, they are at least less than natural; there may be a more natural way of thinking about our concepts and practices. The theoretical diagnostician can even concede that skeptical problems cannot be solved in their own terms while stepping out of the skeptic's game; and this without becoming a skeptic and without acknowledging any truth in the conclusion of the skeptic. As Williams puts it: "There is no danger in conceding that the skeptic cannot be refuted on his own terms if those terms are not ones we are bound to accept" (p. 41).

My discussion in this chapter will be restricted to only one brand of skepticism, namely, *semantic* skepticism. I will concern myself exclusively with skeptical worries concerning whether we know what our words mean, whether our meanings are determinate enough to support genuine communication; and I will leave aside skeptical worries about the external world or about other minds. In the next section I will argue that Wittgenstein's discussions of skeptical problems concerning meaning amount to a *theoretical diagnosis of semantic skepticism* (or at least a sketch of such a diagnosis). I will then identify the similarities between Wittgenstein's diagnosis and Dewey's critique of traditional views of meaning; and I will use these similarities to explain the convergence of their positive views, showing how an alternative picture of meaning emerges from the theoretical diagnosis of indeterminacy problems. According to this theoretical diagnosis, the crucial move in semantic skepticism—"the conjuring trick"—is the demand for a (certain type of) theory to fix meaning, which is claimed to be grounded in our communicative practices. What the theoretical diagnosis tries to show is that the demand for a theory that fixes meaning is not immanent in our ordinary linguistic practices, but it is rather a *philosophical* demand imposed on these practices by a particular theoretical conception of their structure or presuppositions. The theoretical diagnosis is completed with the articulation of an alternative conception of meaning which renders the theoretical demands that give rise to semantic skepticism unnecessary—a superfluous and ultimately distorting add-on. It will be my contention that there is a strong convergence between Wittgenstein's diagnosis of semantic skepticism and Dewey's critique of traditional theories of meaning, and that these critical perspectives are intimately related to a strikingly similar picture of meaning that is at the core of their philosophies. This convergence, I will argue, leads to a minimal philosophy of language that conceptualizes meaning without philosophical additives and strong theoretical demands—a pragmatic conceptualization of meaning that departs from the received semantic views in the philosophical tradition.

Let me begin by identifying clearly what both Wittgenstein and Dewey are reacting against in their critique of traditional theories of meaning. The central theoretical assumption that gives rise to the problem of the indeterminacy of meaning is a well-entrenched assumption that is shared by most (if not all) traditional theories of meaning, namely, the assumption that meaning is *a thing* (whether physical or mental), something *determinate* and *fixed*. We can derive two requirements from this basic assumption: the *Determinacy Requirement* and the *Immutability or Fixity Requirement*. The requirement that meanings be determinate or sharply defined[1] is the requirement that we be able to determine for anything whatever (for any object or idea) whether or not it is part of the meaning of a term. The Immutability Requirement is the requirement that meanings be fixed, that they remain the same over time and across speakers. The basic rationale for these requirements is that without fixity and determinacy communication would be impossible. If meanings were recalcitrantly vague and constantly fluctuating, if they were radically indeterminate and unstable, we could not understand each other, we could never be quite sure whether we mean the same things by our words as others do, or whether each of us means the same things by her words now as she did in the past or as she will in the future. In other words, the received view of meaning suggests that if the requirements of determinacy and fixity were not met, there would be no guarantee for successful communication, for what meanings (if any) are attached to our words would be always up for grabs. The violation of these semantic requirements is precisely what is behind the skeptical challenges that fall under the heading of *the indeterminacy of meaning*.[2] These challenges suggest a disturbing possibility: it is very possible that the semantic determinacy and fixity prefigured by the normative presuppositions of our linguistic practices might be nowhere to be found in these practices.

It is important to note that the Determinacy and Fixity Requirements don't purport to be in any way *factual* or *descriptive* of actual linguistic practices. They are *normative* conditions for communication that may or may not obtain. They can even be conceived as *ideal* conditions that our actual practices can only approximate (conditions that would only obtain for a perfect language, conditions that would be descriptive only of an ideal speech situation). So the claim of the received view is not that the meanings that we find in our communicative practices actually meet these requirements, but that they *should*; not that our meanings are in fact fully stable and determinate, but that they *should* be. The claim is that the demands of communication expressed by the Determinacy and Fixity Requirements set the standards that we have to live up to; that these are the normative standards of communication even if they are only partially met in our less than perfect practices where communication is typically defective (even when successful). More radically yet, the claim is that these are the standards *even if they are never met at all!* Exploiting the demands that are (alleged to be) implicit in our communicative practices the skeptic develops indeterminacy arguments that shake our most basic confidence in everyday communication and uproot our taken-for-granted certainties concerning meaning. The skeptical conclusions that these arguments try to establish is that, for all we know, the semantic requirements of determinacy and fixity, the very conditions of possibility of communication, are never met at all (not even approximately or partially); for all we know, there are only communication failures and no successes in our communicative attempts; for all we know, we do not *really* communicate at all, and our linguistic practices only produce the *illusion* of shared meanings, the *appearance* of mutual intelligibility and understanding.

Are these skeptical doubts about meaning *natural?* The meaning skeptic claims that they are because they are generated simply by drawing the implications of the normative standards implicit in our communicative practices. Although the doubts of the meaning skeptic may seem quite counterintuitive, they are alleged to be doubts that arise naturally because they are rooted in a commonsensical view of meaning and communication. But are the doubts of the meaning skeptic really based on nothing else than on platitudes that we must all accept? Are the semantic assumptions of the skeptic really platitudes? Are they really inescapable? The central target for a theoretical diagnosis of meaning skepticism is the claim that indeterminacy challenges derive from our ordinary concept of meaning, from the standards involved in our ordinary practices of communication. The *naturalness* that the meaning skeptic claims for his doubts can only be substantiated if the normative standards of communication on which he relies are shown to be in fact the standards we unavoidably commit ourselves to in our ordinary linguistic practices. Let's consider one example of how the skeptical problem of the indeterminacy of meaning is alleged to arise naturally from our ordinary semantic intuitions.

According to the skeptic, in clear cases of successful communication (if we could find any), in cases where our words have well-defined semantic contents (if we could find any), our meanings would be fully *determinate* and *fixed*. Given that mathematics has traditionally been considered a paradigm of semantic determinacy and fixity, it is not surprising that skeptics typically use this semantic domain to shake the foundations of our semantic certainties. With its clearly defined concepts and its fully articulated system of rules, mathematics seems better equipped than any other domain to offer paradigmatic cases of determinate and fixed meanings. So, if the skeptic succeeds in showing that not even here is it possible to establish that the most basic semantic requirements are met, then it should not be difficult to generalize his skeptical conclusions and transfer them to other domains. Thus, for instance, in his interpretation of Wittgenstein, Kripke (1982) develops indeterminacy arguments concerning the meaning of the word "plus" and the symbol "+" (pp. 7ff). Here, he contends, we seem to have a clearly fixed and fully determinate meaning, namely, the mathematical function of addition, which can be captured in a rule that determines the correct application of "plus" and "+" in every instance. According to Kripke, we ordinarily rely on our grasp of this rule in our computations in everyday practices. Relying on my grasp of the rule for addition I can claim that in a "metalinguistic sense" I am certain that "'plus,' as I intended to use the word in the past, denoted a function which, when applied to the numbers I called '68' and '57,' yields the value 125" (p. 8). But the skeptic challenges this metalinguistic certainty and questions whether there is any way at all in which we can justify the claim that the correctness of "68 + 57 = 125" is uniquely determined by our grasp of the meaning of the terms involved. Kripke introduces the following skeptical possibility: perhaps "+" does not mean addition or the plus function, but *quaddition* or the *quus* function. He defines the latter as follows: the numerical value of the quaddition of two numbers is the same as that of the addition of these numbers when they are smaller than 57, and 5 otherwise. This is the challenge that this skeptical possibility raises: "The sceptic claims (or feigns to claim) that I am now misinterpreting my own previous usage. By 'plus,' he says, I always meant quus; now under the influence of some insane frenzy, or a bout of LSD, I have come to misinterpret my own previous usage. Ridiculous and fantastic though it is, the sceptic's hypothesis is not logically impossible" (p. 9).

The burden that this skeptical possibility imposes on us is to *isolate* a fact that can uniquely determine the meaning of "+" so that we can settle whether the correct solution to "68 + 57" is 125 or 5, for "if [the skeptical hypothesis] is false, there must be some fact about my past usage that can be cited to refute it" (p. 9). The meaning skeptic argues that this is a burden that cannot be met, for, as it turns out, we are unable to isolate facts that can endow our words with fixed and definite meanings, that is, facts that can ground our normative assessments and allow us to deem every application of a term either correct or incorrect. The skeptic's gamble is that in the search for meaning-determining facts we will come out empty-handed, that any candidate fact will fall short of the demands derived from the normative presuppositions of our practices. Thus Kripke goes on to argue that appeals to intuitions, dispositions, and the like, will not do because, for any intuition, disposition, etc. for adding there is a corresponding, indistinguishable intuition, disposition, etc. for quadding; and, therefore, all these facts about the speaker and her linguistic usage fail as candidates for the fact that determines the meaning of her words and the correctness of her claims.

From the standpoint of a theoretical diagnosis, the most contentious point in Kripke's indeterminacy argument occurs at the very beginning, in setting the stage, when Kripke appeals to our assumptions concerning the meaning of the word "plus" and the symbol "+." In this vein, Gary Ebbs (1997) has argued that "Kripke plays the role of a *dialectical skeptic* [who] begins with our firmly entrenched judgments about some topic, and draws a skeptical conclusion from his analysis of those judgments" (p. 11). As Ebbs points out, in order to succeed the dialectical skeptic "must convince us that prior to encountering his arguments we were already committed to the requirements that lead to his skeptical conclusion" (p. 11). Therefore, it all hinges on the starting point of the skeptical argument: how persuasive the conclusions of the dialectical skeptic are depends on how persuasive is his interpretation of our common-sensical assumptions. As Ebbs observes, "the most important ingredient in Kripke's dialectical strategy is his interpretation of our ordinary understanding of meaning" (p. 11).

The premise of Kripke's skeptical argument is the postulation of well-defined semantic rules as the basis of meaning. Kripke's initial assumption is the idea that the meaning of our claims and the outcome of our normative assessments are determined by semantic rules that speakers grasp and follow. He takes it to be part of our ordinary understanding of communication that it is *because* we grasp and follow rules that our words have meaning, that we can agree or disagree, and that we can make assertions and assess their validity. And since his skeptical argument shows that we can't grasp or follow rules in a way that determines the meaning of our claims and the outcome of our normative assessments, Kripke concludes that our words are meaningless and our communicative exchanges, our agreements and disagreements, our assertions and their evaluation, groundless. As Ebbs remarks, "Kripke's skeptical conclusion is an inevitable consequence of his tempting interpretation of our naïve first thoughts about meaning and assertion" (p. 10). In a book-long theoretical diagnosis quite congenial with the one I develop in this chapter, Ebbs argues that "Kripke's picture of meaning leads us unknowingly to accept an objectifying perspective that obscures our understanding of meaning and assertion" (p. 11).

It is this objectifying perspective which requires that we be able to isolate those elusive meaning-*determining* facts. The core of this objectifying or reifying perspective is the assumption that meaning is a definite *thing*, fixed and determinate, and the semantic requirements that derive from these assumptions. The discussion that follows tries to challenge this perspective through a theoretical diagnosis of semantic skepticism derived from Wittgenstein.

I will not develop my discussion of the indeterminacy problem as an examination of Kripke's skeptical arguments concerning meaning and rule following, either in their own right or as an interpretation of Wittgenstein's arguments. Many critics have done this quite adequately already.[3] My discussion will have a broader focus than the skeptical doubts of a Kripkean variety. My goal is to articulate an interpretation of Wittgenstein's indeterminacy arguments as a theoretical diagnosis of meaning skepticism. My interpretation tries to show that Wittgenstein's discussions of indeterminacy diagnose semantic skeptical challenges as arising from a distorted and distorting picture of our communicative practices (i.e., from a misconception about our ordinary concept of meaning and the semantic assumptions implicit in our linguistic practices). It may seem surprising that I want to interpret Wittgenstein as offering a theoretical rather than a *therapeutic* diagnosis of skepticism, since he has been considered by most commentators as the therapeutic diagnostician par excellence. Williams, for one, has argued that Wittgenstein's strategy to deal with the skeptic is not to dig out the theoretical presuppositions of the skeptical hypotheses, but to show that they fall into incoherence and unintelligibility, being thus committed to a definitive refutation of skepticism. It is important to note, though, that Williams's interpretation refers to Wittgenstein's discussion of skepticism about the external world in *On Certainty*. Similar therapeutic interpretations have been offered to account for Wittgenstein's treatment of the skeptical problem of other minds.[4] However, for the purposes of this book, I am interested only in Wittgenstein's diagnosis of *semantic* skepticism and it is this diagnosis that I will interpret as theoretical, putting aside his diagnostic treatment of other kinds of skepticism.[5]

1.2. Wittgenstein as a Theoretical Diagnostician: Overcoming the Temptations of Reification and Decontextualization

It is important to observe that the reifying perspective that conceives of meaning as a (fixed and determinate) thing can have many different faces, leading to many different kinds of reification. Perhaps the most natural form of reification is to think of meaning as a *thing out there* in an *objective* realm, whether this is the physical domain of natural entities or the notional domain of ideal entities. This form of semantic reification is at the heart of both naturalism and Platonism, which—though radically opposed metaphysical views—are nonetheless different versions of the same semantic view: a semantic *objectivism* that locates meanings in a *mind-independent* realm. On the other hand, meanings can also be reified in a rather different way by projecting semantic shadows inward instead of outward. This perhaps more subtle but equally problematic form of semantic reification consists in conceptualizing meaning as a *thing in here*, in a *subjective* realm, that is, as a mental entity of some kind: a disposition, an idea, an image, a schema, a rule formulation or interpretation, or the like. This subjectivist reification is shared by a wide variety of perspectives from nativism and intuitionism to associationism and dispositionalism. All these views can be considered as different versions of semantic *subjectivism*; what they all have in common is the idea that meanings reside in a *mind-dependent* realm. In my discussion of objectivist and subjectivist reifications below, I will try to identify, following Wittgenstein, the common assumptions on which both objectivist and subjectivist views of meaning rely.

In the *Investigations* Wittgenstein identifies many different ways in which meaning can be conceived as a thing. In his critical discussions of semantic reifications he tries to show that, in all the different forms it can take, the reifying perspective has as its natural companion the problem of semantic indeterminacy: objectivist and subjectivist views of meaning face similar skeptical challenges concerning the fixity and determinacy of semantic content. Moreover, there is one particular argumentative form that the indeterminacy problem takes for all of these views, namely, *the Regress Argument*. On my reading, the Regress Argument shows that the reifying perspective on meaning fails according to its own standards, for any form of objective or subjective reification fails to satisfy the basic semantic requirements it presupposes. This failure would be inescapable if the reifying perspective were the only game in town; that is, the skeptical conclusions about meaning that derive from the Regress Argument would be unavoidable truths about semantic content if meanings could not be thought of in terms other than those that prompt indeterminacy arguments such as the Regress. The antiskeptical move here cannot be simply to insist that meaning ought to be conceived in some other terms, for in this sense "ought" does not imply "can." In order to use the Regress Argument (or any other indeterminacy argument for that matter) as part of a theoretical diagnosis of semantic skepticism rather than as the basis of a tacit agreement with the skeptic, we are required, at the very least, to sketch an alternative semantic perspective, to articulate a different conceptualization of meaning. The task of theoretical diagnosis is, therefore, twofold: first, to identify the theoretical presuppositions of the reifying perspective that invites the indeterminacy problem; and second, to suggest an alternative perspective that doesn't rely on those presuppositions. Only in this way can the reifying perspective and its skeptical implications be shown to be, at best, optional and avoidable. In what follows I try to elucidate how the Regress Argument, as developed in

Wittgenstein's discussions of meaning and rule following, can help us identify the presuppositions of objectivist and subjectivist reifications and thus contribute to a theoretical diagnosis of semantic skepticism.

Wittgenstein's first critical discussion of semantic objectivism can be found in the opening sections of the *Investigations*. What he terms "the Augustinian picture of language" is an objectivist, denotational approach according to which meanings are things out there that can be pointed at. This objectivist reification is the target of Wittgenstein's critique of ostensive definition. He begins this critique by emphasizing that an ostensive definition is always ambiguous, for ostensive definitions are used to introduce very different kinds of words: "one can ostensively define a proper name, the name of a colour, the name of a material, a numeral, the name of a point of the compass and so on" (1958a [PI] §28). So, for example, if pointing with one hand to something I am holding with my other hand I say "apple," how can someone who doesn't already know the meaning of the word, determine whether "apple" means the kind of fruit I'm holding, its color, its material, its number, or whatever? Far from fixing meaning, Wittgenstein claims, "an ostensive definition can be variously interpreted in *every* case" (PI §28).

There are two possible responses that can be given at this point. But far from solving the indeterminacy problem, these responses call for further elaborations that make the indeterminacy argument sharper and more lethal: these elaborations can be found in Wittgenstein's Regress Argument and Quine's Argument for the Indeterminacy of Translation. One response is to suggest that the indeterminacy of an ostensive definition can be dispelled by disambiguating the ostension with a *sortal*, that is, with a classificatory term that specifies what *sort* of thing the word defined is supposed to name, saying for instance "This *colour* is called so-and-so" (PI §29). But Wittgenstein replies that sortals can also be variously interpreted according to different classificatory systems; and since they are not self-explanatory, "they just need defining [. . .] by means of other words!" (PI §29). But in order to guarantee the univocity of these further words, more defining is needed. So we are thus led to a regress. "And what about the last definition in the chain?" Wittgenstein asks (PI §29). We can always interpret the terms used in the last definition in different ways. So the upshot of the Regress Argument is that meaning cannot be fixed by an ostensive definition, for no matter how much is added to the definans, the definiendum remains indeterminate.[6]

But there is another possible response to the indeterminacy of ostension. The defender of ostensive definition can reply that the trick is not to take the defining to different levels of abstractions (as sortals do), but to different situations in order to diversify the evidential basis that can facilitate the correct understanding of the definition through an induction. The idea here is that repeated ostensive definitions of the same term, say "apple," can progressively enable us to rule out competing interpretative hypotheses until we are left with the correct one. We can address this response by supplementing Wittgenstein's discussion with Quine's Argument for the Indeterminacy of Translation.[7] This indeterminacy argument shows that the correct interpretation of an ostensive definition cannot be uniquely established on inductive grounds because we can always concoct alternative interpretative hypotheses that fit the available evidence equally well. As with Quine's "gavagai," we can always wonder whether "apple" refers to apples, or perhaps to undetached apple parts or to the time slices of an apple. One way in which interpretative alternatives can be produced is by projecting past usage into the future in an unexpected way. These alternative interpretative hypotheses that exploit the temporal dimension of language use typically have the disjunctive form "so-and-so up to this point in time and so-and-so thereafter," and try to drive home the point that future use is underdetermined by past use.[8]

Wittgenstein's Regress and Quine's Indeterminacy of Translation are very different indeterminacy arguments,[9] but they have at least this much in common: they both try to establish that the meanings of words do not simply attach themselves to self-identifying objects out there, that the world around us does not divide itself into kinds, that there is always room for alternative conceptualizations. These indeterminacy arguments teach us that *if* meaning is an object out there (as some referentialist views contend), it remains forever elusive which object in particular it is, for there are always skeptical hypotheses that can reinterpret our ostensive definitions in new ways. The indeterminacy that afflicts objective reifications casts doubt on the identification of meaning with a thing in the world, that is, on the idea that the world has self-indicating powers, that it contains self-identifying objects.[10] Meanings are not simply out there waiting to be pointed at. They are not *pure* objects, *mind-independent* objects unaffected by our conceptualizations and our ways of dealing with the world. Even in its extensional sense, word meaning seems to be deeply mind dependent: it seems to require the mediation of our ways of looking at the world and our practices. How else are we going to identify language-world correlations? At this point there is the temptation to take the reifying perspective in a different direction by appealing to *mental reference*. Mental reference is what I have called "subjective reification," which takes place when the denotational approach turns inward and claims that meanings are not things out there, but things in here, mental things. But subjective reifications are open to the same indeterminacy problems as objective reifications, for nothing is intrinsically self-interpreting, neither mind nor the world. Neither the objective world nor the subjective world have special powers of indication: neither the things out there nor the things in here can interpret themselves.

Wittgenstein's critique of subjective reification is developed in his discussions of meaning and rule following. In these discussions the Regress Argument is used to establish that there are no privileged mental representations (such as pictures, schemas, rule formulations, or interpretations) which, *by themselves*, can univocally determine the meaning of a word and its correct use. Mental representations can always be interpreted and applied in different ways; and, therefore, we are led from one representation to another indefinitely when we attempt to fix the correct use of a word or the correct application of a rule by means of mental representations. This Regress Argument is first developed by Wittgenstein in the discussion of the meaning and correct use of the word "cube" (PI §§139–42). He argues that the correct use of the word "cube" cannot be fixed by a mental representation of the object designated by this word, for instance, by a picture or drawing of a cube. For, even if we suppose that this picture "comes before our mind" every time we use the word, it is still up for grabs what accords with this representation and what doesn't: "In what sense can this picture fit or fail to fit a use of the word 'cube'?" (PI §139). One may think that if you apply the word to a triangular prism, "then this use of the word does not fit the picture" (§139). But this is a mistake, for whether it fits or not depends on how the picture is to be interpreted and projected onto the prism, and "it is quite easy to imagine a *method of projection* according to which the picture does fit after all" (§139). So Wittgenstein concludes that although the picture of a cube can "indeed *suggest* a certain use" of the word, it is always "possible for me to use it differently" (§139).

Similar argumentative moves and similar conclusions can be found in the discussion of the continuation of a numerical series according to the rule "+ 2" (esp. §§186–98). In this part of the rule-following discussion Wittgenstein calls into question the idea that the *meaning* of a rule determines what we do with it, as if the entire range of applications of the rule were somehow contained in its meaning. Thus he accuses the interlocutor of being "inclined to use such expressions as: 'The steps are *really* already taken, even before I take them in writing or orally or in thought.' And it seemed as if they were in some *unique* way predetermined, anticipated—as only the act of meaning can anticipate reality" (§188). But what is this meaning with such magical powers? What does the meaning of a rule consist in? One natural suggestion is to say that the meaning of a rule is to be found not simply in its formulation (such as the algebraic formula "+2"), but in an *interpretation* that reads the rule formulation in a particular way. It may appear that if we fix the interpretation of the rule, we thereby fix its meaning and hence its applications. We may think that how the formation rule "+ 2" is to be applied to the series of natural numbers can be fixed by giving the following interpretation: "Write the next but one number after *every* number"; and we may think that all the numbers in the series follow from this sentence. To this suggestion Wittgenstein responds: "But that is just what is in question: what, at any stage, does follow from that sentence. Or, again, what, at any stage we are to call 'being in accord' with that sentence (and with the *mean*-ing you then put into that sentence—whatever that may have consisted in)" (§186). The interpretation of the rule does not really get us any further, for it can in turn be understood in different ways. It is in fact just another formulation of the rule, like the algebraic formula, and it can also be variously interpreted. Interpretations are themselves open to interpretation. No interpretation interprets itself. So Wittgenstein concludes at §198 that "any interpretation still hangs in the air along with what it interprets, and cannot give it any support. Interpretations by themselves do not determine meaning."

It is important to note that in this negative conclusion that Wittgenstein draws from the Regress Argument the emphasis should be put on "determine." The point is not that interpretations are always useless, but that they cannot accomplish the function assigned to them by certain philosophical theories of meaning: the function of definitely determining semantic content once and for all. This was also the conclusion of the Regress Argument used in the critique of ostensive definition: Wittgenstein did not deny that ostensive definitions can have a role to play in language learning (in fact, he acknowledges this at PI §§30–31); his point was, rather, that it is mistaken to think of ostensive definitions as semantic foundations, to conceive of bare pointings as fixing the meanings of words once and for all unambiguously. The Regress Argument, therefore, offers an incisive critique of the philosophical search for *definite fixers and determiners of meaning*, trying to show that this search is misguided and we will come out of it empty-handed. For all the candidates found in this search for semantic foundations, the Regress Argument can be used to reach the same conclusion; namely, that the alleged semantic fixers and determiners by themselves do not fix and determine meaning. Wittgenstein has nothing against ostensive definitions or against interpretations per se (as he has nothing against mental images, schemas, rule formulations, etc.). All these things have a role to play in our communicative practices. The problem, the indeterminacy problem, arises when these ordinary ingredients of our communicative practices are elevated to the status of an *isolable foundation*, the be all and end all of meaning.

The upshot of Wittgenstein's Regress Argument in all its formulations is that indeterminacy arises because in all these cases meaning is assumed to be an isolable thing, whether in an objective or in a subjective realm. Wittgenstein's different formulations of the argument show that the medium in which the reification of meaning takes place is quite inconsequential. What matters is that meanings are isolated or detached from specific contexts of use, and they are thought of as having definite and fixed boundaries (i.e., as having "rigid limits" or being "everywhere circumscribed by rules," PI §68; see also §§71, 76, 79, 99). Thus Wittgenstein's diagnosis identifies as the source of the indeterminacy problem the theoretical assumption that there must be *isolable semantic foundations*, that is, fixers and determiners of meaning which constitute the isolable facts that can satisfy the Determinacy and Fixity Requirements. These are the semantic facts that Kripke was looking for and could not find. What Wittgenstein's theoretical diagnosis shows is that this search is misguided, that it starts from a theoretical assumption that constitutes a significant departure from our ordinary understanding of meaning and communication. My interpretation of Wittgenstein's arguments thus strongly disagrees with Kripke's skeptical reading. While Kripke's Wittgenstein thinks that it is reasonable and natural to look for the fixers and determiners of meaning that make communication possible (although they are nowhere to be found), what Wittgenstein's arguments actually show (I contend) is that these sought fixers and determiners of meaning are mere theoretical constructs—philosophical fictions—that play no role in our actual communicative practices or language games. While Kripke's Wittgenstein thinks that the normative presuppositions of any linguistic act lead to semantic skepticism, that the very act of using a term commits us to the requirement that there be semantic facts that unambiguously fix and determine the meaning of the term in all contexts, what Wittgenstein's diagnosis actually shows is that this requirement, far from being an unavoidable normative presupposition, is in fact an unnatural theoretical demand imposed from outside on our practices, a demand that is only motivated by and grounded in a distorting philosophical picture of language.

The crucial philosophical move in this theoretical departure from the ordinary use and understanding of our semantic notions, from the commonsense view of meaning and communication, is *decontextualization*. The theoretical assumption that there must be isolable semantic foundations forces us to abstract from particular contexts of use in a vain attempt to distil the semantic essence of our words from those contexts. This assumption and the decontextualizing or reifying perspective it gives rise to require that we be able to isolate something or other that gives complete determinacy to our meanings and sustain it over time, that is, something that enables us to draw a fully determinate and unchangeable boundary around the meaning of our words. This constitutes the theoretical common ground shared by the meaning realist and the meaning skeptic. I will refer to this theoretical common ground as *semantic foundationalism*, for what is at its core is the assumption that meaning requires isolable semantic foundations. Both meaning realists and meaning skeptics are foundationalist at heart. But while the meaning skeptic argues that the required semantic foundations are nowhere to be found, the meaning realist (whether of an idealist or a naturalistic persuasion) claims to have found the fixers and determiners of meaning that the foundationalist assumption demands (be it in a Platonic realm or in the natural world).

Wittgenstein's indeterminacy arguments try to persuade us that, considered in their own terms, the semantic foundations proposed by meaning realists do not work: they do not satisfy the Determinacy and Fixity Requirements as they were supposed to. However, the conclusion we should draw from Wittgenstein's indeterminacy arguments is not that meaning is radically indeterminate, but rather, that it *looks indeterminate* when we adopt a detached semantic perspective, when we depart from specific contexts of use and abstract from their particularity and messiness. The indeterminacy of meaning is inescapable only from the perspective of a philosophical theory that demands absolute determinacy and fixity. This philosophical theory is not a harmless reconstruction of commonsensical intuitions. By decontextualizing meaning in the search for isolable semantic foundations this theory posits unreasonable semantic standards of determinacy and fixity, standards that cannot be met even if considered in the foundationalist's own terms. So when meaning is construed in foundationalist terms, it becomes radically indeterminate. But construing the concept of meaning in that way is optional; and, as it turns out, that philosophical construal is not a very promising option, but a blind alley. Fortunately, we can abandon the decontextualizing and reifying perspective of semantic foundationalism that Wittgenstein's theoretical diagnosis identifies as the basis of meaning skepticism. This diagnosis is only part of the story of Wittgenstein's engagement with semantic skepticism, and not the most interesting part but only a preliminary part, a prolegomenon to an alternative view of meaning. But it is important to note that the alternative semantic view that emerges from Wittgenstein's critical discussions is not a theory (as traditionally conceived), but an approach, a strategy, a piecemeal way of elucidating meanings *in context*.

The alternative approach Wittgenstein sketches to resist semantic decontextualization and reification is developed around the idea of our "consensus of action" or our "agreement in forms of life." As I have argued elsewhere,[11] this perspective on meaning emerging from Wittgenstein's later philosophy can be described as a *pragmatic contextualism*. I will develop the central ideas of this perspective in the next section through an examination of Wittgenstein's and Dewey's semantic views. In later chapters I will put to use this semantic contextualism in ways Wittgenstein never anticipated (and even in ways he might not approve of). But it is important to keep in mind that in Wittgenstein's own philosophy this contextualist perspective has mainly a deflationary point: its central point is to dissolve metaphysical disputes about meaning. Wittgenstein's semantic contextualism is developed as a reconstruction of our commonsensical intuitions about meaning and communication. He thought that when made perspicuous, semantic platitudes can shed light on our philosophical problems concerning meaning and can have an extraordinary (even devastating) critical impact on our semantic theories. The semantic contextualism that emerges from Wittgenstein's reconstruction of ordinary intuitions is at the service of his critique of meaning skepticism and meaning realism. The central philosophical task of this contextualism is to show the gratuitousness and unnaturalness of semantic foundationalism and its assumptions, shared by meaning realists and meaning skeptics alike.

1.3. Contextual Determinacy:
Wittgenstein and Dewey on Meaning and Agreement

Any discussion of semantic skepticism should distinguish between meaning's being *underdetermined* and its being *radically indeterminate*. This distinction between underdetermination and indeterminacy is suggested by Laudan's (1990) argument against relativistic views of science, although Laudan does not draw this distinction explicitly. Using my terminological distinction, what Laudan's argument shows is that in philosophy of science indeterminacy arguments such as the ones developed by Goodman, Quine, and Kuhn only establish that theories are underdetermined by evidence, but not that they are radically indeterminate. Laudan argues that unless we wrongly identify what is reasonable to believe with what is logically possible, indeterminacy arguments are not as troublesome as they seem. These considerations only play with logical possibilities. Most (if not all) of the logical possibilities considered by indeterminacy arguments are equally valid candidates for the interpretation of a theory in the abstract, but not in particular situations where the state of the discipline and the body of evidence available, as well as various sociohistorical circumstances affecting scientific research, impose all kinds of interpretative restrictions. So, contextual factors heavily constrain the interpretation of theories,[12] rendering many logical possibilities unreasonable. As Laudan (1990) puts it, indeterminacy arguments establish the *thesis of nonuniqueness* (p. 271), that is, the thesis that for any interpretation of a theory or hypothesis there is always the *possibility* of an alternative interpretation that is logically compatible with our entire body of knowledge. But these arguments fall short of establishing the *thesis of cognitive egalitarianism* (p. 270), that is, the thesis that *all* rival interpretations are equally belief-worthy or equally rational to accept.

So, the upshot of Laudan's argument is that the classic indeterminacy arguments in philosophy of science prove that scientific theories and their interpretation are underdetermined by evidence, but not that they are radically indeterminate. There isn't an infinite (or even indefinite) number of equally plausible hypotheses that we can choose from in the interpretation of our theories. But there can be a constrained set of competing alternatives with equal or similar epistemic support.[13] This set may be narrowed down by future research, but it may also grow by the inclusion of new competing hypotheses (whose consideration is after all contingent on the available conceptual resources and the imagination of scientists). As Laudan's argument suggests, underdetermination is simply one aspect of the *limited* and *fallible* nature of our epistemic practices, but it doesn't constitute an insurmountable obstacle to scientific research or to the various investigative activities of ordinary life, as the skeptic would have us believe. Underdetermination can be inflated into radical indeterminacy only if we buy into the mistaken assumption that what is logically possible and what is reasonable are coextensive.

Laudan's objection against indeterminacy arguments in philosophy of science is also valid in the philosophy of language: *underdetermination does not warrant indeterminacy*. The auxiliary assumption that enables us to go from underdetermination to indeterminacy is the assumption that there must be isolable semantic foundations that render our meanings fully determinate and fixed; and if we fall short of that—the assumption suggests—anything goes, any semantic interpretation is equally valid and, therefore, meaning is radically indeterminate. It is only when we have been antecedently persuaded by semantic foundationalism that it makes sense to argue that in the absence of semantic foundations there is no determinacy whatsoever. As we saw in the previous section, Wittgenstein's theoretical diagnosis of meaning skepticism unmasks this foundationalist assumption and questions its plausibility or reasonableness. In order to show how gratuitous this assumption is, the next step is to sketch a nonfoundationalist picture of meaning in which *underdetermination does not warrant indeterminacy*. This picture blocks the inferential moves that meaning skeptics want to make with their indeterminacy arguments, showing that the impossibility of semantic fixers and determiners of meaning by itself—that is, without relying on foundationalist assumptions—does not warrant semantic skepticism. At the core of this nonfoundationalist picture is what I term the idea of *contextual determinacy*, which accepts and integrates the thesis of underdetermination while rejecting the thesis of radical indeterminacy. According to this idea, our meanings do not live up to the standards of absolute determinacy and fixity of semantic foundationalism, but they are not radically indeterminate: they are *contextually determinate*, that is, they acquire a transitory and always imperfect, fragile, and relativized form of determinacy in particular contexts of communication, given the purposes of the communicative exchanges, the background conditions and practices, the participants' perspectives, their patterns of interactions, and so on, I contend that this idea of contextual determinacy is developed by Wittgenstein and Dewey in their elucidations of the relation between meaning and *agreement in action*. This section will examine the *pragmatic contextualism* that results from those elucidations. The challenge of this contextualism is to develop a nonfoundationalist view of meaning based on underdetermination, as opposed to unqualified determinacy or indeterminacy.

Before I start developing the idea of contextual determinacy and elucidating the pragmatic contextualism of Wittgenstein and Dewey, I want to address a worry that is likely to be entertained by those who are familiar with the analytic literature in philosophy of language. Analytic readers may wonder what is particularly new or interesting about this response to indeterminacy arguments. They may think that the semantic holism developed by a legion of analytic philosophers in the second half of the twentieth century[14] has already established that semantic facts are not isolable and detachable from particular contexts. Isn't the core idea of semantic holism that meanings cannot be decontextualized and encapsulated in atomic packages? And so, what's the fuss about? Isn't this "pragmatic contextualism" a fancy way of delivering old news? Many may think that an examination of contextualism as a nonfoundationalist and nonskeptical view of meaning is unlikely to yield insights that are new or even controversial.[15] However, this is not so. To begin with, it would be a mistake to simply identify contextualism and holism. The demands of contextualization go well beyond what is typically understood by semantic holism. Contextualism certainly involves a holistic insight insofar as it asserts the priority of the whole over its parts. However, on the contextualist view shared by Wittgenstein and Dewey, the whole-part relation is understood in a way that is rather different from standard holistic views of language. On standard holistic views, there is no qualitative difference between the whole and its component parts. Following Meredith Williams (1998), we can describe these views as *homogeneous holisms*, that is, views in which what is required in order to understand a word or a sentence is "more of the same," more words or sentences. By contrast, a *heterogeneous holism* holds that the whole in which words and sentences have to be inscribed is composed of qualitatively different elements.[16] Both Wittgenstein and Dewey qualify as heterogeneous holists, for their concept of *context* does not refer to a homogeneous whole—a system of signs, a network of sentences, or a calculus of propositions—but rather, to a heterogeneous whole that contains verbal and nonverbal elements.

Wittgenstein's and Dewey's emphasis on contextualization underscores that words are inextricably interwoven with nonverbal actions and with the surroundings in which both verbal and nonverbal actions take place. Both Wittgenstein and Dewey call our attention to the embodied nature of speaking subjects and the material conditions of language use. Wittgenstein argues that our linguistic practices are supported by stable regularities in the environment, and that if these natural regularities changed so would our practices (PI §142 and PI II.xii). On the other hand, the embodiment of speaking subjects and the material aspects of communicative contexts figure prominently in Dewey's "naturalistic" account of language as "the tool of tools" (1988a [EN], p. 134). This first point about the heterogeneous character of communicative contexts can be described as the thesis of the *materiality* of language and discursive contexts, which is repeatedly emphasized by Wittgenstein and Dewey. They stress, even more emphatically, that language and its contexts of use are action oriented. The intimate bond between words and actions is precisely what the

Wittgensteinian notion of a language game is supposed to underscore: "I shall [. . .] call the whole, consisting of language and the actions into which it is woven, the 'language-game'" (PI §7); "the term 'language-*game*' is meant to bring into prominence the fact that the *speaking* of language is part of an activity, or of a form of life" (PI §23). In a similar vein, Dewey refers to language use as *agency* and to speakers as *agents* (EN p. 137 and p. 139). On his view, "language is primarily a mode of action" (EN p. 160). Therefore, the relevant contexts in which language use has to be understood are practical contexts of action. This second point about the heterogeneous character of Wittgenstein's and Dewey's holism can be described as the *performativity* of language and discursive contexts, which thematizes the inseparability of words and actions. As Wittgenstein puts it, "words are deeds" (1980a [CV], p. 46).

Materiality and performativity are only two of the crucial features of language and discursive contexts that Wittgenstein's and Dewey's contextualism brings to the fore. Two other central dimensions that we have to take into account are *sociality* and *temporality*. Both Wittgenstein and Dewey underscore the social character of the contexts in which words and sentences acquire meaning. For Wittgenstein, only in the context of a shared practice does a word have meaning (PI §§208ff). Similarly, Dewey emphasizes that the context in which words gain meaning is a context of social cooperation. In order to be able to reconstruct the meaning of words and sentences, he tells us, "we have to be able to re-instate the whole *social context* which alone supplies the meaning" (EN p. 160; my emphasis). Furthermore, both Wittgenstein and Dewey emphasize the temporal dimension of discursive contexts of communication. Wittgenstein argues that the meaning of a term cannot be derived from a single application or instance of use, and that we cannot understand the meaning of a term unless we consider the use of the term over time (PI §§141ff). The meaningful use of a word is not something that can happen only on one occasion; rather, it is something that requires "a regular use," "a custom" (PI §198; see also §199). Similarly, for Dewey, communication takes place in cultural and natural contexts that have a history and exhibit a temporal structure: a temporal context of interaction that can be described as "a scene of incessant beginnings and endings" (EN p. 83). It is important to note that communicative contexts are temporally structured and temporally extended, that they have a past and a future. Although it may seem trivial, this temporal point is worth emphasizing because it runs against the *temporal fixity* that afflicts many standard views of language. This diachronic and historical view calls into question the fixing glance of the reifying or decontextualizing perspective, which tries to freeze meaning in an instant, in a frozen time slice that encapsulates all possible uses and ossifies semantic content.

When the contexts of language use are thought of as heterogeneous wholes that are material, performative, social, and temporal, they are the *pragmatic contexts of communication* to which Wittgenstein and Dewey call our attention. Not only the rest of this chapter, but also the rest of this book, is an elucidation of these four central dimensions of pragmatic contexts of communication. These features of discursive contexts are crucial to understanding the idea of contextual determinacy, that is, to understanding how meanings acquire (transitory and imperfect) determinacy when contextualized. Both Wittgenstein and Dewey explain the contextual formation and transformation of meaning in a strikingly similar way. They both argue that the meaning of words and sentences becomes contextually determinate through the *tacit agreement in action* of the participants in communicative practices. This notion of tacit agreement in action brings together the four central dimensions of language use and discursive contexts (to repeat: materiality, performativity, sociality, and temporality). In what follows I examine Wittgenstein's and Dewey's accounts of contextual determinacy through practical agreement.

For Wittgenstein, communication and rule following presuppose "a consensus of action" or "an agreement in forms of life." This claim brings out a *contextualist* point about intelligibility: what we say and do acquires significance only against a *background* or in a *context*, namely, the background or context provided by a *practice*, a shared way of doing things. As early as 1939 Wittgenstein argues that the contextual determinacy that our words acquire depends on the practical agreement underlying our practices. This agreement, he emphasizes, is not "a consensus of opinions" but "a consensus of *action*: a consensus of doing the same thing, reacting in the same way" (1975 [LFM], pp. 183–84). Communication involves the coordination of action and requires a particular kind of *social bond*: it requires seeing others as partners, that is, as engaged in a joint activity (whether the activity involves cooperation, competition, or any other kind of intersubjective relation). On Wittgenstein's view, a linguistic practice always has a practical point that normatively structures the communicative exchanges that take place in it. Wittgenstein emphasizes that it is "immensely important" that our uses of language have "a *point*" (LFM p. 205), that is, that they play a role in regulating our dealings with the world and with each other, that they be integrated in our forms of life. But having a point, he remarks, is always "a matter of degree"; and the extent to which a use of language has a point depends on the context in which that use figures. Thus meaning becomes determinate in particular contexts of action. What we say and do acquires significance only against the background of a tacit agreement in action. When this background agreement is lost, actions and utterances become incomprehensible. Wittgenstein argues that if we were to encounter activities in which we could not see any underlying practical agreement among the people engaged in it, we would not be able to see any meaning in them, but only nonsense, unintelligible movements and noises: "*the whole point* of what they are doing seems to be lost, so that we would say, 'What the hell's the *point* of doing this?'" (LFM p. 203).

In the *Investigations* too Wittgenstein emphasizes that the lack of agreement "would make our normal language-games lose their point" (PI §142).

On Wittgenstein's view, meaning depends on the normative structuration of linguistic activities according to the practical agreement of their participants. The agreement in action underlying a language game is exhibited in what Wittgenstein calls "a technique of use," a shared way of doing things (cf. e.g., 1978 [RFM] I.143ff). It is important to note that the techniques of use that render a meaning contextually determinate cannot be captured in a list of rules or, we could add, in a network of interconnected sentences or a translation manual. A technique of language use is something that necessarily remains in the background: it is not a further set of propositions or rules; it is a skilled activity, something that can only be *shown* in actions. Techniques are embodied in what practitioners do "as a *matter of course*" (PI §238). On Wittgenstein's view, our shared techniques of use simply do not leave room for radical indeterminacy. These techniques do not draw a sharp boundary around the meaning of terms, but they make meaning *as determinate as it needs to be* for the purposes of particular activities. Whether the term "rabbit" refers to rabbits, to rabbit stages, or to undetached rabbit parts is a doubt that simply does not enter into the minds of those who use this term to coordinate their actions (for instance, rabbit hunters). But should it enter? Is it a *reasonable doubt*? The skeptic[17] will insist that what is in question is not whether as a matter of empirical fact these alternative interpretations are in fact considered, but rather, whether they should be. Ignoring nonstandard interpretations of our words, or pretending that they don't exist, won't do if these interpretations have a legitimate claim to be considered. Our refusal to consider these interpretations out of mere stubbornness would undermine the normative validity of our claims concerning meaning.

The crucial argumentative move here is to shift the burden of proof onto the shoulders of the skeptic. Wittgenstein's contextualist considerations show that the normative structure of our practices *excludes* certain interpretations from the meaning of our words; and this *normative exclusion* constitutes a prima facie reason against considering them, for their consideration runs against the agreement in action underlying our practices and threatens these practices with "losing their point." So, with a prima facie reason *against* interpretations that don't fit the background consensus of action of a practice and in the absence of any reason *for* them, the balance tips against the skeptical semantic hypotheses and, therefore, they should be considered an illegitimate intromission in our appraisals of meaning. But it is important to note that these interpretative hypotheses are deemed unworthy of consideration—an illegitimate intromission in our semantic evaluations—only insofar as they are mere logical possibilities, that is, *until reasons for them are given*. It is important to note that this is a shift of the burden of proof and not a direct and final refutation of semantic skepticism. For indeed, on the contextualist view under consideration, we cannot exclude the possibility of the skeptical hypotheses (or of any interpretative hypothesis for that matter) becoming relevant and reasonable to entertain. To rule out these interpretative hypotheses from consideration once and for all simply because they can threaten our consensus of action and the intelligibility of our practices, would be to say that we refuse to consider them because we are *afraid of nonsense*, that is, because we do not want to face the possibility of our practices "losing their point." Philosophical problems concerning the normative exclusion of certain interpretations as part of the meaning of our words will be discussed in later chapters (see esp. my discussion of censorship in chapter 3). But I want to acknowledge here already that this normative exclusion is indeed problematic and has to be handled in such a way that we do not simply stick to the current background agreement and preserve the status quo come what may. I will argue that there is no room in pragmatic contextualism for a conservative attitude toward semantic innovations and eccentricities.[18]

Like Wittgenstein, Dewey argues that the primary function of language is the coordination of human action. For Dewey, to use language is to participate in an intersubjective enterprise (or social practice) mediated by signs. The opening remarks of Dewey's account of language in *Experience and Nature* make it clear that the core of communication is "participation, sharing" (p. 132). Dewey emphasizes that communication involves "partaking in a common, inclusive, undertaking" (p. 141). He argues that communication should be understood in terms of *partnership*: "The heart of language is not 'expression' of something antecedent. [. . .] It is communication; the establishment of cooperation in an activity in which there are partners, and in which the activity of each is modified and regulated by partnership" (EN p. 141).

Dewey contends that most philosophical problems concerning meaning arise from not taking seriously the interactional nature of language. On his view, meanings emerge from concerted action; they are the result of social cooperation by means of signs. He argues that when this basic insight is overlooked or forgotten, we fall into different kinds of mystifications. Like Wittgenstein, Dewey criticizes different kinds of semantic reification. On the one hand, he argues against the objective reification of Platonism, which conceives of meanings as "forms and essences" utterly removed from actual contexts of communication and concerted action (EN p. 133). This reification of meaning proposed by idealist thinkers fails to acknowledge that meanings are based on "natural interaction in the form of communication" (p. 133). The detachment from actual communicative contexts indulged by these idealist thinkers creates a "gulf between existence and essence" that is "factitious and gratuitous"; and with this gulf meanings become untenable abstractions that are ultimately empty, idle wheels that play no role in our practices. On the other hand,

Dewey also criticizes the subjective reification of meaning that we can find in mentalism (pp. 134–35). He argues that empirical thinkers miss the real significance of language by conceiving of meanings as ossified mental structures that precede our communicative exchanges. As Dewey puts it, on this mentalistic view, "language acts as a mechanical go-between to convey observations and ideas that have prior and independent existence"; and "speech is thus regarded as a practical convenience but not of fundamental intellectual significance" (p. 134). Dewey contends that we cannot make sense of meaning in abstraction from the social use of language in communicative contexts. These prior and independent mental contents postulated by empirical thinkers have a spurious existence. For, Dewey argues, social communication precedes soliloquy and the articulation of mental contents; and, therefore, we cannot understand these contents prior to and independently of linguistic social interactions: such priority and independence render these alleged meanings vacuous. As Dewey points out, this argument against mentalism rests on his genetic account of the natural emergence of human mentality from the use of language in social interaction. This account is sketched in chapters 5 and 6 of *Experience and Nature*; and it bears a striking resemblance to the more detailed account offered by Mead in *Mind, Self, and Society*.[19]

It is important to note that Dewey's critique of idealism and empiricism (i.e., Platonism and mentalism) and his development of a pragmatist alternative are based on his theory of language and communication. This reveals the centrality of Dewey's philosophy of language which, rather than being simply derived from his metaphysics, as traditionally thought, is in fact the basis for it, the foundation of Dewey's pragmatism and naturalism. Against the traditional metaphysical interpretation of Dewey's philosophy, Sleeper (2001) has argued that *Experience and Nature* should be read first and foremost as providing a naturalistic theory of communication and meaning, that is, as "an attempt to discover the relationship of communication to nature, to disclose the traits of nature that support it as well as those that impede it" (p. 117). Therefore, Sleeper claims: "If anything should be regarded as Dewey's first philosophy, it is his genetic account of communication" (p. 118). My interpretation here is in line with Sleeper's claim, although I depart from his reconstruction of Dewey's philosophy "as a radical form of realism" (p. 3). Containing residues of traditional metaphysical interpretations, Sleeper's realist reading ontologizes Dewey's account of language and communication and makes it impossible to recognize the crucial convergence between Dewey's and Wittgenstein's philosophy of language. Since the contrast with Sleeper's interpretation can render mine more perspicuous, I will briefly discuss some of the central interpretative claims of his realist reading.

While acknowledging certain affinities between Wittgenstein and Dewey, Sleeper argues that from a Deweyan perspective Wittgenstein's view of meaning as use is "still beholden to the classical habit of thinking that grammar controls our way of knowing things, as opposed to seeing that it is our way of knowing things that ought to control our grammar. Instead of deriving his ontology from the forms of discourse, Dewey derives his forms of discourse from his ontology" (Sleeper p. 119). I take issue with Sleeper's depiction of Wittgenstein as a linguistic idealist. But I will not address here[20] the idealist interpretation of Wittgenstein's philosophy that Sleeper simply assumes without providing any argument for it. This interpretation has come under heavy attack in recent years and does not enjoy much support today.[21] But there have been linguistic idealists indeed, whether or not Wittgenstein can be counted among them. Is Sleeper correct in his account of Dewey's reaction to linguistic idealism? It is not true that Dewey's philosophy simply reverses the order of explanation of linguistic idealism, giving priority to ontological structures over discursive ones and trying to derive the latter from the former. Dewey's critique of linguistic idealism is developed on existential grounds through his account of "experience." The Deweyan notion of experience can be said to have an ontological dimension. But, for Dewey, the ontological aspects of human experience (i.e., of our pragmatic engagements and existential activities) are not distinct and apart from discursive structures; and, therefore, it is impossible to establish a relation of priority between ontological structures and discursive structures that enables us to derive one from the others. Rather than establishing a relation of derivation in one direction rather than another, Dewey's critique of the metaphysical tradition goes deeper and attacks the very possibility of establishing that relation. His transactional view emphasizes the interrelations between discursive and experiential structures in such a way that any kind of derivation is rendered impossible, for these structures are dialectically bound up with each other and cannot be neatly extricated.

Sleeper's realist interpretation forces Dewey's philosophy to remain closer to the metaphysical tradition than it really is. On Sleeper's reading, while traditionally ontological structures have been derived from grammar, "what Dewey contends, rather, is that the structures of discourse are *derived* from the structures, relations, and properties of things" (p. 118; my emphasis). There is no room in Dewey's view for this ontological perspective. The realist language that Sleeper uses misconstrues Dewey's position, for this language invites the reification of meaning and the postulation of language-independent structures, relations, and properties. However, in his critique of linguistic idealism Dewey does not call our attention to the things in themselves, but rather, to our pragmatic engagements with things in cooperative activities that make use of language and are discursively structured.

For Dewey, there are no meanings independent of language use in particular communicative contexts, as Platonism and mentalism contend: meanings are not ossified objective or subjective structures that can be detached from communicative practices; they emerge from our concerted interactions and pragmatic engagements with the environment through language. Dewey emphasizes that we should not conclude from the insight that there are *no meanings without language* that meanings can be reduced to mere relations between signs. This is at the core of Dewey's critique of nominalism: "The idea put forth about the connection of meaning with language is not to be confused with traditional nominalism" (EN p. 145). Against nominalism Dewey contends that meanings are not purely linguistic (or semiotic) constructions. He argues that the principal flaw of nominalism is that it neglects the interactive nature and social significance of language and turns language into a mere system of noises or marks devoid of practical significance: "The defect of nominalism lies in its virtual denial of interaction and association." "Nominalism ignores organization, and thus makes nonsense of meanings" (p. 145). Nominalist views fall into the kind of homogeneous holism which, as discussed above, is rejected by both Dewey and Wittgenstein. Similar to the contrast between homogeneous and heterogeneous holism is the contrast that Sleeper draws between Peirce's and Dewey's views of language and meaning. Sleeper correctly identifies the central difference between these pragmatist views in Dewey's claim that, pace Peirce, "the 'interpretant' of a 'sign' is not just another 'sign'" (p. 138).[22]

On Dewey's view, what nominalism misses is the central idea of pragmatic contextualism, namely, that "[a word] *gains meaning when its use establishes a genuine community of action*" (EN p. 145; my emphasis). Like Wittgenstein, Dewey argues that meaning acquires contextual determinacy through practical agreement, through a "concerted consensus of action" (p. 145). It is the practical contexts provided by our common activities and undertakings that render our words significant. In the development of his view of communication as partnership, Dewey argues that the success of communication depends on the "agreement in action" among participants: "To fail to understand is to fail to come into *agreement in action*; to misunderstand is to set up action at cross purposes" (EN p. 141; my emphasis). In order to explain how this practical agreement is formed by communication partners and the kind of sharing that results from it, Dewey develops an example that is strikingly similar to the celebrated language game of the builders that Wittgenstein discusses in the *Investigations* (§2, §8, and §§18–21). The example concerns a very primitive linguistic activity between two partners that consists only of simple words and pointing gestures, as well as certain responses to these words and gestures. In this activity the words and pointing gestures are used by one partner (A) to issue orders that can be met by appropriate or inappropriate responses from the other partner (B). This is how Dewey describes the activity and its development through a learning process:

A requests B to bring him something, to which A points, say a flower. There is an original mechanism by which B may react to A's movement in pointing.

But natively such a reaction is to the movement, not to the *pointing*, not to the object pointed out. But B *learns* that the movement *is* a pointing; he responds to it not in itself, but as an index of something else. His response is transferred from A's direct movement to the object to which A points. (EN p. 140; emphasis preserved and added)

In their discussions of this simple language game of commands and responses, both Wittgenstein and Dewey make similar points about the kind of *learning* required and its effects. Wittgenstein remarks that this language game requires more than "ostensive definitions"; it requires an extensive "ostensive teaching" (PI §6 and §9). This teaching, Wittgenstein remarks, involves a process of conditioning or associative training; but it goes well beyond that: it involves a training in the use of the term directed toward instilling a particular communicative attitude, an attitude that is responsive to the perspective and the normative assessments of others. The successful completion of this training yields more than the establishment of mere associations between words and things; it results in a consensus of action, a shared practical orientation or joint perspective through which speakers coordinate their behavior. Like Wittgenstein, Dewey also argues that there is a particular kind of learning process that makes agreement in action possible and, therefore, constitutes a precondition for the emergence of meaning.[23] Dewey's remarks on learning are supposed to illustrate how the *intersubjective mediation*[24] characteristic of language emerges. According to Dewey, by learning to respond appropriately to A's commands and acts of pointing, B learns to adopt A's perspective. B's responses become mediated through "A's *relationship*, actual and potential, to the thing": "The characteristic thing about B's understanding of A's movement and sounds is that he responds to the thing from the standpoint of A. He perceives the thing as it may function in A's experience, instead of just ego-centrically" (EN p. 141). And, of course, this intersubjective mediation is reciprocal and enjoyed by both partners in communication: each must learn to look at things from the perspective of the other. Thus A's utterances are also mediated by B's perspective: "A in making the request conceives the thing not only in its direct relationship to himself, but as a thing capable of being grasped and handled by B. He sees the thing as it may function in B's experience" (p. 141). Dewey concludes that "the essence and import of communication, signs, and meaning" consist in coordinating action in a way that makes possible the *sharing of experiential perspectives*: "Something is literally made common in at least two different centers of behavior. To understand is to anticipate together, it is to make a cross-reference which, when acted upon, brings about a partaking in a common, inclusive, undertaking" (p. 141).

In their discussion of learning both Wittgenstein and Dewey make clear that their practical approach to language should be distinguished from behaviorism and automatism. The establishment of a consensus of action through training processes has a normative and cognitive dimension that goes beyond setting up mechanisms of intersubjective stimulations that trigger mechanical responses. According to Wittgenstein's and Dewey's practical approach, communication and meaning involve the *tacit sharing of perspectives*. This peculiar kind of sharing is instituted by normatively structured communicative exchanges that take place in cooperative contexts of action. Dewey points out that meaning can be conceptualized and explained in behavioral terms, but only insofar as we make clear the very special kind of behavior it involves, namely, *intersubjective normative behavior*,[25] a peculiar coordination of action that makes the behavior of each participant sensitive to the perspective and normative assessments of others. This is precisely the kind of behavior which, according to Dewey, is specifically human. Dewey's account of the contrast between animal and human languages elaborates this point (EN pp. 139–42).

As Sleeper (2001) points out, for Dewey there is a genetic continuity "between natural events (animal sounds, cries, etc.) and the origin and development of meanings" (p. 123). However, he also stresses that there is a substantive difference between animal signals and human languages: animals respond to signals and develop signaling reflexes and habits; but these are qualitatively different from the verbal responses and habits that humans are capable of. The qualitative difference resides in the kind of participation and association that humans become capable of by means of language. For example, he remarks, "by habit, by conditioned reflex, hens run to the farmer when he makes a clucking noise," and they learn to respond to many other signals (p. 140). But language is more than "signaling acts": "While signaling acts are a material condition of language they are not language nor yet are they its *sufficient* condition" (p. 140). Dewey emphasizes that the complex patterns of behavior that hens exhibit in response to signals do not amount to linguistic behavior in the human sense. There is no communication in these behavioral patterns; there cannot be, for hens are incapable of a participatory activity that involves a shared perspective: "The hen's activity is ego-centric; that of the human being is participative. The latter puts himself at the standpoint of a situation in which two parties share. This is the essential peculiarity of language, or signs" (EN p. 140). In the so-called animal languages there are no *meanings* (in Dewey's sense), for there is no *social normativity*, that is, no agreement in action among participants that structure and regulate their conduct. Animal behavior remains purely and exclusively "ego-centric." By contrast, for humans, communication through signs makes possible a particular kind of participation or sharing, which involves the ability to see things from the perspective of another. "*This community of partaking is meaning*" (EN p. 146, my emphasis).

We need to ask: What is the relation between "this community of partaking" and the context of action from which it emerges? Is the sharing in which meaning consists rigidly tied to the originating context? And whatever its tie to the originating context happens to be, how does meaning travel to new contexts?

1.4. Meaning in Context: Semantic Stability and Semantic Change

For Wittgenstein and for Dewey, there is no fixity or rigidity in the connection between meanings and the particular contexts of use from which they emerge. Meanings are dynamic structures; and they cannot be rigidly tied to particular contexts and fixed once and for all. This is expressed in Dewey's magnificent claim: *"Meanings are self-moving to new cases"* (EN p. 148; my emphasis).[26] But this dynamic view raises the issue of the continuity of semantic content over time and across contexts. How do we account for the durability of meaning? How come the meaning of a word is not lost outside its context of use, and it does not have to be reinvented anew in new contexts? How come we don't have to start from scratch with each new context? Dewey remarks that "a stick even though once used as a lever would revert to the status of being just a stick, unless the *relationship* between it and its consequences were distinguished and retained" (EN p. 147). He goes on to argue that it is precisely through language ("the tool of tools") that we are able to mark and retain this relationship between things and their consequences: "Only language [. . .] serves to register the relationship and make it fruitful in other contexts" (p. 147). But how is this done? How do words codify those relationships with consequences? And how do they manage to retain their significance over time and from context to context?

On Dewey's view, what is most characteristic of human praxis is the *semiotic mediation* of our agency: signs mediate the relationship between our practical engagements with things and their consequences. That mediation is established and maintained through *repetition*. On Dewey's view, semantic continuity is produced by the repetitive character of our linguistic agency: "only repetition through concerted action" can produce and sustain semantic links from contexts to contexts (EN p. 147). The repeatability of signs through our reiterative agency is of the utmost importance: there is semantic continuity because we repeat each other's uses of signs, because there is a performative chain of utterances that refer to and rely on one another. The crucial importance of repetition will be further discussed later, but it is important to note here, with Dewey, that the semantic durability of meanings has to be constantly maintained by the discursive agency of speakers through repeated use. The consensus of action of language users must be *constantly renewed*: it must be maintained from context to context and preserved over time through the repetitive agency of speakers. This constant renovation of the background consensus of action is at the same time the source of semantic stability and continuity and the source of semantic innovation and change. For, paradoxically as it may seem, repetition does not leave things the *same*: in our attempts to repeat the same use of a sign, there are always differences that become new semantic ingredients. Our repetitive agency *reproduces and yet transforms* the consensus of action of our linguistic practices and the meanings that emerge from that consensus. So in its performative regeneration, the consensus of action of language users is always being reconstructed and rearticulated.

A similar view is developed by Wittgenstein in his discussion of what counts as *doing the same* when we follow rules (see PI §§143ff). In order to determine what counts as following the rule correctly we need to be able to determine what counts as following the rule at all, that is, what counts as being engaged in the *same* activity, as doing the *same* thing. In this sense, criteria of correctness presuppose criteria of identity or sameness. But the criteria of sameness underlying our practices cannot be algorithmically derived from abstract specifications of rules. Wittgenstein's discussion shows that it is a mistake to think that rule-following behavior flows automatically from a list of rules, as if it were a matter of mechanically applying an algorithm. For rules can always be interpreted and applied in many different ways. And this *multiple applicability* cannot be stopped, for any particular interpretation that is proposed to fix the application of the rule can in turn be variously interpreted and applied; and thus we are led to a regress of interpretations. On Wittgenstein's view, linguistic practices are indeed subject to rules or norms, but they are not rule governed in the way that has been traditionally thought: rules and their interpretations "do not determine meaning" (PI §198). Explicit rules and interpretations can play a role in our practices, but they are not the normative foundations of these practices; on the contrary, they presuppose and remain parasitic on "a regular use," "a custom" (PI §198). So, far from being derived from rule formulations and interpretations, our normative actions precede them. *Action comes first*: "'obeying a rule' is a *practice*" (PI §202; my emphasis). What counts as *doing the same thing* in our rule-following practices "is exhibited in what we call 'obeying the rule' and 'going against it' in actual cases" (PI §201). What counts as following a rule in a language game can only be shown in concrete cases: "*This is what we call a chair.*" These instances of use, these demonstrations, constitute exemplars that can shape our *sense of similarity* and guide our practice, although they never determine our behavior in a unique way. Wittgenstein's use of emphatic demonstratives ("*This* is an X") underscores the importance of exemplars and demonstrations as guides for our practice. But he points out that "one does not define a criterion of identity by emphatic stressing of the word 'this.' Rather, what the emphasis does is to suggest the case in which we are conversant with such a criterion of identity, but have to be reminded of it" (PI §253). This suggests an immanent perspective according to which there are no criteria of identity and correctness outside (or in abstraction from) our actual practices. The only criterion of identity is what as a matter of contingent fact counts as the same in the practice. There is no criterial authority for what counts as the same beyond what is actually taken as such by rule followers, beyond what they do in their repeated performances.

This contextualist account of the reiterative agency that reproduces our practices can be supplemented with contemporary performative views of language. Especially congenial to the contextualist perspective I have sketched are the discussions of language use developed by Joseph Margolis (1996, 1999) and Judith Butler (1993, 1997). Although Margolis and Butler are certainly unlikely partners, their views of predication and resignification can help us clarify the intrinsic malleability of meanings which are produced and reproduced through our reiterative agency in language games.

In Margolis's constructivism we find an ally of the pragmatic contextualism developed in this chapter. Margolis emphasizes that predication does not proceed on criterial or algorithmic grounds: "general predicates [. . .] cannot be extended to new instances, except informally, in terms of what, consensually, may be tolerated as effective or incremental extensions from acknowledged exemplars" (1999, p. 63). Following Wittgenstein as well as Goodman, Margolis argues that "the perception of predicative similarity lacks, in the last instance, adequate criteria or algorithms of application," but it is not entirely arbitrary: "it escapes utter arbitrariness only by appealing to the *sittlich*, the actual practices of a society of apt speakers" (1999, p. 64). Our linguistic practices can always be extended in different ways, but these possible extensions are constrained by contextual factors. In the application of a term to new contexts, Margolis points out, we are confronted with a "choice among various lines of extension amid an indefinite run of such possibilities" (p. 64). But our learned linguistic skills make this choice manageable by narrowing down the set of relevant possibilities: "our aptitude for discerning relevant similarities in a run of would-be cases—any cases—signifies our mastery of the same *sittlich* practices within whose bounds such similarities obtain or are reasonably extended" (p. 64). Margolis endorses what I have termed the thesis of the contextual determinacy of meaning when he says that meanings are "determinable" even though they are "not determinate" (1999, p. 58 and p. 65). In this way he draws a distinction between the relative determinacy achieved in particular contexts (what I have called "contextual determinacy") and the absolute, context-independent determinacy that is an impossible semantic ideal. Our meanings do not (cannot) enjoy the fixed determinacy of the latter kind. For us, there is only the context-dependent determinacy achieved through consensual practices. But for Margolis, as for other pragmatic contextualists, the lack of absolute determinacy does not indicate the demise of meaning—as the skeptic claims—but its instability and plasticity.

A performative account of the instability and plasticity of meaning can be found in Butler's view of discursive agency.[27] She explains discursive agency in terms of *citationality*, arguing that every utterance or meaningful performance cites previous ones and at the same time takes up their meaning in a new direction. For Butler, citation is always *resignification*; discursive agency always redirects meaning. On Butler's view, the meanings of our signifiers have a temporal structure built into them: they are *constrained* by past uses, but they remain *open* to future uses. The future of a signifier depends on a "citational chain," that is, a chain of signification that operates through an insistent citing of the signifier. Butler explains the *openness* of signifiers in terms of the semantic *excess* of our speech acts, which cite or invoke indefinitely many past and future speech acts. As Butler puts it, any speech act in a performative chain has "a condensed historicity: it exceeds itself in past and future directions, an effect of prior and future invocations that constitute the instance of utterance" (1997, p. 3). The performative iterability of signifiers, Butler argues, necessarily involves *resignification*, that is, "a repetition that fails to repeat loyally, a reciting of the signifier that must commit a disloyalty [. . .] in order to secure its future" (1993, p. 220). Although Butler's account is more deconstructive than reconstructive, her view also points in the direction of the rearticulation of meanings and the formation of new meanings through the changing citational chains of speakers' performances, in Wittgenstein's and Dewey's terms, through the changing consensus of action of speakers.

The point of convergence between Margolis's and Butler's semantic views, as well as between those of Wittgenstein and Dewey, consists in the self-transformative character of the performatively sustained agreement of a linguistic community. This background agreement is incessantly renewed by the repetitive agency of speakers. There is a constant performative regeneration of the underlying consensus shared by the members of a linguistic practice. According to pragmatic contextualism, meanings are as stable as the background consensus that sustains them. So, given the constant reconstruction and rearticulation of the consensus of action of language users, the meanings emerging from this consensus always point to new contexts, that is, they are "self-moving to new cases." On this contextualist view, meanings are durable but they do not remain the same; they are in a constant process of transformation, no matter how minute and unnoticeable these transformations may be. Absolute sameness is impossible and unnecessary for the continuity of semantic contents. The contexts of use in which a term finds application can be expanded and diversified; or they can be narrowed down and homogenized; and, accordingly, meaning *can* grow or shrink, become enriched or impoverished. But what a meaning *cannot* do is to become absolutely static, frozen in time.

Of course it does not follow from the intrinsic malleability of meaning that all terms are equally open to semantic fluctuation. The meaning of some terms may be more unstable because they are less heavily controlled in the practices in which they are used, or simply because their use is spread out across so many and such diverse practices that their meaning is much harder to control and semantic variations are bound to occur. As I have argued elsewhere (see my 2003c), this is exactly what happens to heavily used binary categories for the description of identity, such as "man/woman," "homosexual/heterosexual," "white/nonwhite," and so on. On the other hand, the meanings of some terms are made very stable by a number of social institutions and practices that restrict the uses of these terms very strictly. The restrictive forces of many different practices and institutions can converge and contribute to the semantic fixity of terms by rigidly reinforcing a narrow range of uses and discouraging (or even prohibiting) all others. A good example is the term "marriage," whose use has been heavily and clearly restricted by legal, political, religious, and cultural practices and institutions. The application of this term and consequently its meaning have become restricted to same-sex couples. But as these practices and institutions are challenged, the possibility of expanding the meaning of "marriage" arises; and this shows how substantial semantic changes can be brought about by the transformation of the relevant practices and institutions. It is worth noting that the example of "marriage" has been the focus of attention in the philosophy of language for quite some time (at least since Austin), presumably because it underscores the normative dimension of meaning and its clear link to social and cultural practices and institutions.[28] But are there terms that are immune to semantic fluctuations? What about the so-called logical or grammatical connectives? Don't they constitute a special case? Those terms that play a purely syntactic or grammatical role—such as "and," "or," "but,"—do seem to exhibit a special kind of semantic fixity. It is no accident that they have been called "logical constants." It is undeniable that there is something special about grammatical meanings, but their special semantic stability can be explained pragmatically by reference to their dependence in all or most of our linguistic practices and on their normative presuppositions (what Wittgenstein called "rules of grammar"). So the so-called grammatical or logical meanings do not constitute a counterexample to the semantic approach of pragmatic contextualism, for semantic fluctuation cannot be ruled out a priori even in this case, and we can offer a pragmatic explanation of how the special semantic stability of these terms derives from our practices and contexts of use.[29]

In short, meanings can be very stable or very unstable, but the important point is that their stability always comes in degrees and can never be absolute, for it is always dependent on the relevant practices of use and their underlying consensus of action. These practices can be quite rigid and their background consensus of action quite strict, but the possibility of change can never be ruled out completely. It is important to note that this account of semantic continuity in terms of the constant regeneration of the consensus of action of language users rejects the notion of *semantic extrapolation* that is often invoked in philosophical discussions of the durability of meanings across contexts. It is misleading to depict the temporal life of meaning as a process of semantic extrapolation from context to context, for this gives the impression that meanings are fully formed in one particular context and subsequently transplanted to other contexts, but this is not how the formation and transformation of meanings in and through contexts takes place. We need an account of semantic continuity that can accommodate both the stability and the variability of meanings across contexts. Dewey's discussion of meaning contains helpful considerations for understanding the semantic connections between contexts.

On Dewey's view, every meaning has a "generic or universal" aspect, "for a meaning is a method of action [. . .], and method is general" (EN p. 147). But there are different levels of generality at which the semantic content of our words can be considered, depending on whether (and how much) we expand or narrow down our semantic gaze: we may want to focus on the immediate context in which a word is used and the significance it acquires in that context; or we may be interested in a collection of overlapping contexts. To illustrate this point about the variable generality and the flexible context dependence of meanings, Dewey uses the example of a policeman directing traffic by holding up his hand and blowing his whistle (EN pp. 149–50). The gestures and noises of the traffic policeman function as signals to direct movements. The movements thus produced are part of the meaning of the gestures and sounds of the traffic officer, but so are also the "arrest, fine or imprisonment" and other consequences that may follow from failing to respond to these signals as expected (EN p. 149). Dewey argues that we have to take into account the relation of the gestures and sounds in question to more distant consequences that, though more or less removed from the immediate context in which the gestures and sounds are produced, are nonetheless implicated in their meaning. There are legal and penal contexts in which those gestures and sounds have particular consequences and acquire a specific meaning. In fact, Dewey remarks, there is an entire network of social contexts that supports the "orderly arrangement of persons and vehicles established by social agreement" (p. 149). In order to acknowledge the semantic relevance of these different contexts, Dewey distinguishes between two different aspects of the semantic content of a word: what he calls the *proximate* meaning and the *ultimate* meaning.[30] He explains this distinction through the example of the traffic signal of the police officer: "Its proximate meaning is its nearby consequences in coordination of movements of persons and vehicles" (p. 149); "The ultimate meaning [. . .] is the total consequent system of social behavior" (p. 150).

Dewey emphasizes that the ultimate (or more generic) meanings of our words are not formed through generalization, but rather, through the pragmatic and semiotic interconnections between contexts. These contexts become inter-related by means of the practical consequences they have on one another, but also by the use of the same term or signal across contexts and in some cases also by the explicit references of one context to another. Some connections are forged by the echoing of one context in other contexts. This *echoing* phenom-enon is a form of semiotic *repetition* that fuels a constant dynamism in the tem-poral life of meaning. In using the same term to refer to a previous context of use, something is added to or subtracted from the semantic dependence of the term on the prior context. In this way, the contribution that one context makes to the meaning of a term is subsequently modified and transformed in other contexts. For different purposes, we may want to impose some order on this wild mess of interrelated contexts. For different purposes, our semantic elucida-tions may restrict the meaning of a term to one context or to one type of con-text. But a more comprehensive semantic analysis should take into account the plurality of contexts that contribute to the meaning of a term. In this respect Dewey calls our attention to the restrictive semantic perspective offered by sci-ence. In science, he remarks, meanings are ascertained in abstraction from the social situations of ordinary practices: for example, the natural phenomenon of fire is considered in abstraction from its significance "in the scheme of human activities, in the experience of social intercourse, the hearth and domestic altar, shared comfort, working of metals, rapid transit, and other such affairs" (EN, p. 150). The scientific perspective focuses on the causal aspects of objects and events and neglects the role of these objects and events in our ordinary, every-day practices. Dewey emphasizes that we have to be aware of the semantic restrictions imposed by this perspective. He illustrates this point by drawing a contrast between the ordinary use of the term "water" and the scientific use that makes the term semantically equivalent to "H_2O":

> "Water" in ordinary experience designates an essence of something which has familiar bearings and uses in human life, drink and cleansing and the extin-guishing of fire. But H_2O gets away from these connections, and embodies in its essence only instrumental efficiency in respect to things independent of human affairs. (EN p. 151)

For Dewey, there is no problem in using "water" in a restrictive sense in scientific contexts, focusing exclusively on the causal and mechanistic aspects of the substance designated by the term. (He remarks that this is not only "legitimate," but in fact "indispensable"; EN p. 150.) The problem arises when this scientific meaning is claimed to express the essence or semantic core of the term. Every time one part of the semantic content of a term is privileged as the essence or the semantic core of that term, some contexts are privileged over others: one context (or set of contexts) is thought to *contain* the meaning of the term, and the term's semantic connection to any other context is either denied or deemed accidental. Thus, to claim that "Water is H_2O" captures the essence of the term "water," as Kripke (1972) and Putnam (1975) would do decades later, is to fall into an unacceptable semantic reductionism that privileges scientific contexts over ordinary contexts and prioritizes instrumental efficiencies over other forms of engagement and their values and objectives.[31] This scientism and semantic reductionism are the product of "a modern philosophy that makes reality purely mechanical and which regards the consequences of things in human experience as accidental or phenomenal byproducts" (EN p. 151). Dewey's argument against the conception of meaning defended by scientific realists has critical force against contemporary versions of scientific realism,[32] as well as against any kind of semantic reductionism, whether scientific or not. When a meaning is elevated to the special status of the semantic core or essence of a term, it is treated as divorceable from other (accidental) meanings that the term may have and, therefore, as radically detachable from certain contexts of use. But Dewey argues that this radical separation between contexts of use is untenable. In particular, he observes, severing abstract contexts of use, such as scientific or philosophical contexts, from ordinary contexts of social intercourse and everyday experience results in semantic emptiness. Meanings become vacuous when they are radically decontextualized in this way. If after decontextualization the term preserves some meaning, it is because some tie to the ordinary experiential contexts of interaction has been preserved: "Water still has the meaning of water of everyday experience when it becomes the essence H_2O, or else H_2O would be totally meaningless, a mere sound, not an intelligible name" (EN p. 152).

Both Dewey and Wittgenstein emphasize that, no matter how far removed from ordinary contexts of action, human signs always have a relation (no matter how indirect) to these contexts. Our signs depend on these contexts for their significance: they have meaning only against the background of the consensus of action underlying our practices; only this tacit background agreement makes possible the kind of sharing of perspectives in which meaning consists. Dewey remarks that "mathematical symbols have [the] least connection with distinctively human situations and consequences" (EN p. 150). But even mathematical symbols—as long as they are not considered uninterpreted squiggles—have a crucial semantic dependence on our practical activities and their underlying consensus of action. It is not accidental that both Dewey and Wittgenstein include a discussion of mathematical symbols and their meanings in the development of their contextualist views. Both philosophers recognize that mathematics, being the most abstract and apparently acontextual semantic domain, can be considered an exception or a counterexample to their practical and contextualist approach to meaning. But they both emphasize that mathematical meanings are also contextual and crucially dependent upon a tacit agreement in action; and they both use mathematical examples to illustrate their pragmatic contextualism.[33] Talking about the dependence of meaning on a background agreement in action and in "forms of life," Wittgenstein remarks: "This consideration must apply to mathematics too. If there were not complete agreement, then neither would human beings be learning the techniques which we learn" (PI II p. 226). Wittgenstein emphasizes that although it is a branch of knowledge, mathematics "is also an *activity*" (PI II p. 227), and not an isolated one, but an activity related to many other human activities, an enterprise that is supported by and is also the support of many practical endeavors. It is their nondiscriminating and multipurpose character, their being usable in so many different contexts and for so many different purposes, that makes mathematical signs unusually portable. Dewey too emphasizes that it is a mistake to treat mathematics as an autonomous system without practical consequences and independent of concrete human activities (cf. EN pp. 150–51). The common insight of Dewey's and Wittgenstein's philosophy of mathematics is that we cannot understand mathematical meanings in complete abstraction from shared practices and ordinary contexts of action.[34]

In conclusion, according to Dewey's and Wittgenstein's pragmatic contextualism, all meaning is ultimately rooted in the consensus of action of our practices. Radical indeterminacy arises when we detach language from its techniques of use and the background agreement in action of language users. But, on this view, indeterminacy is not a final and inescapable feature of language; it is the artifact of philosophical theories that lose sight of the contextual character of language. There is no radical indeterminacy when the use of a term is contextualized and considered against the background of the tacit agreement in action of its users. But it is crucial that we make clear the exact nature of the relationship between meaning and agreement in order to avert misunderstandings. The most important misconception to unmask here is the idea that *agreement can fix meaning*. It would be a mistake to understand agreement as playing the role of the fixers and determiners of meaning that meaning realist and meaning skeptics debate about. On Dewey's and Wittgenstein's contextualist view, the semantic content of words is not decided by the consensus of language users. Their view is not that our words mean whatever the linguistic community chooses. This naïve semantic conventionalism or collectivism would make meanings utterly arbitrary and, therefore, it would be open to a social version of the Humpty Dumpty objection of semantic vacuity; namely, when a word means whatever we want it to mean, it does not mean anything in particular, because anything whatever can be or not be part of its meaning if the community so decides. On this view, there is no room for semantic constraints of any kind; linguistic communities have an absolute and arbitrary discretion and are not bound by anything. Interestingly enough, this semantic collectivism is not without adherents:[35] it is the semantic view behind social behaviorism, which depicts speakers as clonic Humpty Dumptys rocking back and forth on their wall and babbling at unison. But, on Dewey's and Wittgenstein's view, the meaning of words is not whatever is agreed upon by their users. The relation between meaning and agreement is more indirect: agreement in practice is the *background condition* for the emergence of meaning. This relation is analogous to the relation between agreement and correctness as explained by Wittgenstein. He argues that a tacit agreement in action is the requisite background for our normative assessments, but that does not mean that "human agreement decides what is true and what is false" (cf. PI §241). As he repeatedly emphasizes, the agreement in question "is not agreement in opinion but in form of life" (PI §241; cf. also PI II p.226). On Wittgenstein's view, correctness is not a matter of decision—by majority vote as it were—of the linguistic community. Our tacit agreement in action does not determine the correctness of our claims, but it is the precondition for our ability to assess correctness.[36] A complete failure in the coordination of action among the participants in a language game would dissolve the game, making it impossible to identify the moves in the game and to assess their significance and correctness. It is in this sense that our assessments of intelligibility, just like our assessments of correctness, depend on our tacit agreement in action, without being determined by it. There is indeed room for disagreement in our semantic interpretations; but this disagreement can happen only against the background of a practical agreement[37] that restricts the semantic possibilities that we consider as candidates for the meaning of our words. So, according to the pragmatic contextualism developed in this section, meaning is *constrained but not determined* by the tacit agreement of our practices. Our semantic interpretations are channeled in particular ways by this agreement, but they are not fully determined and fixed once and for all.

This nondeterminist contextualism will be further elaborated in the next section through an examination of the temporal life of agreement, that is, of how agreement in action is established and sustained over time. So I will close this chapter with a discussion of temporality and its implications for a contextualist approach to meaning. Putting meaning, agreement, and their relation in a temporal or historical perspective will bring to the fore what is most characteristic of the contextualist view I develop and defend in this book.

1.5. Sustaining Agreement in Action: Normalcy and Eccentricity

The consensus of action on which our discursive practices or language games are based is not something that simply happens, but something that is achieved by a long history of efforts on the part of individual speakers, of particular linguistic communities, and even of the entire species in its adaptation to its natural surroundings. These efforts have to be constantly sustained in order to maintain the required tacit agreement, whose achievement is always in progress. And they are typically not intentional efforts, not even necessarily (perhaps not even often) conscious efforts. We need to examine how tacit agreements in action are produced by human agency (both intentionally and unintentionally, consciously and unconsciously). Wittgenstein sketches an account of the formation and preservation of practical agreement in and across contexts. This account has two distinct levels: a *phylogenetic level* that studies how the coordination of action is established in human communities through biological and cultural processes of evolution and adaptation, and how it is transmitted from generation to generation; and an *ontogenetic level*, which examines how people are brought into a consensus of action (and hence into shared practices) during their lifetime. These levels correspond, respectively, to Wittgenstein's remarks on "natural history" and his remarks on learning. It is no accident that these remarks follow his discussions of indeterminacy arguments. For, as suggested above, this genetic account is part and parcel of Wittgenstein's contextualist alternative to the semantic foundationalism that gives rise to the indeterminacy problems.

Wittgenstein's phylogenetic and ontogenetic account makes clear that the tacit consensus of action of our practices operates as a *constraining background condition*, but not as a fixer and determiner of meaning. That is, the account shows how our background agreement makes meaning contextually determinate without thereby rigidly determining it and fixing it once and for all. Our situated semantic interpretations are made possible—but not determined—by this agreement. The *contingency* of the relation between meaning and agreement is part of what Wittgenstein tries to convey by calling our attention to the phylogenetic and ontogenetic development of our practices and their consensus of action.

On the one hand, at the phylogenetic level, Wittgenstein repeatedly argues that the facts of our "natural history" could have been different and, accordingly, our concepts and language games would have been different (cf. PI II p. 230; RPP I §46). And Wittgenstein makes clear that there is no strict correlation between these counterfactual possibilities and, therefore, we cannot simply derive the meanings embedded in our linguistic practices from the facts of our "natural history." He presents these facts as *contingent preconditions* for human intentional activities and the development of human concepts, but these facts are not absolute determinations that dictate the shape of our concepts and the way in which our activities are to be conducted. Wittgenstein's rationale for viewing linguistic practices and their meanings as springing from our "natural history" is a contextualist one. He argues that our linguistic intentional activities can only be understood when properly situated; and he emphasizes that the situations in which they are inscribed include both cultural and natural aspects: "Commanding, questioning, recounting, chatting, are as much a part of our natural history as walking, eating, drinking, playing" (PI §25); "An intention is embedded in its situation, in human customs and institutions" (PI §337).

As I have argued elsewhere,[38] Wittgenstein's notion of "natural history" brings together the natural and cultural aspects of the evolution of human communities and their practices. As Nalini Bushan (2002) has pointed out, this notion intentionally blurs the distinction between nature and culture and defies the sharp separations established by many naturalists and social constructivists. The overcoming of the nature-culture dichotomy in Wittgenstein's later philosophy has been emphasized by Rupert Read's (2002) interpretation, which characterizes Wittgenstein's view as a *cultural naturalism* very similar to Dewey's. On Read's interpretation, very congenial to my own, this naturalism tries to dissolve the debate between nature and culture and, instead of referring to natural and cultural contexts in isolation from each other, proposes that we speak of *ecosystems* as hybrid niches or heterogeneous contexts in which the cultural and the natural are fused together. In Wittgenstein's remarks on "natural history" human beings are depicted as always inhabiting an environment that is inextricably cultural and natural. These remarks emphasize that our linguistic practices are contingent not only on the biological history that we share as members of the same species, but also on the historically constituted "form of life" that we share as members of the same culture. The "natural history" of our shared practices brings to the fore their *social* significance. Like Dewey, Wittgenstein conceives of sociality as a natural aspect of human beings and their activities; and he underscores the importance of customs that are produced and maintained over time, and the development of a *second nature*[39] formed through common activities transmitted from generation to generation in the history of the group. In stressing that human activities are constrained—though not determined—by their past, Wittgenstein also emphasizes their variability and fluctuation. Thus, for example, he contends that an elucidation of "measuring" as part of "human natural history" can "make the concepts of measuring, of exactness, etc., intelligible to us in their variations" (1980b [RPP] I §1109).

Similar points are made by Wittgenstein's historization of our linguistic activities and their meanings at the ontogenetic level in his discussions of learning. Just as the historical evolution of the species and the linguistic community constrains the significance of our utterances and actions, the historical development of the individual also constrains the meanings that can be ascribed to what she says and does. Without falling into a social determinism, Wittgenstein's remarks on learning emphasize the *constraining* effect of the ontogenetic development of our agreement in action. This background agreement is ontogenetically established through training processes: "instruction effects [. . .] *agreement in actions* on the part of pupil and teacher" (RFM

VI.45; my emphasis). The goal of the training process is to bring the pupil into the practice. This process is under the control and normative guidance of a teacher or master who plays the role of a mediator between the learner or novice and the linguistic community of which the teacher-master is a representative. Bringing the novice into the practice is achieved by effecting a consensus of action between the pupil and the teacher and hence, by the same token, between the pupil and the community of practitioners. Through all kinds of drills, tests, normative assessments and corrections, the master structures the behavior of the novice so that she can participate in the consensus of action that characterizes the behavior of competent practitioners. In the light of that consensus the regularized behavior of the novice becomes significant and can be considered indicative of her understanding.

As made clear in Wittgenstein's discussion of the acquisition of understanding in linguistic practices (PI §§139–54), the ability to grasp and express meanings is a temporally extended ability that requires a successfully completed training process. Although Wittgenstein pays special attention to formal, well-structured, intentional, and explicit processes of training, it is worth noting that most of our linguistic skills are picked up through a casual exposure to unceremonious linguistic practices. Indeed most of what we say and do is picked up in a variety of informal settings: on the street, in the schoolyard, at home, in games of all sorts, and so on. And although it is rarely the focus of his discussions, Wittgenstein does call attention to the initiating and formative role of informal activities of language use. Whether formal or informal, the process of initiate learning that Wittgenstein elucidates is a process of enculturation in a practice that leads to the development of reactions and attitudes that become *natural* to the initiate learner. Wittgenstein emphasizes that this learning process aims not only to produce a behavioral regularity, but also to instill a *normative attitude*: the learner acquires not only a particular way of proceeding but also a "*way of looking at things*" (PI §144). The most characteristic normative attitude that results from initiate learning is what Wittgenstein describes as *blind obedience*, or as acting "under the compulsion of a rule" (PI §231): "When I obey a rule, I do not choose. I obey the rule *blindly*" (PI §219). This compulsion and blindness are especially hard and difficult to escape in some of our basic linguistic activities such as counting, adding, and naming colors. The training required by these activities is so strict that it produces the *illusion of necessity*, that is, the illusion that things could not be otherwise. From the perspective of those who have been trained in these activities, there is nothing indeterminate—or even underdetermined—about the meaning of the terms that appear in them. From their perspective the meaning of a term such as "two," "plus," "red" is *overdetermined*: it is "overdetermined," Wittgenstein remarks, by "the way we always use it, the way we are taught to use it" (RFM I.2 and VI.16). But, of course, the meanings that look overdetermined from the perspective of those trained in the relevant practices may appear utterly indeterminate from the perspective of those who do not participate in the consensus of action underlying those practices. As we saw in the previous section, if we break the connection between language use and shared techniques of use, indeterminacy will ensue. For it is only against the background of a practical agreement in form of life that contextually determinate meanings become possible: "Words have meaning only in the stream of life" (RPP II §687).

Overdetermination is the basis of blind obedience. It is important to note the normative significance of the Wittgensteinian notion of *blind obedience*. This notion cannot be understood independently of Wittgenstein's account of initiate learning and the kind of overdetermination that can result from it. Blind obedience is the product of the *normative exclusions* that are instituted in the training processes through which we are acculturated in linguistic practices. These training processes, if successful, make the learner *blind to alternatives*:[40] the learner is taught to follow rules blindly, without considering alternative courses of action as possible applications of the rules. The alternative blindness that according to Wittgenstein is characteristic of the mastery of a technique should not be confused with the blindness of reflexes and conditioned responses. The blind rule following of competent language users is not the product of causal mechanisms; it results from the internalization of standards of correctness, it is informed by normative considerations as to how things *ought* to be done. Wittgenstein describes the adoption of normative standards through training with the image of the learner going "in a circle." He remarks that when the pupil sees how things *must* be done, "he has gone in a circle" (RFM VI.7). The "circle" created by the process of training consists in this: what the learner is trained to do becomes the criterion that defines what she is doing.[41] This is how a *normative attitude* is inculcated: through repeated practice the novice internalizes the normative standards of the linguistic community; and by the end of the learning process the novice regards the way she has been taught to go on as the only way to proceed (cf. RFM I.1–2 and VI.7). Thus, through training processes, the shared procedures and techniques of a practice become *second nature*. Through intiate learning speakers become *blindly* committed to a particular way of talking and acting, which is regarded as *nonoptional*.[42]

We are now in a position to say in exactly what sense the background agreement in action produced by learning processes constitutes the *precondition* of the contextual determinacy of meaning. This tacit agreement establishes a *normal* way of proceeding, a *normal* way of using words and responding to them, and deems all other possibilities *abnormal*. And thus, against the background of the agreement of those who have been acculturated in the practice, we can say "we have here a normal case, and abnormal cases" (PI §141). Particular ways of speaking and acting fit the consensus of action underlying a practice; others do not. As participants in a consensus of action, we share normative expectations about what counts as normal; and it is only when these normative expectations about normalcy are in place that words have a rule-governed use and acquire a contextually determinate meaning: "It is only in normal cases that the use of a word is clearly prescribed. [. . .] The more abnormal the case, the more doubtful it becomes what we are to say" (PI §142). Discussing the language game of ascribing colors to objects, Wittgenstein makes explicit the *crucial connection between agreement and normalcy*: "There is in general complete agreement in the judgments of colours made by those who have been diagnosed *normal*. This characterizes the concept of a judgment of colour" (PI II p. 227).

The assumed normalcy of certain uses of words and courses of action and the assumed abnormality of others provide the requisite normative background in which we can negotiate our semantic interpretations, that is, the normative context in which semantic possibilities are endorsed or rejected. As Wittgenstein emphasizes, a sense of normalcy is a crucial component of linguistic competence. Our competence in a language game requires that we develop a sense of how to continue the practice, that we be able to preserve its background consensus of action. Our normative expectations about normalcy structure our interactions in the language game. These expectations constitute a kind of trust or mutual reliance that makes the continual coordination of action possible. These shared normative expectations amount to the presumption that people will speak and act in accordance with the norms of the practice, that is, in ways that conform with the established consensus of action. This *presumption of normalcy* on which our discursive practices depend can be compared with the *presumption of innocence* that is at the basis of our legal system and of civil society. There is an interesting analogy between the normative foundations of civil society and those of language games. In a civil society we take for granted the citizens' respect for the law. Someone's condition as a citizen would be immediately jeopardized if we arbitrarily assumed that she is in violation of the law. Moreover, if allowed, this arbitrary suspicion would threaten the stability of the entire society, for it would shake the *trust* that we have deposited on one another as fellow citizens, a trust that we need in order to regulate our interactions according to the law. Similarly, a community of speakers and rule followers must take for granted that its members act and talk in conformity with the rules of the game, respecting the background consensus that the community has established. We must have faith in the competence of fellow players in language games so that we can rely on one another in the coordination of our actions. We must assume that the future actions and utterances of fellow speakers will proceed as before, that is, that they will be *normal* and continue the consensus of the practice as expected. This reciprocal reliance and presumption of normalcy are required in order to regulate our communicative interactions according to shared norms. Our communicative exchanges require mutual trust; there is no genuine sharing of perspectives, no genuine intersubjectivity, and no meaningful conflict, disagreement, or debate, without this trust.

Just as in order to live under the rule of law people must be presumed innocent until proven guilty, in order to live under the rule of communication, so to speak, our speech and behavior—our participation in a language game—must be presumed normal until clear indication to the contrary is shown. Otherwise our condition as speakers and actors, our competence, would be arbitrarily called into question and, therefore, undermined. So in the same way that the presumption of innocence is one of the pillars of civil societies, the presumption of normalcy is a central pillar of linguistic communities. As we shall see, the presumption of normalcy is not always extended to all the members of a linguistic community (and indeed never to those excluded from it), just as the presumption of innocence is, unfortunately, not always granted to all citizens. There are people who are deemed *unable to mean what they say or to say what they mean*; and by being excluded from the ranks of the normal language users their speech acts are systematically under suspicion. Here the political analogy is not hard to make, for there are indeed many contemporary contexts in which the presumption of innocence is systematically lifted for certain subjects who become second-class citizens in those contexts: Arabs at the airport, Mexicans at the Southern U.S. border, and those who commit the "offense" of "Driving While Black" are suspected of being up to no good and treated as guilty until proven guilty.[43] But what does it mean to be presumed abnormal and incapable of articulating meanings properly? An example of subjects who are deemed abnormal in certain respects and whose speech acts are suspected of being unintelligible in those areas, are *transgendered subjects* who have been and still are (though less often) depicted as suffering from a pathological "gender confusion" that handicaps their ability to express gender meanings.[44] Talking about the pathologization of her transgendered identity under the diagnostic rubric of "gender dysphoria," Susan Stryker (1994) describes as follows the systematic suspicion of *nonsensicality* to which her speech acts are subject: "Through the filter of this official pathologization, the sounds that come out of my mouth can be summarily dismissed as the confused rantings of a diseased mind" (p. 244).

Even for subjects who are not considered abnormal, it is of course the case that the presumption of normalcy is often lifted. Our normative expectations about what is normal are often violated (even by the most normal subjects). The violation of these expectations does not automatically disqualify a speaker as incompetent and render her speech acts unintelligible. What a violation of expected normalcy does is to *shift the burden* onto the shoulders of the eccentric user, who must now prove the meaningfulness of her speech acts. We can call it "the burden of eccentricity." This burden involves a twofold task: showing that there is a connection between the new use of the word and previous ones, a link between the novel course of action and the prior standard behavior deemed normal; and also showing that this link or connection is fruitful and promising. A departure from a well-entrenched normative expectation is redeemed by demonstrating exactly how the new use or behavior is a legitimate extension of the prior consensus of action, and a continuation of the practice that is worth pursuing, a productive and rich way to go on. The more entrenched the normative expectation violated is, the more difficult this task becomes.

It is important to note that this contextualist analysis inspired by Wittgenstein and Dewey does not suggest that the normative expectations speakers share, or the violations they incur and the burdens they take up, are conscious moves in our language games that require the explicit recognition of speakers. On the contrary. This analysis tries to make explicit the tacit normative attitudes exhibited in speakers' actions and reactions. Often unknowingly, speakers frequently take up the burden of eccentricity. Whether they know it or not, they use terms in ways that depart, to a lesser or greater extent, from standard usage. Eccentric speakers may use language with the intent of conforming to accepted uses; they may even be convinced that they in fact do so. But if their speech acts expand the repertoire of available uses of a term and establish new semantic connections, they qualify as eccentric and transformative. As we saw in the previous section, semantic extensions and transformations are taking place all the time in the repeated use of terms, whether speakers notice it or not. Even the linguistic community as a whole may proceed unaware of the eccentric character of new uses and the semantic transformations they produce. If the eccentricity is quickly covered up with enough clear connections with prior uses, it may not even be noticed (i.e., recognized as an eccentricity) and it may be quickly integrated as part of standard usage.

The opportunity for eccentricity is everywhere. But productive eccentricities—those that result in the extension or transformation of the use of a term and affect its semantic content—require more than an opportunity to depart from previous uses. In Wittgenstein's discussions of language use, every time he considers a fixer and determiner of meaning that is supposed to dictate the use of a term, he objects: "but it was possible for me to use it differently" (PI §139). We can also say this when we consider the use of a term in relation to the consensus of action of its users (no matter how rigid the consensus may be). For indeed, as I have argued, this consensus is not a fixer and determiner of meaning. But we need more than a mere possibility in order to have an eccentric use that can be considered a candidate for semantic innovation and transformation. Outside particular contexts and histories of use, all possibilities have equal value; and as long as we remain in that detached and acontextual perspective, keeping company with the meaning realists and the meaning skeptics, radical indeterminacy will be uncontestable. But in a particular communicative context and against the background of a history of use, the possible uses of a term are heavily constrained—though not determined—by the normative expectations of normalcy shared by language users. Only when our linguistic uses and semantic interpretations are contextualized can we distinguish between normal and eccentric uses, and subject the latter to normative assessments leading to their rejection or integration in our practices.

The eccentricity of novel uses may range from minimal deviation to a radical departure that may look, on the face of it at least, like pure nonsense and madness, mere noise articulated by the babbling mouths of those who otherwise appear to be normal speakers. (Concrete examples will be considered later in my discussions of subversive agency and marginalized subjectivities in the last two chapters.)[45] Eccentric uses must advance from mere possibilities to contextualized opportunities to enrich our practices. Whether the burden of eccentricity is met successfully ultimately depends on the response of the community. Whether unconventional novel uses amount to new semantic ingredients for the meaning of terms depends on whether these uses are accepted and repeated in future utterances by other speakers. This is what I termed the semiotic phenomenon of *echoing* in my analysis of Dewey's emphasis on repetition as a crucial mechanism for sustaining agreement. How much echoing a novel use produces is a good measure for how well the burden of eccentricity has been met. Echoing thus functions as a mechanism of normalization: the more a use is echoed, the better accepted it becomes. By being echoed the new use affects the performative chains of repetitions in which word meanings are gestated. Besides echoing, there is another measure of the long-lasting effects of an eccentric new use and that is whether or not it has an impact on how the use of the term is taught subsequently. As suggested by Wittgenstein's discussions, the deepest, most extended, and most durable semantic transformations are those that are integrated in learning processes and are thus transmitted from generation to generation. Through learning processes what may originally appear to be eccentricities can become institutionalized as part of the normal use and the standard meaning of the term.

Only those uses sanctioned by initiate learning come to be considered normal by most (if not all) members of the linguistic practice. In the learning situation the novice may come up with creative ways of using language. For instance, in the language game of the builders, the learner may respond to the command "Slab!" by bringing a hammer, or by jumping up and down, and she may even insist that that is an appropriate response, that it should be considered the correct way of obeying the order. But if these possible uses that the novice tries out are dismissed by the teacher, they do not become part of the normal application of the term. For, as Wittgenstein points out, the teacher or master—as a competent practitioner and representative of the linguistic community—has the capacity and authority to distinguish between "a normal and an abnormal learner's reaction" (PI §143). The differential authority between master and novice is crucial for the learning process to play its structuring role in regularizing the learner's behavior and inculcating a normative attitude in her. By normalizing speech acts the process of initiate learning accomplishes the critical function of sustaining the tacit agreement in action of practitioners. It is in this sense that learning should be thought of as a process of enculturation. Through the learning process, if successful, the learner becomes an autonomous practitioner who can engage in regulatory activities on her own. But initially the learner depends on the assistance of the master, who structures and regulates the learning environment (this is Wittgenstein's point about "stage setting"; cf. PI §257). But the normative background that the master brings to bear upon the behavior of the novice is progressively made available to the learner through the training. Thus the learning process consists in a gradual transfer of authority and responsibility from the hands of the master to the novice's own hands.[46]

This gradual process of acquiring autonomy and control over one's behavior through another is implicit in Wittgenstein's discussion of the builders and in Dewey's discussion of an equivalent language game of simple orders. It is not accidental that in their discussions the person who issues the orders has the prerogative of assessing the responses to her commands as correct or incorrect. It is not accidental that the person who is in a commanding position (undoubtedly a position of power) is at the same time depicted as the one who exhibits mastery of the practice and plays the role of the teacher in instructing the other as to how things should be done. Even if Dewey is right that an equal partnership is the desired and natural result of communicative processes, we need to pay attention to the fact that these processes require a preliminary learning stage that is based on inequality, that is, on an unequal distribution of power and authority. So in communicative practices a relation between equals is not at all something given, but something that we have to work hard to attain. It is important to note that communicative processes start from a structure of differential authority. This is because there is a preestablished agreement, an already existing consensus, which invests with authority only those who participate in it. As members of this consensus, the masters have the prerogative of participating in normative assessments and semantic negotiations while novices do not. It is by the hands of the masters that new speakers and agents are constantly being brought into the existing consensus; and this continual process of bringing people into the practice constitutes a process of *renewed consolidation* of the existing consensus, which is necessary to maintain it. But through this process of consolidation and renewal the consensus of action of a practice is at the same time constantly extended and transformed. Let's not forget that what is stigmatized as abnormal in one context may become a normalized way of speaking in other contexts, or in other historical moments of the same context. For example, the use of certain terms for self-definition, such as "Nuyorican" or "queer," is considered eccentric in some contexts and normal in others; and while black slang and Ebonics are considered as appropriate language[47] by some people in some contexts, they are also considered as deficient and defective English by some in other contexts. We have to pay attention to the diversity and variability of linguistic contexts as well as to how these contexts and their normative assumptions are formed and consolidated.

1.6. A View from *Elsewhere*

In the last section I discussed the stabilization of the background agreement of our language games through phylogenetic and ontogenetic developmental processes. I argued that the contextual determinacy of meaning is crucially dependent on the constraints that shape our discursive agency, which include our "natural history," the "overdetermination" and "blind obedience" produced by initiate learning, and the normative presumption of normalcy. But although for the most part I have focused on the stabilizing aspects of our constrained agency, it must be noted that the uncontrollable dynamic nature of this agency always exceeds the constraints imposed on it and the stabilization to which it is subject. The discursive agency of speakers requires domestication precisely because it is wild; and its wildness is never lost. The transformative potential of our agency can be tamed, but not eliminated. Given the innumerable variations and transformations (big and small) that can occur in the agency of speakers, the stability of their background consensus in action is always deficient and frail. I will discuss the *destabilizing* aspects of speakers' agency and the *precarious* nature of their tacit agreement in later chapters. It is sufficient to note here that the agency of language users is always moving to new contexts and, therefore, the contextually determinate meanings emerging from their concerted interactions are always slipping and undergoing transformations; in Dewey's words, they "are self-moving to new cases" (EN p. 148). This unpredictable adaptability to new contexts and the semantic slippage that results from it are of the utmost importance. The intrinsic dynamism of our linguistic practices and of the meanings produced in them reveals an important feature of our discursive contexts. I want to close this chapter with some remarks about the dynamic aspect of contextuality, which brings to the fore what is most peculiar about the contextualism that I defend.

No matter how well consolidated and rigidly structured they may become, discursive contexts are always *unfinished or incomplete*. The contexts in which our language games are played are not rigidly delimited and self-contained spaces. The normative space for the agency of speakers that a discursive context provides always exhibits some amount of *openness*. The porosity of these contexts is due to the fact that there are always paths of communication among them, that they are not sealed off from each other. This porosity is not an accidental feature that contexts may or may not have, an added bonus for well-behaved contexts as it were. Rather, it is an intrinsic feature of discursive contexts: what I call "constitutive intercontextuality." A discursive context always has some ties to other contexts; and these ties are not mere accidental connections, but constitutive relations that collectively shape the context in a particular way. Discursive spaces are intrinsically interconnected.

There are two sets of considerations that support my thesis of constitutive intercontextuality. On the one hand, when considered *diachronically*, it is clear that discursive contexts have a *temporal structure* built into them: they are preceded and followed by other contexts. Discursive contexts have a historical existence. They cannot be produced by spontaneous generation, nor can they vanish into thin air without leaving any trace. They are created and destroyed by the situated agency of speakers which is (why not say it) always already situated and, therefore, has to be understood by reference to anterior and posterior contexts. On the other hand, when considered *synchronically*, in carving out its own space for linguistic interaction, a discursive context always presupposes other contexts (whether actual or possible). There are many different ways in which contemporaneous contexts rely on one another: they may logically presuppose one another; they may feed and support each other; they may be in tension or in competition; they may even exclude each other, and so on. A context is in various ways defined by its dependence on other contexts. Contemporaneous contexts are situated vis-à-vis one another and they become constituted through their *mutual positioning*: they occupy a particular position in the network of our practices; and their particular place in the "stream of life" is delineated by their relative position with respect to other contexts. Of course, there can be contexts that explicitly deny any kind of dependence on other contexts. But although they may in fact exhibit considerable degrees of self-sufficiency, this does not undermine their constitutive intercontextuality. Even if there are no explicit relations or open channels of communication between contexts, that does not mean that we can understand these contexts in isolation and independently of each other. My thesis of constitutive intercontextuality does not make *isolationism* impossible, but it shows its limits. Instead of denying the constitutive interdependence between contexts, isolationism is simply a particularly peculiar form that intercontextuality can take. For even the attempt to seal off each context from the rest, even the attempt to block all paths of traffic across contexts, creates a crucial relation of dependence between contexts, albeit a negative, isolationist one. Though purely negative, isolation is itself an intercontextual relation that can become a formative link that defines the relative position of contexts. Thus isolationism demonstrates a form of intercontextuality: it demonstrates how contexts can be shaped through purely negative relations to other contexts (e.g., mutual ignorance, noninterference, etc.).

Intercontextuality can be characterized in two different ways. In a negative sense, intercontextuality can be described as the *constitutive incompleteness* of contexts. In a manner of speaking, discursive contexts are unsaturated spaces: they have holes or cracks in them. These holes or cracks are windows into other contexts. And these windows are not accidental gaps, but congenital fissures, constitutive openings. Contexts are never complete in themselves: they are always undergoing the neverending process of being completed by other contexts; and it is in this sense that their openings to other contexts are constitutive and inevitable. This negative characterization serves to undermine any claim of completeness or autonomy that can be made about discursive contexts. But we need a different characterization to show that these contexts are not vacuous either. The threat of vacuity can arise from the thought that a container with holes is not much of a container. Doesn't the claim that discursive contexts have constitutive openings entail their semantic and normative emptiness? It can be objected that the unsaturated contexts with fissures I have described are not the appropriate receptacles we need to contain meanings, that whatever they may contain won't be enough for meanings to find a foothold in them. My response to this objection is twofold. In the first place, *containment* does not properly capture the normative relation that exists between contexts and the meanings produced in them. It is the central contention of my contextualist view that meanings are intrinsically elusive and cannot be contained in any way at all; and it is precisely in their intrinsic elusiveness or uncontainability that their richness and productivity consist, as later chapters will try to show. But in the second place, we can provide a positive characterization of intercontextuality that shows that contexts are not at all vacuous, that far from being devoid of semantic and normative significance, they exhibit an *uncontainable excess* of meaning and normativity. In a positive sense, intercontextuality can be characterized as the *constitutive excess* of any given context. Each particular context of language use is always exceeding itself, always overflowing, always spilling over other contexts.

Both of these characterizations of intercontextuality underscore the openness of contexts to the unexpected. Whether we understand intercontextuality in terms of incompleteness or in terms of excess, it underscores that the situated agency of speakers is always exposed to unpredictable novelties. Whether through windows or through overflows, surprises are bound to keep cropping up in our discursive contexts. This constant exposure to surprises was already suggested by the unpredictable adaptability of our discursive agency to new contexts, and it is now further emphasized by intercontextuality, that is, by the incomplete and yet excessive character of contexts. The porous and open nature of discursive contexts and the uncontrollable dynamism of our agency as it travels across contexts strongly suggest that the consensus of action underlying our practices is always open and provisional. Given the features of contextuality and agency I have examined, it is clear that this consensus cannot be finalized and established as a fixed axis around which the practice will perpetually revolve. The tacit agreement of the members of a practice is always in the making and therefore remains always an unfinished task. This means that although the background consensus of language users shapes the meanings that emerge from their communicative exchanges, its constraining force is *always shifting*, however minutely. This is suggested by Wittgenstein's emphasis on the variability and intrinsic instability of what counts as "doing the same thing" in the rule-following discussion (cf. PI §226). Our tacit agreement in action is subject to a constant process of transformation, and therefore, our semantic negotiations are *always constrained but never determined and fixed*.

The thesis of the contextual determinacy of meaning that I have derived from Wittgenstein's and Dewey's pragmatic contextualism thus provides an alternative to meaning realism and meaning skepticism. And this alternative semantic view, it is important to note, is *not* an *intermediate* position, a *moderate* view between two extremes, but rather, a view that is *beyond* the dichotomy between semantic realism and skepticism, a view that is in a different conceptual space where the common assumptions about determinacy and fixity shared by realists and skeptics are overcome. This contextualist view insists that we lose sight of meaning when we abandon particular contexts of language use and adopt a detached perspective in our semantic elucidations. Meanings have to be contextualized as emerging from specific chains of communicative interactions situated in particular contexts of action. And yet, it is the signature claim of my Wittgensteinian and Deweyan contextualism that *meanings are not contained in contexts*. In Deweyan language, meanings are *transactional*: they are formed by practical engagements that are contextually entangled in a dynamic way and always continued in new contexts that are yet to come. As my thesis of intercontextuality suggests, there is a constant displacement of meanings to new contexts. In virtue of the open nature of discursive contexts and of the consensus in action of those who inhabit them, contextually determinate meanings are intrinsically unstable and elusive. The constitutive instability and elusiveness of meaning consist in this: situated meanings always point *elsewhere*, that is, they point to other contexts in which they are further delineated, elaborated, extended, or simply transformed. This *elsewhere* orientation shows that our situated meanings remain always transient, provisional, unfinished, for they are always undergoing reconstruction across contexts. In other words, contextually determinate meanings are always to be completed, always to be continued *elsewhere*. And this semantic dependence of contextual meanings on *other* contexts cannot be eliminated. It would be a mistake to think that the determinacy of meanings can be holistically completed by providing a composite image of these meanings in *all* the contexts in which they figure, for this composite image cannot be had: there are always new contexts that can make new contributions to the meanings of our words. There is always an elusive *elsewhere* on which the semantic determinacy of our words depends, an unpredictable *elsewhere* with semantic ties to the familiar contexts of use available to us.

Unlike other internalist and contextualist views, the contextualist perspective I have articulated shows the impossibility of encapsulating meaning in a single and self-sufficient context (or a collection of them). There are no finished, autonomous, and isolated contexts. On my view, meanings can only be found in contexts, and yet they are not *contained* in contexts. This apparently paradoxical claim tries to convey that meanings are not free-floating structures, and yet they are not *things* that can be fixed to a particular context (or a closed series of contexts). (Even a short-lived meaning that seems to figure only in a well-defined set of contexts is dependent on many other possible contexts that could have obtained, or could obtain in the future if the use of the term in question is recuperated.) Meanings are not *outside* contexts but, in an important sense, they are not *inside* them either. They are not containable things. In fact, they are not things at all. It is precisely this ontological assumption about the *thing-ness* of meaning that was presupposed by both meaning realists and meaning skeptics, and that is rejected by my contextualist perspective. On my view, meanings do not belong to the ontic domain of the physical or of the mental, but to the social and practical domain of *the interactional*.[48] The original claim of my contextualism, which distinguishes it from more traditional contextualist perspectives, is that meanings are not susceptible of localization: they cannot be confined to *anywhere in particular* and always remain constitutively elusive. There is always more to meaning than what a single context by itself can offer. And this is not a claim made from *nowhere*, a claim that requires that we abandon the situated perspective of language users and adopt an impossible acontextual view. Rather, it is a claim made from *elsewhere*, that is, a claim about particular contexts made from the perspective of other contexts. The elusive and dynamic nature of situated meanings, their *elsewhere* orientation, is an important qualification of traditional contextualist views of meaning. This qualification acknowledges the importance of intercontextual connections and points in the direction of a new kind of contextualism: *a view from elsewhere.*

There is always an elsewhere to which any given context is oriented; in fact, there is always a multiplicity of *elsewheres*, composed of past, future, and contemporaneous contexts. In this sense intercontextuality can be described as a kind of *elsewhereness*. And since my contextualism puts the emphasis on intercontextuality, I call it "a view from elsewhere." This label is supposed to draw a *twofold contrast*: first, a contrast with externalist and absolutist views, that is, with *the view from nowhere* of acontextual perspectives; but secondly also, a contrast with internalist and contextualist views that appeal to the insider's perspective as the unified standpoint of our practices, *the view from here*. My *elsewhere* contextualism tries to overcome the dilemma between internalism and externalism by articulating a dialectical perspective that transcends the dichotomy between the inside and the outside of language. This perspective will be developed in the forthcoming chapters through a contextualist account of the identity of speakers (chapter 2), their discursive agency (chapter 3), and discursive processes of exclusion and inclusion (chapter 4). In the next chapter the *elsewhere* orientation of our contexts and practices will be further discussed in an examination of the way in which speakers' identities and voices are interwoven and dialectically entangled with each other in discursive practices. This and subsequent discussions will pay special attention to the specific role of transgressive, resistant *elsewheres*—that is, to the critical and transformative power of politically, socially, economically, and culturally marginalized groups and practices. It is for this reason that I draw on critical race theory, feminism, and queer theory.

As far as semantic skepticism is concerned, it would be naïve to think that this is the end of the story, the complete account of contextual determinacy and the complete dissolution of indeterminacy problems. The appeal to shared practices and their contexts of action faces problems that may be as serious and as deep as the appeal to objects, ideas, images, rule formulations, and dispositions of semantic realists.[49] I will address some of these problems and challenges in chapter 3. But first, let me arm myself with more ammunition by recruiting the sociological perspectives of Mead and Bourdieu for my contextualist cause.

Chapter 2

Contextualizing Identity

T HERE IS A COMPLEX two-way relation between meaning and identity. On the one hand, shared meanings certainly make a substantial contribution to the identity of the speakers of a language. It is through the meanings available in their language that speakers make sense of their experiences, actions, and thoughts to themselves as well as to others. (Some have gone as far as to say that "the limits of my language are the limits of my world.") And it is through their linguistic articulations that speakers develop a sense of who they are: they find a *voice* of their own through the process of making sense of themselves as experiential subjects, thinkers, and agents. So it appears that there can be *no identity without shared meanings*, that is, that the development of speakers' subjectivity, the formation of their voice, is parasitic on the availability of previously formed meanings. On the other hand, the identity of speakers also makes a crucial contribution to the formation and transmission of meanings. As we saw in the previous chapter, the determinacy of meaning is crucially dependent on the background consensus of action of the linguistic community and, more specifically, on the convergence of perspectives of the particular participants in communication. Meanings become contextually determinate through the negotiations of situated speakers in particular communicative interactions. Which meanings can be articulated in a given communicative context depends not only on what the context allows speakers to say, but also on what their own voices allow them to say. Although we have focused on the constraints that spring from communicative contexts, there are equally important constraints emerging from the identity of the speakers situated in those contexts. So it seems also plausible to claim that there can be *no meanings without previously formed identities*, for the emergence of meaning requires speakers who put language to use from their particular standpoints, that is, from the perspectives of their identity as experiencing, thinking, and acting subjects.

So we have the following two theses: "no identities without meanings" and "no meanings without identities." The combination of these theses results in a dialectical claim about the conceptual inseparability and mutual dependence of meaning and identity: these concepts are interwoven in such a way that we cannot understand one without the other. But this dialectical claim may leave many dissatisfied and asking "if you cannot have one without the other, how do you get started?" In order to avoid running into a vicious circle, they would argue, we cannot assign equal weight to the notions of shared meaning and individual identity; rather, a clear relation of priority has to be established between them. So a dilemma is forced on us: either meanings preexist speakers' identities and have an independent existence, that is, they somehow subsist (for example, in the tradition) independently of particular speakers; or, alternatively, speakers have an (at least incipient) identity that is prior to and independent of the meanings they articulate and use—which can be captured in a formal notion of identity that does not rely on or presuppose any semantic content. But is this a real dilemma? Do we have to choose between shared meanings and individual identities? Do we have to assign priority to one of them? Do we have to explain one as the product of the other?

That this is a real dilemma has been widely assumed in the philosophy of language. It is this assumption that has sustained the dispute of *semantic* meaning versus *speaker's* meaning.[1] We can illustrate this dispute with the debate between Michael Dummett and Donald Davidson. Following a particular interpretation of Wittgenstein, Dummett (1994) argues that communication must be grounded in fixed social conventions, and that it is this grounding that accounts for the stability of meaning. Arguing explicitly against Dummett's Wittgensteinian view, Davidson (1994) maintains that communication does not require that a speaker mean the same thing by her words that others in the linguistic community mean. On Davidson's view, the concepts of *idiolect* and *speaker's meaning* are primary, while the concepts of shared language and shared meaning are derivative and, in fact, dispensable. Davidson defends this view through a critique of the role traditionally assigned to semantic conventions in communication (1984a and 1984b), and through his account of the interpretation of malapropisms (slips of the tongue, intentional or nonintentional misuse of words, as well as the use of nonwords, etc; see Davidson, 1986). On Davidson's view, any instance of language use, no matter how idiosyncratic, is interpreted holistically by mapping the speaker's idiolect on to the interpreter's idiolect; and no intermediaries such as social conventions are needed for the construction of such mapping.[2] According to Davidson, shared meanings are simply the transitory byproducts of the communicative encounters between individual speakers; they are nothing more than the fleeting result of the passing contact between idiolects. Thus Davidson gives primacy to idiolects and the always changing meanings that emerge from them.

So where can we find the well of meanings, in idiolects or in social conventions? Do meanings enjoy an intersubjective stability based on fixed conventions? Or are they the unstable foci of streams of consciousness? Are meanings essentially shared and social, or essentially subjective and idiosyncratic? They are both and they are neither. My contextualism aims at the dissolution of the debate between semantic meaning and speaker's meaning and, more importantly, at the overcoming of the *false dilemma* between social conventions and individual's subjectivity.[3] The task of assigning conceptual priority to one of these elements seems to be motivated by the attempt to lay down a secure foundation for communication. But if there is anything at all that functions as such a foundation, it is the very dialectic between shared meanings and individual speaking identities, not one of its poles. It is this dialectic that makes communication possible. Communication does not rest on a single pillar. The flow of semantic contents in communication does not spring from shared conventions or from idiolects (or from any other single and static source); it consists, rather, in the movement back and forth between individual standpoints and shared perspectives. In this way my contextualist account of meaning and identity differs from standard positions in the field, and it should not be assimilated to collectivist or individualist views as traditionally conceived.

Although based on an interpretation of Wittgenstein, my contextualism takes issue with the (allegedly Wittgensteinian) claim of the fixity of semantic conventions and the strong stability of shared meanings. The traditional collectivist position is wrong in assuming that the social nature of communication precludes there being any individualistic or idiosyncratic element in our semantic contents. But, on the other hand, my contextualism does not support the Davidsonian claim that communication does not require that one person speak as others do. There is something right and something wrong about this claim. What is wrong is that this claim disregards that communication presupposes and relies on the background consensus of our practices. As we saw in the previous chapter, this tacit and practical kind of sharing is a background condition, not a determination, of communication. But we should not underestimate the importance, the *normative* significance, of what passes for "normal" or "standard" in our linguistic practices. Communicative interactions are based on and demand social commonalities; and in these interactions *deviant* behavior can be seriously and severely punished, sometimes to the point of being rendered *nonsensical*. And yet, Davidson is right that deviations from what is considered to be standard and normal happen all the time without interrupting communication. Although this phenomenon is quite common, it would be a mistake to think that all instances of linguistic deviation are of this sort. A deviation from standard usage sometimes interrupts communication and sometimes does not, depending on the nature of the deviation and on the context on which it appears. Eccentric uses are treated differently in different contexts because of the different normative structures of those contexts and the negotiations that take place in them. However, when all kinds of differences and deviations happen without even being noticed, this does not occur because of the primacy of idiolects and the absence or dispensability of sharing in the linguistic community. In some cases these deviations are silently *corrected*, often automatically and unconsciously. In other cases these deviations are left uncorrected and accepted as alternatives (no matter how idiosyncratic) to standard usage. The former reaction (tacit correction) shows the *invisibility* of deviations and underscores the *strength and inviolability* of shared usage. The latter reaction (tacit acceptance) indicates that there is room for *internal dissent* in our practices (which contain shared and yet divergent ways of acting); and it highlights the *precariousness and instability* of the underlying consensus of action that sustains these practices.[4] But in either case the absence or dispensability of social coordination does not follow.

According to my contextualist view, meanings are not fixed social entities, but they are more than ad hoc constructs that leave no trace behind in the fleeting subjectivity of speakers. Davidson is right that meanings come alive only in the communicative interaction of particular subjects. However, they are not momentary constructs that can be understood in terms of mappings between idiolects; they are inscribed in communicative situations and have a lasting impact on the participants in the communicative exchange and on subsequent semantic configurations. Contextually determinate meanings are parasitic on a prior sharing in which speakers participate and, at the same time, they renew and contribute to this sustained sharing: they enrich it or impoverish it, adding to it or subtracting from it; or they simply consolidate what was already part of the consensus. So there is a *feedback loop* that communicates the background consensus of speakers and the particular interactions between individual speakers: this is a circular movement between the We and the I-Thou, in which each draws from the other and sustains the other. In this circular dynamic of the communicative process, my contextualist view suggests, we should situate the dialectic between shared meanings and individual identities.

Some of the complex issues concerning the interrelations between meaning and identity will be discussed in this chapter, but they will be further explored in the discussions of agency and censorship of subsequent chapters. Drawing on the argument from the previous chapter, my contextualist account of identity in this chapter will apply the idea of contextual determinacy to the identity of speakers and their voices. This account will try to clarify the interrelations between the collective and individual aspects of identity and their formation and transformation in and through language. As in chapter 1, I will exploit the convergence between Wittgenstein's views and pragmatism. However, while before my discussion drew on Dewey's view of meaning, now it will draw on Mead's view of the self. Dewey's and Mead's views of meaning and identity are complementary (and, in fact, they mutually influenced each other); but given their different thematic foci, Dewey's philosophy of language is more elaborated than Mead's, whereas Mead's account of the sociological and psychological constitution of the self is more detailed and comprehensive. So, for the most part, it is Mead's view (rather than Dewey's) that I will put in dialogue with Wittgenstein's view in this chapter. I will supplement my Wittgensteinian and pragmatist account of identity with Bourdieu's view of the identity of speakers as constituted by their agency and constrained by the practices in which they act. As Shusterman (1995) and I (2003a) have argued, Bourdieu's philosophy of practice has important ties to pragmatism and to Wittgenstein's philosophy of language. What Bourdieu's discussions will add to this chapter is an elucidation of the role of power, authority, and institutional control in discursive practices, and their impact on the identity of speakers and their agency.

Whereas in the previous chapter the convergence of different philosophical perspectives (Wittgenstein's and Dewey's) was facilitated by a common enemy (meaning realism and skepticism), in this chapter different philosophical views will be brought together through a common precursor: Hegel. It seems fairly uncontroversial to depict Dewey, Mead, or Bourdieu as Hegelian philosophers: they all hold a self-professed dialectical approach, and they all have important Marxist or neo-Marxist elements in their philosophy. However, it may seem outrageous to claim that Wittgenstein's philosophy exhibits a Hegelian orientation. Am I going to deny the break of early analytic philosophy with the Hegelian tradition? And where is the evidence that Wittgenstein was inspired by Hegel or Hegelian philosophers? Where does he cite Hegel? Well, he doesn't. And we may not find much historical evidence of a direct Hegelian influence on Wittgenstein (although he was indeed familiar with German idealism through Schopenhauer and probably received some Hegelian influence through Kierkegaard). But Hegel's influence, like God's power, works in mysterious ways. And although I don't want to deny that there are obvious anti-Hegelian elements in Wittgenstein's philosophy such as his hostility to systematic philosophy and totalizing thinking, I do think that there is an awkward but interesting convergence (or at least proximity) between Wittgenstein's views of meaning and identity and Hegel's in important respects. However, I do not want to take up the exegetical burden of showing that Wittgenstein was a Hegelian. Instead what I will try to do is to show how Wittgensteinian ideas can contribute to the development of Hegelian themes.

2.1. The Hegelian Connection:
Identity, Difference, and Polyphony

177. A self-consciousness exists *for a self-consciousness*. Only so is it in fact self-consciousness; for only in this way does *the unity of itself in its otherness* become explicit for it. [. . .] *'I' that is 'We' and 'We' that is 'I.'*

178. Self-consciousness exists in and for itself when, and by the fact that, it so exists for another; that is, *it exists only in being acknowledged*. [. . .] The detailed exposition of the Notion of this spiritual unity in its duplication will present us with the *process of Recognition*. (*Phenomenology of Spirit*, pp. 110–11; emphasis preserved and added)

Thinking that keeps to external reflection [. . .] fails to attain to a grasp of identity [. . .]. Such thinking always has before it *only abstract identity, and apart from and alongside it, difference*[:] a *positing of likeness* and then also again a *positing of unlikeness*—likeness when abstraction is made from difference, and unlikeness when abstraction is made from the positing of likeness. [. . .] The truth is rather that a consideration of everything that is, shows that in its own self *everything is in its self-sameness different from itself and self-contradictory*, and that in its difference, in its contradiction, it is self-identical, and is in its own self this movement of transition of one of these categories into the other [. . .]. The notion of identity [as] *self-related negativity* is not a product of external reflection but has come from being itself. Whereas, on the contrary, that identity that is aloof from difference, and difference that is aloof from identity, are products of external reflection and abstraction, which arbitrarily clings to this point of indifferent difference. [. . .] distinguishing is present as self-related negativity, as a non-being which is the non-being of itself, a non-being which has its non-being not in another but in its own self. What is present, therefore, is *self-related, reflected difference*. (*Science of Logic*, pp. 412–13; my emphasis)

Identity falls apart within itself into diversity [. . .]. Diversity constitutes the otherness as such of reflection. [. . .] The *moments of difference* are identity and difference itself. They are diverse when they are reflected into themselves, that is, when they are *self-related*; as such, they are *in the determination of identity*. (*Science of Logic*, pp. 418; my emphasis)

As illustrated by these quotes, Hegel's reflections on identity contain two crucial dialectical themes. One is the *dialectic of mutual recognition* (or *misrecognition*). On Hegel's view, this dialectic is constitutive of the process of identity formation (as exemplified by Hegel's account of the master-slave dialectic). No one has an identity as a subject capable of speech and action (as "a self-consciousness") without acknowledging and being acknowledged by other speakers and agents, no matter how tacit or indirect this acknowledgment may be. Bracketing for the moment the cognitivist and voluntaristic aspects of the Hegelian dialectic of mutual recognition, what this dialectic shows is the constitutive *sociality* of the identity of speakers and agents. As we shall see, how we understand the social nature of identity will depend, crucially, on how we understand the dialectic of mutual recognition (or of *misrecognition*) in our discursive practices. On the other hand, the second dialectical theme that Hegel's reflections on identity bring to the fore is the *dialectic between identity and difference*. According to Hegel, "identity" and "difference" are not independent and mutually exclusive categories; on the contrary: they are *internally related* and they cannot be properly conceived in isolation from each other (that is, they can be so conceptualized but only in an abstract and empty way). Identity is constituted through differences, and these differences in turn presuppose identities. Identity and difference are inextricably interwoven because "likenesses" and "unlikenesses" (similarities and differences) that set people apart and bring them together, far from being external to one another, are actually bound up with each other.

An identity finds "the unity of itself in its otherness." On Hegel's view, an identity is not something given, but something achieved through "diversity," that is, through "moments of difference" that become "determinations of identity" when integrated in the life of the subject. For an identity to be determinate it must have differences which are not merely external, but in fact *constitutive*. As Hegel puts it, "determinate beings" are those beings that "have within themselves the moment of difference" (*Science of Logic*, p. 93). These "moments of difference" are encountered dialogically, in our interactions and transactions with others. In this sense the dialectic of identity and difference and the dialectic of mutual recognition are inseparable. On Hegel's view of identity, the idea of internal, constitutive difference (or "self-related negativity," in his terminology) is at the same time the idea of the social bond, of the constitutive relation to others. In other words, the claim that identity is bound up with difference and the claim that one's identity is bound up with the identity of others are two sides of the same coin. My discussions of Mead and Wittgenstein in this section (as well as my discussion of Bourdieu in the next section) will elucidate these Hegelian dialectics of identity and difference and of mutual recognition. In conversation with contemporary views of identity in the literature on gender, sexuality, race, and ethnicity, I will try to show how these two Hegelian dialectics go hand in hand and together produce contextually determinate identities. Drawing on my argument for the contextual determinacy of meaning from the previous chapter, I will argue here that identity is abstract and empty (radically indeterminate) when considered outside particular contexts of action and interaction, but it becomes contextually determinate in relation to particular communities and practices. My pragmatic contextualism will provide an account of how our identities acquire certain degrees of determinacy in relation to particular contexts and how this relational determinacy undergoes transformation from context to context. As applied to identity, the contextualist view I have developed will lead to what I term the thesis of "the polyphony of identity." On my contextualist view, identity is conceived as a heterogeneous space where multiple voices not only coexist but also interact in complex ways. The *polyphony* thesis underscores the thoroughgoing heterogeneity of identity; it is a contextualist version of the Hegelian thesis of the inner diversity of identity.

2.1.a. The Dialectics of Recognition

For Mead, there is more than a structural analogy between the determinacy of meaning and the determinacy of identity: there is a common root, a common genesis; and it is this genetic connection that explains why meaning and identity have the same constitutive features and exhibit an isomorphic structure. On Mead's view, language is the basis for the emergence of the human mind and human subjectivities. In order to get inside Mead's sociogenetic view I propose to start on familiar ground, going from meaning to identity.

As pointed out above, Mead and Dewey hold strikingly similar views of meaning and identity. Like Dewey (and Wittgenstein as well), Mead in *Mind, Self, and Society* attacks semantic reifications and develops a dynamic and contextualist view of meaning, which constitutes the basis of a dynamic and contextualist view of identity. Against the subjective reification of meaning, he argues that meaning is not an "idea" or mental content as traditionally conceived (1934 [MSS] p. 76). In an important sense the emergence of meaning precedes the consciousness or awareness of meaning. But meanings cannot be identified with unconscious mental contents either. Meanings go beyond the purely "psychical"; they belong to *the interactional*, to the processes of communicative interaction between subjects. Against the objective reification of meaning, Mead argues that it is a mistake to identify meanings with language-independent objects as denotational approaches do, for the objects of our experience are linguistically constituted, that is, they are disclosed through communicative processes. We cannot perceive or in any way identify objects independently of language. The social process of communication is responsible for the appearance of objects in the experiential fields of speakers: "Language does not simply symbolize a situation or object which is already there in advance; it makes possible the existence or the appearance of that situation or object" (MSS, p. 78). However, Mead remarks that meanings are "objectively there" (p. 76). This observation does not institute a new kind of reification, but simply underscores that meanings are more than a mere illusion; they constitute a reality, an *interactional* reality which has an objective basis. There is an interesting convergence with Wittgenstein here: both Mead and Wittgenstein oppose ontological reductions and reifications of meanings without thereby becoming eliminativists, that is, without denying the reality and objective basis of semantic contents.

Mead's interactionism yields a *relational* view of meaning. On this view, meaning is a relation among certain phases of social interaction: a relation between a communicative action, a reaction to it, and the resulting act that completes the interaction. For Mead, the function of meaning is to bind together the different phases of the process of communicative interaction. Even before symbols are developed, meanings emerge in what Mead calls the "conversation of gestures" in which each gesture is a stimulus that triggers a reaction, which is in turn another gesture that becomes the stimulus of another reaction (cf. pp. 42ff). Drawing on Wundt's research on gestures, Mead illustrates this "conversation of gestures" with his famous example of the dog fight: one dog moves forward and barks, showing its readiness to attack; the other dog refuses to engage by moving backward, which stimulates more forward movement and barking in the first dog until the second dog escapes. The meanings involved in this pattern of interaction consist in the anticipation of an attack and the anticipation of a flight: the gestures of the first dog intimate a threat, and those of the second dog a withdrawal. Another illustration Mead offers is a baby's cry and the comforting response of the parent (p. 44). In this pattern of interaction the sounds emitted by the baby and the parent express certain emotions and at the same time arouse those emotions in the other. Obviously things become much more complicated with the appearance of symbols and entire symbolic systems, but the basic interactional mechanism for the production of meaning remains the same. For Mead, symbols are first and foremost repeatable gestures (initially vocal and later written) that stabilize the patterns of action and reaction between subjects. For example, the term "rabbit" may have different meanings corresponding to different processes of communicative interaction. Each meaning of the term will consist in the functional unity that the term produces in particular interactions: for instance, one hunter shouts "rabbit!" and the other one aims and shoots, killing the animal, resulting in a successful completion of the activity of rabbit-hunting.

Mead summarizes his account of the formation of meanings through communicative interactions as follows: meanings are constituted through "the mutual adjustment to one another of the responses or actions of the various individual organisms involved in that process, an adjustment made possible by means of a communication which takes the form of a conversation of gestures in the earlier evolutionary stages of that process, and of language in its later stages" (MSS, p. 77). According to this interactional account, "the logical structure of meaning" consists in "a threefold or triadic relation between gesture, adjustive response, and resultant of the social act which the gesture initiates"

(p. 80). Thus, Mead concludes, we find "the basis of meaning [. . .] objectively there in social conduct" (p.80). And this, he contends, solves "the problem of the meaning of meaning": "It is not necessary, in attempting to solve this problem, to have recourse to psychical states, for the nature of meaning [. . .] is found to be implicit in the structure of the social act" (p. 81)

Mead emphasizes that the specifically human forms of communication that require meanings involve a very peculiar kind of cooperation. He points out that cooperation without meaning is indeed possible: we find cooperative activity without "common meaning," for example, in the movement of a crowd, or in the concerted behavior of ants and bees (MSS, pp. 55–56). But what characterizes the kind of cooperation made possible by human language, what defines communicative interaction with symbols, is that it requires *reflexivity*: that is, the capacity to take the attitude of the other toward oneself, to adopt the point of view of the other toward one's behavior. For Mead, in order to have meaning in a communicative interaction it is not enough to have gestures that call out appropriate responses; we need more than purely mechanical reactions; we need a certain degree of awareness of the significance of each gesture, of each phase of the interaction, from the perspective of the different participants.[5] All gestures are tools for the coordination of action. But what distinguishes gestures with meaning is that they carry with them an attitude that is *mutually recognized* by sender and recipient. This is how Mead puts it:

> The function of the gesture is to make adjustment possible among the individuals implicated in any given social act [. . .] the significant gesture or significant symbol affords far greater facilities for such adjustment and readjustment than does the non-significant gesture, because it calls out in the individual making it the *same* attitude toward it [. . .] that it calls out in the other individuals participating with him in the given social act, and thus makes him *conscious* of their attitude toward it (as a component of his behavior) and enables him to adjust his subsequent behavior to theirs in the light of that attitude. (MSS, p. 46; my emphasis)

The terms "same" and "conscious" in this passage need to be clarified. In the first place, "conscious" should not be understood in a strong sense as indicating that meanings must be the explicit focus of one's attention or self-consciousness. This would be an overly intellectualistic reading that would rule out all the unconscious aspects of meaning. The consciousness of meaning that Mead talks about refers only to the *reversibility* of communicative perspectives, that is, to being able to adopt the point of view of the other toward oneself: "the individual's consciousness of the content and flow of meaning involved depends on thus his taking the attitude of the other toward his own gestures" (MSS, p. 47). Taking the attitudes of others toward oneself is something that can be done quite automatically and unconsciously; but even if it is not done self-consciously, it is something that depends indirectly on the attention and control of the participant in the communicative process. This reflexivity or reversibility makes the communicative interaction flexible and dynamic; and it constitutes a more effective and powerful mechanism of mutual adjustment than any wired-in mechanism that operates autonomically.

In the second place, we also have to be careful in interpreting what Mead means by "the same" as applied to meaning. Mead sometimes seems to over-emphasize the identity of attitudes and contents. He claims, for example, that the gestures we internalize are "significant symbols because they have the *same* meanings for *all* individual members of the given society or social group" (p. 47; my emphasis). But when he goes on to explain the sameness of meanings in terms of the sharing of perspectives, it is clear that these perspectives do not have to be *the same in every respect*, but only sufficiently similar, where the sufficiency of the similarity is tested by the successful coordination of action. Thus Mead explains the identity of a semantic content in terms of the common responses that a gesture or symbol evokes (cf. p. 73). Meanings require a certain commonality of response, but not strict identity. And here again what is crucial is the reflexivity or reversibility of communicative perspectives: the commonality or sharing that meaningful gestures or symbols presuppose is required so that they can have sufficiently similar effect in speaker and hearer and thus the participants in communication can reverse their positions. (However, although Mead does not make such strong claims about the homogeneity of semantic contents as it may seem at first sight, his semantic view does have a dangerous tendency toward unification that can go overboard. I will come back to this later in my discussion of the unity of the self.)

The centerpiece of Mead's account of communication is reflexivity. As Aboulafia, for one, has put it, Mead's account shows that "an ability to reverse positions or perspectives is built into the fabric of our symbolic interaction" (2001, p. 65). The claim about the mutual recognition of communicative attitudes involved in the thesis of reflexivity or reversibility seems fairly intuitive and uncontroversial. What is far more problematic, though, is the claim about similarity of response in speaker and hearer which Mead also includes in his account of reflexivity. It seems wrong to say that meaningful gestures have the *same* effect on issuer and addressee. If I issue a verbal threat, my threatening noises don't scare me and I don't feel threatened. For, indeed, to *recognize* is not to be similarly affected. One can reply that the claim about similarity of response that Mead's reversibility thesis makes only involves that the speaker must know (or have some sense of) what it is like to be the recipient of the address—for example, what it is like to be the object of a threat, even if she doesn't feel threatened. This is indeed more plausible, but still problematic in some cases: for example, must the harasser know what it is like to be harassed? Must the abuser know what it feels like to be mistreated? Do slaveholders really have an inkling of what it feels like to be dominated? Mead seems to go too far when he claims that meaningful symbolic interaction requires "an arousal in the individual himself of the response which he is calling out in the other individual, a taking of the role of the other, a tendency to act as the other person acts" (MSS, p. 73).

However, some of the claims of Mead's account of reflexivity still hold. According to this account, the path to the development of reflexivity goes *from others to self*, not from self to others. In learning to respond to one's own gestures or symbols as others do, one becomes aware of the attitudes and perspectives of others toward oneself; and this awareness inaugurates the articulation of a mind or consciousness and eventually of a self. The use of meaningful gestures or symbols in communicative interaction is therefore responsible for the emergence of mind and self: "Only in terms of gestures as significant symbols is the existence of mind or intelligence possible" (p. 47). Reflexivity—the ability to take the role of the other toward oneself—is for Mead the common root in the genesis of meaning and the genesis of mind and self: "the same procedure which is responsible for the genesis and existence of mind or consciousness—namely, the taking of the attitude of the other toward one's self, or toward one's own behavior—also necessarily involves the genesis and existence at the same time of significant symbols, or significant gestures" (pp. 47–48).

As we have seen, for Mead, symbolic interaction involves the reversibility of roles or communicative perspectives. He develops his distinctive symbolic interactionism through his theory of roletaking. This theory provides a genetic account of the formation of identity in terms of the Hegelian dialectic of mutual recognition. On Mead's view, the self is constituted through the perceptions of others. The organism acquires individuality and becomes a self by being recognized by others in particular ways and by internalizing these perspectives of others on oneself. The participant in symbolic interaction learns to put herself in the position of others and to anticipate their responses; and thereby she learns to address herself and to respond to herself *as if it were the other*. By thus internalizing the perspectives of others the individual acquires *inner diversity*, to use Hegel's terms. With the internalization of the perspectives of others (and the resulting "inner diversity") the subject can now continue the communicative interaction internally. And thus emerges *thinking* as an introjected process of symbolic interaction,[6] as "an internalized or implicit conversation" (MSS, p. 47). This becomes possible when the individual's mind is diversified into different perspectives and roles. Elsewhere Mead describes these internalized perspectives or roles as "dramatis personae" which, with their peculiar "features and intonations," participate in the dialogue of voices that constitutes the inner life of the subject (cf. 1913, p. 378). He thus develops a performative view in which the identity of a self is essentially *dramatic*, for the dramatization or performance of roles is an essential part not only of its development but also of its dialogical constitution or inner structure: "self-consciousness remains dramatic" (p378). On this view, the recognition of the other takes a performative—in fact "dramatic"—form: it is achived through enactments and reenactments, which take first an external and overt form and later an internal and covert form. We develop the capacity to recognize the perspectives of others by inhabiting them (often adopting them unconsciously toward our own selves), that is, by enacting or playing their roles, whether in real life or in pretend play: "to be aware of another self implies that we have played his role or that of another with whose type we identify him for purposes of intercourse" (1913, p. 377). And this awareness of the other is prior to the awareness of one's own self, for the recognition of the self passes through the recognition of the other, that is, through the recognition of the perspectives of others as directed toward oneself. Therefore, the formation of a reflexive self, of a self-consciousness, rests on a prior alienation or identification with the other that has an everlasting consequence in one's identity; namely, the ineludible mark of *internal fracture or inner diversity*. To become oneself one must first become the other by playing her role and internalizing her perspective or stance in such a way that the other becomes part of one's own self. [7] As Mead puts it in *The Philosophy of the Present*: "The individual is an other before he is a self. It is in addressing himself in the role of an other that his self rises in experience" (1932, p. 168).

In a truly Hegelian fashion, Mead thus shows that there is no self unless it is acknowledged by others and recognized in particular ways. On his view, one recognizes oneself first and foremost as reflected in the other. The development of the self is such that it unavoidably leads to the *constitutive presence of others* inside oneself, a presence that is for the most part unconscious: "We are more or less unconsciously seeing ourselves as others see us. We are unconsciously addressing ourselves as others address us" (MSS, p. 68). Mead emphasizes that those others that are part of our own selves, those internal presences of our inner diversity, can be particular others as well as "generalized others." Through our communicative interactions we internalize the perspectives of particular people (Peter's and Mary's, Chao-Li's and Pedro's) as well as the perspectives of particular groups or communities. In communicative interactions we always face concrete individuals in the flesh and blood, but these individuals also act as members of particular communities and can be taken as representatives of those groups. Thus the perspectives one internalizes can range from very idiosyncratic perspectives that are tied to the personalities and peculiarities of particular individuals, to very impersonal, communal perspectives, with the possibility of all kinds of intermediate and mixed cases in between. The crucial difference is that in some cases one learns to see oneself and address oneself as someone in particular would, and in other cases as an entire group or community would. Different mechanisms are at play here. In one case the mechanism in question is the internalization of (and differentiation through) a *second-person perspective*, the perspective of a *Thou*; and in the other case, it is the internalization (and differentiation through) a *first-person-plural perspective*, the perspective of a *We*. These different mechanisms result in different kinds of diversification, that is, in different internal presences, in different kinds of inner diversity. Mead's account of these different others and the different processes of internalization associated with them can be elucidated through his distinction between *play* and *game*.

Mead points out that our first experiences at roletaking take place in what he calls "playing at something": for example, playing at being a mother, a teacher, or a policeman. Through simple activities of pretend play the child learns to adopt a variety of roles, mastering reversible attitudes that can be applied to others as well as to oneself. Play, Mead points out, is "the simplest form of being another to oneself" (MSS, p. 151). This simple form of roletaking already enables the child to engage in conversations with herself. In these conversations, which initially take place out loud, "the child says something in one character and responds in another character" (p.151.). After particular roles are mastered, the next developmental stage comes with the "organized game." Mead emphasizes that the different roles and positions in a game are arranged and coordinated according to rules. The rule-governed activity of a game involves highly structured interactions and the hierarchical organization of roles. For Mead, the transition from play to game is a transition from taking one role after another to taking a set of organized roles: "the essential difference [is] that the child who plays in a game must be ready to take the attitude of everyone else involved in that game, and that these different roles must have a definite relationship to each other" (p.151). Using baseball as an illustration, Mead contends that what a baseball player does is "controlled by his being everyone else on that team" (p. 154), that is, by playing his role in coordination with all the other roles being played. In the structured activity of a game there appears an abstract "other" which is not anyone in particular, but "the organization of the attitudes of those involved in the same process" (p.154). The child must internalize this communal perspective, this abstract "other," and submit to it in order to become a competent player in the game. Through the mastery of a game the child develops an organized self; and what holds this organization together is what Mead calls the "generalized other" of the game or practice in question. The generalized other is the perspective or normative standpoint of the collectivity that unifies those who cooperate in the game or practice. In the case of baseball, for example, the team is the generalized other that organizes and controls the experience and behavior of each of its members; a more abstract generalized other would be the community of baseball players, which encompasses not only one's own team but also the rival team as well (and even all possible baseball players if the abstraction is pushed to the limit). This is how Mead explains the notion: "The organized community or social group which gives to the individual his unity of self may be called 'the generalized other.' The attitude of the generalized other is the attitude of the whole community" (p. 154).

Corresponding to the activities of play and game Mead's account distinguishes between two different developmental stages of the self. As a result of the roletaking mastered in play activities, a self is constituted by particular, disconnected attitudes, namely, the internalized attitudes of particular others toward oneself in specific social acts (cf. MSS, p. 158). Mead emphasizes that we do not yet have here a full, complete self. This primitive self is nothing more than a collection of features and attitudes, a repertoire of roles. It has no unity and it is full of conflicts; and what is most revealing is that these conflicts are not (and cannot be) played out, for they are conflicts that the self remains insensitive to because it lacks the kind of organization and coherence required to register them as conflicts. By contrast, through the organized activity of games and the communal perspectives underlying their organization, a whole, organized self is formed. What characterizes the second stage in the development of the self, according to Mead, is unification. In this stage the individual's self is constituted "by an organization of the social attitudes of the generalized other or the social group as a whole to which [the individual] belongs" (p.158). On Mead's view, a self does not achieve its full development until it becomes unified by the perspectives and organizing principles of a social group: "the self reaches its full development by organizing these individual attitudes of others into the organized social or group attitudes, and by thus becoming an individual reflection of the general systematic pattern of social or group behavior in which it and the others are all involved" (p.158).

Two problems immediately suggest themselves for this view. The first one is the *problem of individuality*. By focusing on the internalization of social roles, Mead's performative account of the self may appear to be an extreme form of social behaviorism that leaves no room for individuality. But selves seem to bear the mark of individuality; and any satisfactory account of the self must have a story to tell about individuation, that is, about how one self can be distinguished from another. The second problem is that of *social and cultural diversity*. By emphasizing that a self is the product of the socialization in a group or community and the internalization of its collective perspective, Mead's view may appear to involve a monolithic conception of group identities and communities that could only be remotely plausible for highly unified, traditional societies that are organized according to a single set of values and norms and inculcate a common perspective in all the members. But individuals are subject to multiple processes of socialization, and they typically belong to multiple communities or groups with different perspectives and values.[8] How can individuals develop a single self according to Mead's sociogenetic account? The problem of social and cultural diversity is especially pressing for multicultural societies in which individuals can be exposed to different languages, religions, cultural values, and so forth. But it is important to note that this problem is actually present for all societies, even for the most traditional ones, for human societies are messy and include a variety of subgroups and organizations that do not always cohere as harmonic elements in a unified system. No matter how homogeneous they may appear, human communities always contain the possibility of conflicting perspectives, given their internal diversity. Mead's view certainly contains sophisticated conceptual resources to deal (however satisfactorily) with these problems. Let's address one problem at a time.

There is indeed an account of individuality in Mead's sociogenetic view of the self. But it is true, however, that Mead defines the self as "a social structure [that] arises in social experience" (MSS, p. 140). It is only after being socially constituted that we can make sense of a "solitary self," for the fully formed self has then the capacity to "provide for itself its social experiences"; "but it is impossible to conceive of a self arising outside of social experience" (p.140). These claims do not reject individuality as such; only individuality as a given that preexists the social constitution of the self is deemed illusory. For Mead (as for Dewey[9]), individuality is an interactional achievement that remains parasitic on social contexts. What Mead's account opposes is the strong view of individuality as that which defines the self from the beginning, without requiring any work through social processes of communicative interaction. However individuality figures in Mead's view of the self, it will have to be consistent with his strong thesis of *the social constitution of the self*: "What goes to make up the organized self is the organization of the attitudes that are common to the group. A person is a personality because he belongs to a community, because he takes over the institutions of that community into his own conduct" (p. 162).

Mead emphasizes that, within a group, there is "no hard-and-fast line" between one's own self and the selves of others; the selves of the members of a group have a common "structure of attitudes" (MSS, pp. 163–44). He argues that this common structure is required "in order that we may be members of a community at all"; but he goes on to point out that "we are not only what is common to all: each one of the selves is different from everyone else" (p. 163). The internalized attitudes of the community are part of the self but not the entire self. The part of the self that results from taking the roles and attitudes of others and internalizing their perspective is what Mead calls "the 'me.'" By contrast, *the 'I'* is the active part of the self that takes the 'me' as its object and incorporates it in the thoughts and actions of the subject. The 'I' assimilates the 'me' by responding to it in a particular way (accepting it, rejecting it, critically transforming it, etc): "The 'I' reacts to the self which arises through the taking of the attitudes of others" (p. 174). Mead summarizes the contrast drawn by his distinction as follows: "The 'I' is the response of the organism to the attitudes of the others; the 'me' is the organized set of attitudes of others which one himself assumes" (p. 175). The 'me' has a stable structure provided by the generalized other(s) that the individual has internalized. The 'I,' by contrast, has no stable structure: it is a spontaneous, creative, unpredictable, and always elusive part of the self. Let's briefly elucidate these features of the 'I.'

Among the most characteristic features of the 'I' are its *spontaneity* and its *creativity*. These features relate to the 'I's orientation toward the future and its constant encounter with new situations with which it must come to terms and in which it must act: the "movement into the future is the step, so to speak, of the ego, of the 'I'"; "the 'I' gives the sense of freedom, of initiative" (p. 177). As the spontaneous and creative part of the self, the 'I' is the source of novelty. The 'I' has the capacity to contribute novel responses to the life of the individual as well as to the social life of the community. And this brings us to another central feature of the 'I': its *unpredictability or uncertainty*. The 'I's responses are always "uncertain" (p. 176); the "action of the 'I' is something the nature of which we cannot tell in advance" (p. 177). The 'I' is a constant surprise and cannot be pinned down in any way: "It is because of the 'I' that we say that we are never fully aware of what we are, that we surprise ourselves by our own action. It is as we act that we are aware of ourselves" (p. 174). The 'I's uncertainty is thus also related to another crucial feature: its *elusiveness*. The 'I' remains forever elusive. It "cannot turn around quick enough" to catch itself; it is not there until it acts (there is no anticipation for it); and once it acts, it becomes a memory, a 'me': "The 'I' of this moment is present in the 'me' of the next moment. [. . .] It is what you were a second ago that is the 'I' of the 'me'" (p.174). These central features of the I (spontaneity, creativity, uncertainty, and elusiveness) are illustrated in Borges's short story "Borges and I." Giving to its companion 'me' the name of "Borges," the 'I' gives voice to the following lament:[10]

> I know of Borges from the mail and see his name on a list of professors or in a biographical dictionary. I like hourglasses, maps, eighteenth-century typography, the taste of coffee and the prose of Stevenson; he shares these preferences, but in a vain way that turns them into the attributes of an actor. [. . .] I am destined to perish, definitively, and only some instant of myself can survive in him. Little by little, I am giving over everything to him, though I am quite aware of his perverse custom of falsifying and magnifying things. [. . .] Years ago I tried to free myself from him and went from the mythologies of the suburbs to the games with time and infinity, but those games belong to Borges now and I shall have to imagine other things. Thus my life is a flight and I lose everything and everything belongs to oblivion, or to him. (Borges 1981, pp. 19–20)

The difference between the 'me' and the 'I' should not be understood in terms of the difference between a public persona and an intrinsically and unavoidably private self. The 'I' is not the return of the Ghost in the Machine. It is not a mysterious and invisible noumenal entity. It would be a mistake to think of the 'I' as a nonsocial element of the self, or to assimilate the 'me'/'I' distinction to the public/private and observable/unobservable distinctions. One's 'I' is displayed in one's actions and, far from being outside the social sphere, it is constantly being fed by it as well as contributing to it. For the 'I' is an actor, a voice, that participates in social processes and brings novel and spontaneous reactions to them. As Mead puts it, the process of interaction between the 'me' and the 'I' "does not exist for itself, but is simply a phase of the whole social organization of which the individual is a part" (MSS, p. 178). According to Mead's dynamic and interactional view of subjectivity, "the self is not so much a substance as a process," an internalized conversation that reaches outward into other conversations, a social process going back and forth both between the 'me' and the 'I' and between them and the social milieu. Although Mead describes the inner life of the self as an internal conversation, he also emphasizes that this conversation is never self-contained, that no matter how much we retreat to an abstract thinking that feeds itself and stimulates itself, there is always the guiding presence of possible others that extend the internal communication process beyond itself. Whether we know it or not, and whether we like it or not, our selves are always seeking an audience: "One inevitably seeks an audience, has to pour himself out to somebody" (p. 141). In this sense, thinking—no matter how abstract—always remains "preparatory to social action" (p.141).

Although the 'I' is indeed the most distinctive part of one's individuality and uniqueness, it would be a mistake to think that what makes one a unique individual is unrelated to the 'me,' or that the 'me' is only an obstacle to individuality. In the first place, the 'I' and the 'me' are inseparable; they are the integral parts of a single, interactional process that defines the subject. One's identity is the product of the interactions between the 'me' and the 'I.' One's personality resides precisely in the movement back and forth from one part of the self to the other: "The 'I' both calls out the 'me' and responds to it. Taken together they constitute a personality" (p. 178). And, in the second place, although the 'me' is where the common structure of attitudes shared by the members of a group resides, not all 'me's are identical, since there are always variations in the way in which roles and attitudes are internalized. Individuality is also reflected in the 'me.' For internalization is not mere replication. Internalization is more than a passive copying of whatever is out there; it is more than a mechanical and uncritical reception of whatever community standards the subject is exposed to. In this sense Mead calls our attention to the critical role that "subjective experience" plays in the formation of an individual self (see §21 of MSS, pp. 164–73). Our subjective experience has not only psychological significance for the development of individuality, but also crucial social significance for the transformation of the community. On Mead's view, "the subjective" refers to the existential positioning of the individual vis-à-vis the community. This is not a matter of passive adjustment but of transformative interaction, which Mead explains using the model of a *conversation*: "We are not simply bound by the community. We are engaged in a conversation in which what we say is listened to by the community and its response is one which is affected by what we have to say" (p. 168). According to this conversational model, there is a process of constant transformation of the community and its members that takes place unnoticeably through the conversational exchanges of individual selves—exchanges that have practical consequences and can modify the patterns of social interaction. On this conversational view, social changes do not require explicit reforms, let alone upheavals and revolutions: "We are continually changing our social system in some respect" (p.168). There are of course those who try to avoid change at all costs, and even those who refuse to engage in a communicative process that aims at the critique and transformation of the community. But Mead's description of the individual's conversation with the community contains a *normative* point about the critical activity that is expected of mature and autonomous individuals: "the individual has not only the right but the duty of talking to the community of which he is a part, and bringing about those changes which take place through the interaction of individuals" (p.168).

This critical and transformative conversational model makes clear how Mead's view brings to the discussion of identity the same *nondeterministic contextualism* I defended in the previous chapter with respect to meaning. On the one hand, particular communities and their processes of social interaction provide the social context required for the determinacy of the self. As Mead puts it, one becomes "a definite self over against the social whole to which he belongs" (1932, p. 168); "selves can only exist in definite relationships to other selves" (MSS, p. 164). It is through processes of mutual recognition that selves become contextually determinate. According to Mead's interactionism, contextually determinate identities exist only in definite relations with particular and generalized others and in conversation with particular communities. We can make sense of a self only in a particular social context. But, on the other hand, one's social context does not determine one's identity. We are not mere replicants; we do not simply reproduce the attitudes of the community to which we belong. There is always the possibility of going beyond the standards of the community and acquiring a *critical voice*: "the self can get a voice which is more than the voice of the community" (MSS, p. 168). One acquires a critical voice by opposing "the voice of the community" not only in internalized conversations but in conversations with the voices of particular others, that is, not only in thought but in social interaction. Voices are always socially contextualized; they exist only in relation to other voices: the voices of particular and generalized others. Therefore, we can go beyond those voices that have been part of our socialization, we can abandon our conversational partners, but the conversation in which our identity consists remains meaningful only if new voices come in, even if they are the voices of imaginary others. We can disregard "the voice of the community" in which we find ourselves and transcend its normative standards, but only if we posit a new communal voice with its own standards: "The only way in which we can react against the disapproval of the entire community is by setting up a higher sort of community which in a certain sense out-votes the one we find" (pp. 167–68). So a radical departure from one's community does not amount to stepping outside the social context altogether, for it involves the production of a new social context. One cannot meaningfully and successfully depart from one's social environment unless one creates a new social context populated by the voices of new, possible others. On Mead's view, a self that creates its own social context or substantially transforms the one in which she finds herself is an *enlarged self*. The critical process of going beyond one's given environment and community and finding new conversational partners and communities that can support one's individuality is a process of *enlarging* the self. Marginalized subjects can be especially well positioned to make contributions to this critical process, for, although handicapped in some respects, they are especially motivated to *enlarge* their selves and create alternative communities. The lack of comfort and integration of those who live on the fringes of society—their maladjustment and oppression—provides an incentive for social change, for the rearticulation of their own subjectivities, and for the creation of communities in which their selves can be accepted and flourish. Hence the critical and transformative potential of marginalized and oppressed subjectivities for rearticulating both individual and collective identities (we will return to this theme in the last chapter).

Mead's conversational account of the development of an individual self and the ever-present possibility of an enlarged mentality is complicated by the fact that individuals belong to a variety of groups or communities. This brings us to our second problem: the problem of *social and cultural diversity*. Mead acknowledges that individuals find themselves embedded in vast and heterogeneous social networks. But if an individual self is formed in conversation with the community to which the subject belongs, and she belongs to multiple communities, won't she develop multiple selves? Doesn't it follow that the different conversations with different communities that constitute the subject will endow her with a multiplicity of identities? This is in fact Mead's view. For Mead, "a multiple personality is in a certain sense normal" (MSS, p. 142). On Mead's view, the socialization of a subject in each particular group produces an identity structure: a self with a me and an I (an internalized set of attitudes characteristic of the group and subjective responses to those attitudes). On this view, the identity of an agent is composed of diverse and heterogeneous structures, of multiple I/me structures and therefore of multiple selves: "We divide ourselves up in all sorts of different selves with reference to our acquaintances. [. . .] There are all sorts of different selves answering to all sorts of different social reactions" (p.142). Each of the processes of socialization that contribute to the formation of identity shapes the subject as a partner in conversation in a particular way; that is, it endows her with a distinctive voice in a particular set of communicative interactions. In this sense an identity structure can be characterized as a distinctive voice. But an individual is the product of many different processes of socialization and, therefore, she is bound to contain many distinctive voices and thereby many identity structures. This is what I term "the thesis of the polyphony of identity"; namely, the thesis that one's identity is composed by a plurality of voices. The polyphony thesis is a way of developing, in conversational terms, the Hegelian idea of "inner diversity," that is, the idea of the internal diversification or constitutive fracture of the self. According to this thesis, an individual subjectivity—a self or ego—, far from being homogeneous and uniform, is composed of multiple voices. But how are these voices related to one another? Is this heterogeneous plurality of voices something final and inescapable?

There is an important tension in Mead's treatment of the polyphonic nature of the self. On the one hand, he characterizes individuality or uniqueness as a particular configuration of voices; and this seems to suggest that he subscribes to an unqualified version of the polyphony thesis. According to this view of unqualified polyphony, one's identity consists in the dynamic relation or movement, the internal conversation, among one's voices. An identity is a heterogeneous aggregate of selves or voices; and only in very specific contexts, under very restricted conditions of communication and social interaction, can we talk about a singular self or unique voice. These multiple, heterogeneous selves are in communication, but they are not subsumed under or unified by an overarching identity structure. Mead seems to endorse this view when he talks about multiple personality as the normal human condition. But on the other hand, the polyphony thesis becomes substantially qualified by Mead's appeals to "a unified self" (cf. e.g., MSS, p. 143). For Mead, a multiplicity of selves is unproblematic as long as the multiple selves are in communication and connected through memory, so that they can in principle be unified. But he describes the recalcitrant divisions of the self as pathological. According to Mead, the pathological phenomenon of *dissociation* arises with the establishment of disjointed internal mechanisms of communication. This occurs when the individual develops "two separate 'me's and 'I's, two different selves," with no communication between them and no common memory (p. 143). Mead tells us that "the pathological" aspect of this phenomenon resides in "the forgetting," in the "getting rid of certain bodily memories which would identify the individual to himself" (p.143). In Mead's eyes, this phenomenon qualifies as pathological because it constitutes an obstacle for the unification of the self.[11]

Mead's discussion of dissociated personalities leads to a qualified polyphonic view of identity. On this weak polyphonic view, plural selves are conceived as raw materials out of which an identity structure of a higher order, "a unified self," must emerge. So we have, on the one hand, what Mead calls "elementary selves," which result from specific processes of socialization, and, on the other hand, what we could call a *supraself,* which is internally produced, resulting from the unifying powers of internal communication and memory. It is important to note that although Mead relies here on the traditional *memory model of identity,*[12] this model is creatively transformed in his theory. The original and innovative elements that Mead's theory brings to the traditional account of the unity of the self relate to the communicative and social dimension of identity. According to Mead's view, the unity of the different parts of the self is not simply a matter of cognitive access, as the traditional memory model suggests, but also a matter of communicative interaction between the different parts of the self. So a unified self is the practical result of a communicative process; it is the product of symbolic agency and not of passive cognition. On the other hand, Mead's view underscores the social roots and the social consequences of the unity of the self, or of the lack thereof. A unified self is not simply the personal achievement of an individual, but the collective accomplishment of the community or communities involved in the processes of socialization: "The unity and structure of the complete self reflects the unity and structure of the social process as a whole; and each of the elementary selves of which it is composed reflects the unity and structure of one of the various aspects of that process in which the individual is implicated" (MSS, p. 144). Accordingly, on Mead's view, the dissociation of identity structures is treated as a psychological symptom of a social problem that calls not only for psychological treatment but also for social change. Dissociated selves result from a dysfunctional socialization[13] and, therefore, they signal a social problem that can only be remedied by structural transformations of the communities in which individuals are socialized.

Mead's social and communicative account of the unity of the self offers a solution to the problem of social and cultural diversity. This solution makes clear that the tension between a strong and a weak version of the polyphony thesis in Mead's view is resolved in favor of the latter. In the end Mead's theory supports only a qualified version of the polyphonic view of identity. In this theory, a plurality of radically heterogeneous voices is only admitted as a developmental stage of the self that needs to be overcome, whether spontaneously or through therapy and retraining. If the social environment gives adequate support to the development of the self, there will emerge internal conversational processes that put the different selves or identity structures of the individual in communication until a higher level of identity, "a unified self," is achieved. If this unification does not happen spontaneously, the individual will need therapy and processes of resocialization that can set up mechanisms of unification and establish communication between her "elementary selves." The processes of unification that Mead talks about do not seem to eliminate the "inner diversity" of identity, but they tame this diversity and bring it under the subjective organization and control of a unified self. So one's identity can still be said to be composed of plural voices; but these voices are domesticated: they are arranged and organized so that they can be heard at unison or in an orchestrated fashion. The ideal of the unity of the self is the ideal of the harmonization of one's voices. This ideal leads to a *choral version of the polyphony thesis*, according to which the self is understood as a *chorus* of voices. In fact, Mead himself uses the metaphor of the chorus in explaining the dramatic nature of self-consciousness. He talks about the harmonic participation of different "dramatis personae" in one's stream of consciousness and, in this context, he describes the self as "a fusion of the remembered actor and this accompanying chorus" (1913, p. 378).

The choral metaphor is unproblematic and can be in fact helpful if it is used simply to emphasize that in particular contexts the configuration of voices in which one's subjectivity consists can involve a voice in the foreground and a chorus of harmonic voices in the background. But choral polyphony is highly questionable as a normative ideal, that is, if, as in Mead's view, it involves a substantive normative claim about the unity that one's identity or self ought to exhibit. As a normative standard, the choral version of polyphony promulgates a very demanding ideal of unity and harmony that is not supported by an adequate justification. Through my discussions of Wittgenstein and Bourdieu in later sections, I will try to go beyond choral polyphony and toward a more thoroughgoing pluralistic view of polyphonic identity. My view moves toward a polyphonic model in which the tensions, conflicts, and divisions in one's identity are not necessarily pathological and can be fruitful and healthy aspects of the self. But by rejecting the normative ideal of unification as the guide to identity formation, I am not thereby proposing the normative ideal of diversification or division as an alternative. Although my view of identity puts the emphasis on the internal diversity of the self, it also allows for internal unity—a unity that always comes in degrees, contains heterogeneous elements, and requires hard work to be achieved and maintained. Indeed, one can argue that if there are only radical divisions and fractures, polyphony is destroyed, for, although polyphony requires a plurality of heterogeneous voices, it also requires *some degree* of harmony among these voices. Otherwise there would be only cacophony. As we shall see, on my view, the polyphonic unity of the self (when possible and desirable) is always a local, gradual, and context-dependent achievement that, far from erasing inner diversity, actually requires heterogeneous elements. In Mead's view, by contrast, it is assumed that there is an unqualified imperative of unification, that is, that the self should be unified in every respect, in every context, and at all times.

But where does the impetus toward unification come from? Mead gives no justification of the need to unify the different identity structures or selves that compose one's subjectivity, not even a pragmatic justification in terms of the subject's health or well-adjustment.[14] On Mead's view, the ideal of the unity of the self remains an unargued assumption inherited from the Hegelian philosophy of the subject. For Mead, the unity of the self is not the formal unity of a transcendental ego, as Kant would have it, but rather, a concrete historical unity that is the product of a dialectical process and contains the concrete experiential results accumulated in that process. In a Hegelian fashion, Mead conceives of the unified self as the telos that drives the dialectical process of identity formation, being both what completes the process and the underlying guiding principle that organizes and structures it. The Hegelian heritage of Mead's view becomes particularly clear with the emphasis he places on self-consciousness as that which completes the development of the self. Mead contends that while consciousness takes as its object particular experiences, roles, and attitudes and offers responses to them, the self-consciousness of a subject takes as its object an entire self, a complete identity structure. What characterizes self-consciousness, he tells us, is precisely the "recognition or appearance of a self as an object" (MSS, p. 169). Thanks to its synthesizing powers self-consciousness has the capacity to unify the different "elementary selves" that compose the individual subject. This synthesizing power is a cognitive power of reflection, which makes self-consciousness and the unified self that results from it *essentially cognitive phenomena*. "Self-consciousness, rather than affective experience with its motor accompaniments, provides the core and primary structure of the self, which is thus essentially a cognitive rather than an emotional phenomenon" (p. 173). Mead goes on to explain that "the essence of the self [. . .] is cognitive" and that it lies in the "internalized conversation," the "inner dramatization," orchestrated by self-consciousness, which is first and foremost "an intellectual process" (p.173). This "internalized conversation" produced and directed by one's self-consciousness has the potential to supply the subject with self-knowledge and self-control. The development of the self is thus characterized as a process that culminates with an autonomous self-consciousness that knows itself and is in control of its determinations.

Still under the sway of the philosophy of the subject, Mead's account of identity formation contains a residual cognitivism (and perhaps also a residual voluntarism) that becomes explicit with the Hegelian emphasis on self-consciousness and the synthesizing power of reflection. This cognitivism colors Mead's view of the production of an enlarged mentality that goes beyond the bounds of particular communities. For Mead, the process of enlarging the self has an essential cognitive dimension: it is a process of self formation that can take place only through the cognitive and reflective powers of the mind, through what he calls "the voice of reason" (MSS, p. 168). It is "the voice of reason" that makes it possible to transcend all communities, to extend indefinitely the critical process of departing from particular social groups. Because we can address ourselves not only in the voice of an other but also in "the voice of reason," because we can adopt a rational point of view that goes beyond the standpoint of any particular individual or community, there is no limit or stopping point to the process of enlarging the self, which can be continued indefinitely up to the point where the individual is standing over against all existing communities: "A person may reach a point of going against the whole world about him; he may stand out by himself over against it. But to do that he has to speak with the voice of reason to himself" (p.168). What does "the voice of reason" have to offer that cannot be provided by the voice of an imaginary other or the voice of a new, yet to be developed community? Here we reach Mead's *cosmopolitanism*[15]: by adopting a rational point of view, by speaking with "the voice of reason," we appeal to a universal community, a community that opens itself to the members of all communities. In this universal community particularity gets *aufgehoben*, that is, it gets transcended without being simply eliminated or overcome (differences are preserved but taken to a higher level). This is a universal community of partners in conversation, a communication community without limits.

Mead's cosmopolitanism emphasizes that a communication or speech community is the most inclusive community there can be. He distinguishes between concrete social groups and abstract ones (cf. MSS, pp. 157–58): the former are those in which individual members are directly related to one another and in contact through their interactions (e.g., clubs, corporations, etc.); the latter are those in which there is only an indirect and abstract relation among their members (e.g., the class of creditors, the category of taxpayers, etc.). Mead points out that the formation of abstract groups makes possible "the widening and ramifying and enriching of the social relations among all the individual members of the given society as an organized and unified whole" (p. 157). Abstract social bonds allow individuals to enter into "definite social relations (however indirect) with an almost infinite number of other individuals" (p.157). Mead argues that among the abstract social groups "the one which is most inclusive and extensive is, of course, the one defined by the logical universe of discourse" (p. 157). The voice of reason, of a communicative rationality, binds all language users together in a universal community of communication. The abstract social bond that brings us all together into this universal community is a communicative relation, "a relation arising from the universal functioning of gestures as significant symbols in the general human social process of communication" (p. 158).

So at the core of Mead's cosmopolitanism is the idea of a communicative rationality universally shared by all language users. This idea has been elaborated

by Habermas's theory of communicative action and universal pragmatics
(cf. his 1987, 1990, and 1992). Drawing heavily on Mead (among others),
Habermas has developed a postmetaphysical universalism based on a formal-
pragmatic account of communication and its normative presuppositions (see
esp. 1992, pp. 149–204). The Habermasian appropriation of Mead for a universalist perspective presents a problem for the interpretation and use of his
theory in this book: How can Mead's views be incorporated in a contextualist perspective? Isn't Mead's universalism incompatible with a contextualist
approach to meaning and identity? Mead's idea of a universal community
of communication may appear to be contrary to the pragmatic contextualism of this book, but I will argue that it is not so when properly understood.
And even if some of Mead's ideas and theses have to be revised or qualified to be rendered compatible with the contextualist approach defended in
this book, his theory is still for the most part an ally of my pragmatic contextualism. As argued above, Mead's sociogenetic view is not as radical as
it could and should be because it retains some cognitivist elements of the
Hegelian philosophy of the subject. As argued below, my pragmatic contextualism involves a more thoroughgoing pluralistic perspective that is not qualified by the unifying powers of a cognitive (and volitional) subjectivity and its
transcendental communicative rationality.[16] I do take issue with the ideal of
unity and self-knowledge underlying Mead's characterization of the mature
and autonomous self. But the stronger polyphonic view of identity I develop
below through Wittgenstein and Bourdieu retains the central ideas of Mead's
sociogenetic view. Therefore, Mead's interactional account of meaning and
identity remains a central pillar of the pragmatic contextualism developed in
this book. As a conclusion to this section, I will try to explain how Mead's
claims about the "universality" of communication and of an "abstract" speech
community are not only compatible but should in fact be considered an integral part of a contextualist perspective.

Mead's claims about a *universal* community of communication refer
back to his account of the *universality* of meaning previously developed. He
devotes an entire section of *Mind, Self, and Society* to explain what he calls the
"universality" of meaning (§12, pp. 82–90). This account makes clear that for
Mead semantic universality is not at odds with particularity and concreteness.
On Mead's view, meanings arise and remain tied to particular communicative
interactions and the concrete experiential contents negotiated in those interactions: "The significant gesture or symbol always presupposes for its significance the social process of experience and behavior in which it arises" (p. 89).
Mead explains the universality of meanings in terms of their intersubjectivity:
that meanings are "universal" means that they are *shareable*. For Mead, meanings are in principle universally shareable; but this universality does not deny
their particularity and their concrete origins and trajectory. What is crucial

here again is the reflexivity or reversibility of communicative perspectives; this is what makes meanings *universal* in Mead's sense:

> Meaning is that which can be indicated to others while it is by the same process indicated to the indicating individual. [. . .] It must therefore be a universal, at least in the identity which belongs to *the different perspectives which are organized in the single perspective*, and in so far as the principle of organization is one which admits of *other perspectives than those actually present*, the universality may be logically indefinitely extended. (MSS, p. 89; my emphasis)

So by underscoring the "universality" of meaning Mead wants to underscore that a meaning involves a commonality that is not restricted to the particular subjects involved in communicative interaction, but a commonality in which others can, in principle, participate. For Mead, a meaning is a communicative structure that involves the unification of multiple perspectives; and this communicative structure is always open; that is, the unification of perspectives is never finished or complete but always open to new possible perspectives. Thus the universality of meaning refers to the *indefinite* character of its sociality. So to say that meanings are universal is to say that they can contain an indefinite number of different perspectives, that is, that they are indefinitely open to "other perspectives than those actually present," that they have an *elsewhere* orientation. The ever present possibility of another perspective is what defines the peculiar brand of contextualism I defend: what I have called "a view from elsewhere." My contextualist view of communication underscores that what is most important about the semantic structures produced in communicative interactions (as well as about the identities of speaker/agents that develop through those interactions) is their *openness to eccentric standpoints*. No matter how incipiently formed, a meaning always integrates more than one communicative perspective; and, moreover, the integration of perspectives that fuels the semantic life of a meaning structure is never completed: it is a task that remains indefinitely open. The plurality of perspectives or viewpoints to be integrated in a meaning structure cannot be self-contained. No matter how much speakers or their practice may try to contain this plurality (more on this later in my discussion of censorship), meaning structures keep exceeding themselves for as long as they are used in communication; they keep being modified by an unpredictable and uncontrollable dialogue of voices. By analogy with my discussion of identity in this section, we can call this phenomenon "the polyphony of meaning": a meaning always involves a tacit dialogue of voices or communicative perspectives, an open-ended dialogue that can be indefinitely extended.

Mead's view of the universality of a speech community has to be understood in the same way as his view of the universality of meaning. A communication community is universal because it can be extended indefinitely, because it remains always open to new perspectives and voices. This *radical openness* is at the core of Mead's concept of universality. It is important to note that this concept is not a purely formal and logical concept. It is more than a mere extensional or quantificational category. It involves a particular kind of *attitude* and a particular kind of *agency*. A universal community of communication is founded by and based on the attitude of its members: the attitude of striving toward inclusion, the attitude of recognizing an indefinite number of diverse others as equals, as fellow communication partners. According to Mead, this cosmopolitan attitude is already present in the normative attitude that democracy calls for: "democracy [. . .] is an attitude which depends upon the type of self which goes with the universal relations of *brotherhood*" (MSS, p. 286; my emphasis).[17] But this inclusive attitude has to be reflected in our interactional agency as well. Mead emphasizes that our communities must undergo a constant process of "social reconstruction" in order to be rendered more inclusive (cf. pp. 308ff). There is no universal community of communicative partners unless there is an active struggle toward inclusiveness that is constantly sustained and renewed by all participants.

Thus understood, universality is not contrary to plurality and diversity. A universal community of communication, in Mead's sense, is not at all a homogeneous space but, quite the contrary, a space of heterogeneous differences that mutually support each other. On this multicultural version of Mead's cosmopolitanism, diversity is not only formally recognized, but is in fact the social fabric that brings individuals together and becomes part of their own identity. Mead argues that "the implication" of a cosmopolitan democratic way of life is "that the individual can be as highly developed as lies within the possibilities of his own inheritance, and still can enter into the attitudes of the others whom he affects" (MSS, p. 326). It is important to note that our progress toward inclusiveness is achieved both at the social and at the psychological level; that is, it involves the critical transformation of both community structures and identity structures. In this sense, Mead emphasizes that the critical and transformative process of "social reconstruction" goes hand in hand with an analogous critical and transformative process of "self reconstruction" (p. 309). The product of this process of self reconstruction through the recognition of diverse cultural others as conversational partners is an *enlarged self*. So we can now talk about an enlarged self or an enlarged mentality in a different and richer sense. An enlarged, cosmopolitan self is one that recognizes and embraces diversity and is always open to acknowledge new eccentric viewpoints or voices. But such a self is not necessarily one that stands all by herself over against all particular communities (although, as we saw, Mead does occasionally mention this possibility); an enlarged, cosmopolitan self does not have to define herself against all cultural conventions and traditions.

The interpretation of Mead's theory I have articulated makes his cosmopolitan view of identity and community perfectly compatible with my contextualist view from elsewhere. A similar interpretation has been fully developed and defended by Aboulafia (2001), whose account of Mead's cosmopolitan self contrasts sharply with the formal, universalist interpretation of Habermas. Aboulafia and Habermas have antithetical interpretations of Mead's account of postconventional identities or enlarged selves. The crucial issue in their dispute is the following: How are we to understand the appeal to a wider community implicit in a postconventional identity? How are we to understand the universal communication community presupposed by an enlarged self that goes beyond the bounds of particular communities and traditions? In relation to this issue Aboulafia develops two important criticisms of Habermas's interpretation and use of Mead's theory. Both of these critical arguments support my contextualist appropriation of Mead's ideas.

In the first place, Aboulafia criticizes the Habermasian claim that the condition of possibility of genuine individuality is the *formal anticipation* of a universal community of communication. According to Habermas, the solution of the conventionality of the 'me' is given by the 'I,' which draws on its communicative capacities to project or anticipate an ideal speech situation in which the self can be defined in terms that transcend any given community: "The 'I' itself *projects* the context of interaction that first makes the reconstruction of a shattered conventional identity possible on a higher level" (1992, p. 187). Since we cannot step outside our social skin, what the 'I' does is to step into a counterfactual situation, that is, to appeal to an ideal kind of sociality imagined by the counterfactual supposition of a universal communication community. Habermas remarks that individualism has to be considered "the flip-side of universalism," for genuine individuality requires a universalistic idealization: "the idealizing supposition of a universalistic form of life, in which everyone can take up the perspective of everyone else and can count on reciprocal recognition by everybody" (1992, p. 186). Habermas's formal universalism is grounded in the normative structure of communication. He argues that the idealized anticipation or counterfactual projection of an unlimited communication community "is backed up by the structure of language itself" (p. 188). Drawing on the normative presuppositions of communication, a postconventional identity can develop "in the *anticipation* of symmetrical relations of unforced reciprocal recognition" (1992, p. 188: my emphasis). On Habermas's view, the individuality of this enlarged self results from recognizing itself "as the alter ego of *all* others in every community" (1992, p. 187). Aboulafia replies that Habermas "is pressing for an *abstract* approach to individuality that Mead would find inadequate" (2001, p. 69; my emphasis). He emphasizes the interactional dimension of Mead's approach and argues that what has primacy in this approach is not a formal anticipation or projection, but our interactive agency. Our actual interaction with particular others remains primary and there is no substitute for it. Aboulafia agrees with Habermas that in Mead the notion of an unlimited communication community functions "as a guiding ideal of interaction" (p. 66). But he argues that, on Mead's view, what characterizes a postconventional identity is being open for a substantive dialogue with specific others, not a formal and counterfactual relationship to an anticipated unlimited communication community. We need to remember that, for Mead, a self can become determinate only in and through particular interactions with specific others ("selves can only exist in definite relationships to other selves" (MSS, p. 164). So, as Aboulafia puts it, on Mead's view "we do not seek to be assured simply that we are unique, but that we are unique in some specific manner, in relation to a vital community" (p. 69), a community that is more than an idealization or a counterfactual supposition.

In the second place, Aboulafia argues against Habermas's way of linking individuality to personal autonomy. In order to decouple these notions it is important to distinguish between the pursuit of individuality and the practice of individualism.[18] If to be a unique individual is to be autonomous, the fully developed self must transcend her social determinations and return from social mediations to herself. Aboulafia shows that this is at odds with crucial elements of Mead's social theory of the self. To begin with, the idea of the self's return to itself, transcending her social determinations, suggests a kind of purity that our individuality (no matter how *post*conventional) cannot have. On Mead's view, autonomy as a pure return from the social and conventional is an impossible and unproductive illusion. As Aboulafia puts it, "Mead would insist that no return is "pure," and it is possible only by way of the mediation of a 'me'" (2001, p. 67). On the other hand, the Habermasian view of autonomy as central to individuality also runs contrary to Mead's view of the uncertainty and elusiveness of the I, which makes it impossible for the self to acquire self-mastery by means of self-knowledge and self-control. As Aboulafia remarks, "the notion of an 'I' that can return to itself and assure itself of its autonomy and individuality clearly departs from Mead's understanding of [. . .] the 'I' as a 'fictitious 'I' always out of sight of himself.' [. . .] Habermas is sneaking in some sort of a quasitranscendental ego that threatens the *existential* spontaneity of the 'I'" (pp. 67–68). Finally, Habermas's emphasis on autonomy distorts the relationship of a postconventional identity to cultural traditions and communities, and misunderstands the significance of one's relation to cultural others as well as the significance of one's ties to one's own cultural roots. Since for Habermas the main challenge for the process of enlarging the self is the attainment of autonomy, he conceives of cultural conventions and traditions as constraints. By contrast, Aboulafia seems to suggest that the cultural and conventional should be conceived as an enabling condition for the development of the self. In order to develop an enlarged self we do not have to define ourselves in contraposition to cultural traditions and communities, but through them, critically positioning ourselves in diverse cultural environments. Cultural diversity provides the means and the opportunity to develop new forms of identity. The multiplicity of diverse others we face in multicultural societies constitutes the perfect social environment for the formation of enlarged and postconventional selves, for it presents us with the challenge of developing our identity "in the face of having to face so many others, so many mirrors through which we examine and, in part, come to be who we are" (p. 69). In order to achieve a unique individuality we do not have to define ourselves negatively with respect to the multiple others we face, or with respect to the multiple selves we develop in our interactions with them. In order to attain an enlarged postconventional identity we do not have to simply oppose or reject the conventional identities we have assumed, the 'me''s we have developed through different processes of socialization. A postconventional identity does not call for an oppositional relation to cultural selves, but for the dialectical integration of this multiplicity of selves. As Aboulafia puts it, "the major challenge a post-conventional identity must meet is the integration and maintenance of a multitude of selves" (p. 68). Here too what needs to be emphasized is the interactional dimension of Mead's account, which explains the dynamic (and not merely oppositional) relation between the multiple selves that compose one's identity.

In this section we have seen how Mead's interactional theory of the development of the self offers a sociogenetic account of the contextual determinacy of identity: selves become contextually determinate through a dialectic of mutual recognition that is played out in communicative interactions or "conversations." First through overt conversations with others and later through internalized conversations, the self acquires different degrees of determinacy which remain dependent on particular conversational contexts in which the self is recognized. In conversation with specific others one internalizes different forms of address that become different internal voices. Thus through the internalization of social recognition there emerges a definite self that contains inner diversity (i.e., the constitutive, internal presence of others). This diversified self can then engage in conversation with itself since it contains different voices that can enter into dialogue. But we should not assume that this dialogue *always* occurs, or even that its occurrence is *always* desirable. In some cases particular paths of communication among the inner voices of one's self may be heavily constrained or even entirely blocked for good reasons (e.g., to protect the individual from an emotional breakdown). In other cases the failure of communication among one's diverse selves may give rise to pathological personalities and dysfunctional behavior. The optimal form of internal communication for one's identity is something that has to be assessed piecemeal and in context-specific ways.[19] Through the self's inner conversation, through the dialogue between the 'me' and the 'I,' new identity structures develop. These identity structures in turn call for further conversations with others, for they stand in need of recognition, which may require the social transformation of existing communities or the formation of new ones.

In the next section I will focus on a different aspect of the dialectical formation of identity through social recognition. I will use Wittgensteinian ideas to elucidate the *dialectic between identity and differences* that underlies the formation of identity through social interaction and through the membership in communities. The dialectic of identity and differences is indeed a social dialectic that proceeds by means of processes of recognition: identity and differences are formed through intersubjective interactions, through the agents' transactional recognitions (and misrecognitions) of their similarities and differences. But these similarities and differences are not simply emergent effects of intersubjective processes of recognition, mere byproducts. They are, rather, presupposed as well as performatively formed by those processes. There is no recognition of identity without the (tacit) recognition of complex networks of interrelated similarities and differences. This is very messy, but no one said it was going to be neat. There is no reason to expect that our identities as speakers and agents will be neat; nor can we assume (without argument) that such neatness should be a requirement or adequacy condition for a philosophical account of identity. In fact, my Wittgensteinian account below shows that identities are intrinsically and unavoidably messy.

2.1.b. To Be *and* Not to Be: This Mess Called My Identity

In this section, instead of talking about identity in general, my discussion will focus on specific aspects of one's identity: in particular, gender, sexuality, race, and ethnicity. I will argue for two theses. First, I will argue that *identity is bound up with difference* and that all identity categories are intrinsically heterogeneous and necessarily unstable. Secondly, I will argue that identity is a *multifaceted* phenomenon that requires a *pluralistic or multidimensional* logic. On my view, the different aspects of identity are not developed discretely, one at a time or in coordination; the processes that shape gender, sexuality, race, and ethnicity are inextricably interwoven in such a way that their separation (even if only analytic or strategic) is distorting and politically dangerous, for it occludes relations of interdependence and it blocks paths for resistance and subversion. In order to develop both of these theses I will draw on the philosophy of the later Wittgenstein and on a body of literature that is at the crossroads of gender studies, queer theory, and critical race theory. In particular, I will elaborate on ideas derived from the performativity theory of gender and sexuality[20] and on critical challenges raised by feminists of color.[21]

What is the relevant notion of *identity* that is invoked when we talk about gender, sexuality, race, and ethnicity? It is certainly not the absolute identity of indiscernibles: identity in every respect. (It is far from clear that *any* living thing can be identical to itself in this absolute way.) When we talk about people of the same gender, the same sexual orientation, the same race, or the same ethnicity, we are talking about *relative* identity, that is, identity in some respect. But even this notion of relative identity needs to be further qualified if we want to avoid an overly strong reading of identity claims. When identity is relativized to specific respects, it does not preclude difference in other respects. But does a relative identity entail the absence of difference in the relevant respect? It depends. Sometimes we say that two things are identical, for example, in color, in a *strict* sense: they have exactly the same shade of color, with the same brightness, the same intensity, and so on. But sometimes we ascribe identity of color in a *lax* sense even if there are differences in shade, brightness, intensity, and so on. This lax sense of relative identity is intimately related to the notion of *similarity*. Things that are similar in some respect can nevertheless be somewhat different in that respect (let alone in others); but their differences are overlooked in a context in which they are brought close enough to each other so that they can be grouped together and treated as members of the same category or *family*. So similarity operates in a *context of difference* in a double sense: things are regarded as similar against the background of differences in other respects as well as differences in the relevant respect that are considered negligible and are in fact neglected. We can *see* (the relevant) similarities only insofar as we make ourselves *blind* to (the irrelevant) differences. And this sight and this blindness presuppose each other and cannot be understood independently: they are both required by the perception of similarity.

One of the lessons we can learn from Wittgenstein's later philosophy is that most of the concepts we use to describe ourselves and the world around us are not applied according to fixed criteria of strict identity. When we use a concept such as "game" or "chair," we treat all kinds of different things as *the same* although they are not strictly identical in any respect; that is, in our categorizations different things are treated as instances of the *same* category even though there is no feature (or set of features) that they all have in common. Many different kinds of activities are called games and many different kinds of artifacts are called chairs; and we can always add new items to the list of things that fall under these concepts (we can always invent new kinds of games and produce new kinds of chairs). Wittgenstein suggested that these concepts are like *families*, whose members resemble one another in many different ways: some may have similar hair, others a similar nose, others may share a particular way of talking, or a similar laughter. Families are composed of heterogeneous elements; there is nothing in particular that all their members must have: they simply exhibit some similarities, they share certain "family resemblances,"[22] but there is no fixed set of necessary and sufficient conditions that determine membership. As Wittgestein puts it, what brings together and keeps together the members of those categories that function like families is "a complicated network of similarities overlapping and criss-crossing" (PI §66). Wittgenstein's analogy between the strength of a concept and the strength of a thread illustrates this point: "we extend our concept [. . .] as in spinning a thread we twist fibre on fibre. And the strength of the thread does not reside in the fact that some one fibre runs through its whole length, but in the overlapping of many fibres" (PI §67).

Since, as we just saw, similarity is bound up with differences in a twofold sense, this network of similarities in which the familial identity of the members of a concept consists must be accompanied by *two distinct networks of overlapping and criss-crossing differences*: one network of differences that sets apart the members of the family from the members of other families; and another network composed of those differences among the members of the family themselves that lurk in the background and are disregarded for the sake of familial identity. It is important to note that the relationship that holds between these networks is a *dynamic* one: differences that today set apart one family from another may become inconsequential tomorrow; and, on the other hand, internal differences that are considered negligible today may grow to be important differences tomorrow, even to the point of excluding individuals from membership in the family. At the same time, these dynamic fluctuations between the networks of differences correspond to transformations in the network of similarities that sustains familial identity, for all these networks are mutually dependent and they are shaped simultaneously. Thus the analogy between families and concepts underscores change: a family is a living unit whose members come and go; and, similarly, what is covered by a concept is subject to change and must be left open. Moreover, even when the extension of the concept does not change, even when the membership in the family remains the same, the relations among the members of the family (as well as their relations with other families) change as differences become visible and family ties are relaxed.[23]

The familial view of identity based on Wittgenstein's account of categorization suggests two points, namely, that identity can be thought of as something *heterogeneous*, based on diversity, as well as as something *unstable*, subject to fluctuation. This familial view of identity has been recently applied to ethnic identity in order to show that the quest for ethnic purity is misguided. This quest presupposes the homogeneity and fixity of ethnicity; but when ethnic groups are conceptualized as families, it becomes clear that the homogeneity and fixity of ethnic identities are nothing but myths. In this vein, in his familial account of Hispanic identity, Jorge Gracia emphasizes that families are not homogeneous wholes composed of pure elements: "They include contradictory elements and involve mixing. Indeed, contradiction and mixing seem to be of the essence, for a living unity is impossible without contradiction and heterogeneity" (2000,

p. 50). Gracia argues that this is particularly true of the Hispanic family that has been constituted through mixing or *mestizaje* at all levels: it is *mestizaje* that characterizes all aspects of Hispanic life from language, art, and religion to music, cuisine, and clothing. Given this heterogeneous character, it is not surprising that all attempts to reduce the shared identity of Hispanics to common properties fail. These failures have led many to conclude that we should give up Hispanic identity and retreat to national identities (Mexican, Cuban, Argentinean, etc.)—but, as it turns out, these collective identities pose the same problems. This reaction is based on the essentialist assumption that there is no shared identity when there are no common features. But this assumption is a misconception. The unity of Hispanics as an ethnic group cannot be established at the expense of diversity, but on the basis of it. As Gracia (2000) puts it, the unity of Hispanics is "a unity in diversity," not a unity of commonality, but a *unity of community*: the unity of a *family* formed by "a unique web of changing historical relations" (p. 49). This familial-historical view calls our attention to the contingencies of the past that have contributed to the formation of our Hispanic identity; and it underscores that the future of our identity remains open and therefore presents us with a task for which we have to take responsibility. According to this view, an ethnic identity is something dynamic that is always in the making and can never be fixed once and for all.[24]

This familial view can be extended to apply to other dimensions of identity that involve a bond between an individual and a group. Gender, sexuality, and race seem to be amenable to this treatment; they seem to involve a shared identity that can be analyzed in terms of membership in a community or family. But before I try to show how the familial view can be used to shed light on identity categories, two caveats are in order. First, as used in my Wittgensteinian view, the notion of a family should not be understood as a purely biological concept but, rather, as a hybrid notion that contains *social and political* elements as well as biological ones. Families are not just biological groups, but social structures and legal institutions. It would be a mistake to think that only biological features constitute adequate criteria for familial membership. (Indeed, people can gain and lose parental rights on the basis of nonbiological considerations.) Secondly, we have to keep in mind that there are all kinds of family and, therefore, only a *pluralistic* notion of "family" can be useful for the analysis of collective identities. My Wittgensteinian approach does not rest on any specific conception of the family; in particular, it is not dependent upon the patriarchal familial model that has been dominant in the West. As Jacquelyn Dowd Hall (1983), for one, has noted, given the social, political, and legal institutions of the United States, the appeal to family values typically involves a rhetoric of custody and protection that has been at the service of a masculinist ideology. However, power can be distributed among the members of a family in many different ways: there may or may not be a head of the family;

there may or may not be differential authority among family members at all. Far from being complacent with the patriarchal model of family relations, the genealogical approach and the comparative perspective behind my familial view are intended to subvert this model and to be critical of oppressive familial structures in general. In this sense, my familial view connects with ongoing efforts in the literature on identity (esp. in feminist theory[25] and queer studies[26]) to rearticulate the very notion of a family and to subvert what is typically understood by "family values."

With these caveats, I propose to use the metaphorical notion of a family as the guide for the analysis of identity categories. But like all metaphorical conceptualizations, the familial view of identity categories has its dangers and limitations. In her critical review of my essay "Identity Trouble" (2003c), Marilyn Frye (2005) has issued important warnings for the familial metaphor. Frye warns that this metaphor can reinforce certain biases about identity: in particular, an *individualist* bias and a biased tendency toward the *unification and purification* of the raw materials that make up an identity.[27] In the first place, Frye argues that the notion of family resemblance presupposes individualism because it is based on the preexistence of attributes or traits of *individuals* independently of their membership in groups. But, as I argue in my reply (2005a) to Frye, the similarities and differences among the members of a family do not emanate from preexisting individual features, nor are they created ex nihilo by membership in groups or families and then conferred upon individuals. These similarities and differences are fluid, dynamic, unstable, and they involve a constant process of negotiation that involves individuals, groups, and subgroups at different levels and in different contexts (economic, legal, political, religious, cultural, etc.). In the second place, Frye argues that the notion of *resemblance* is ultimately not appropriate for the kind of heterogeneous pluralistic view of identity that I defend because this notion retains the logic of *unity and purity*. Frye's claim is that although the notion of family resemblance admits heterogeneity in the raw materials of identity, it nevertheless privileges unity and purity because it demands the unification of those elements in order to compose a particular configuration of identity. The claim is that resemblance requires unity, harmony, and congruency; and it forces us to work toward the dissolution and overcoming of any kind of tension, conflict, or disunity.

I do not think that the notion of family resemblance requires or presupposes the logic of unity and purity. I do not think it is necessary to unify or purify similarities and differences in order to maintain the familial ties of collective identities. One can enter a familial group in many different ways and these different points of entry are often maintained even when they are in tension: for example, some individuals are included in the category "woman" because of their anatomical features, others because of their reproductive

capacities, others because of their chromosomes, others because of their performance. Familial identities are not threatened (at least not always) by the
existing conflicts (sometimes even contradictions) among familial relations.
The suggestion of my view is that the goal or ideal should not be to erase
the destabilizing differences, excesses, and heterogeneities that create conflicts
and tensions (*identity troubles*) but, rather, to create contexts and practices in
which these differences, excesses, and heterogeneities can be enjoyed without
rejection, exclusion, or stigmatization. There is nothing in my view that suggests that the struggle for solidarity and the fight for (social/political/cultural/
legal) recognition of differences should require the unification and purification of similarities and dissimilarities. In fact, this would be to capitulate to
the homogenizing social forces that try to domesticate our identities, that is,
it would be to accept that nonconforming identities cannot flourish without
sacrificing their differences, that one cannot live properly with conflict, tension, and instability.

As Frye points out, there have been Wittgensteinian researchers in Cognitive Science—most notably Rosch and Mervis (1975)—who have argued
that perceptual filtering and focusing is required in order to make some similarities and some differences salient in perception and cognition. But, pace
Rosch and her colleagues, family resemblances do not have to be conceived
in terms of prototypes or paradigmatic exemplars; and they do not need to
contain focal points which relegate to the *periphery* of the group those members who do not exhibit the stereotypical features that have become salient.
My goal is precisely to sketch a more pluralistic model in which there are
multiple networks of similarities and differences that offer different configurations of familial identity, without these being competing configurations that
we need to harmonize or that we need to adjudicate between and choose
from. But we do have to keep in mind that the resemblances that become stereotypical or paradigmatic typically operate in the unitary way suggested by
Frye; and indeed there are forces—social, political, and cultural forces—that
try to impose that unitary logic on the dynamic life of identity groups. This
last point is emphasized by Peg O'Connor (2005) in her use of my familial
view to explain how *privileged identities* are formed and how they maintain
their privileged status. O'Connor notes that the internal dynamic of group
identity as I describe it is susceptible to being exploited by privileged classes
of subjects to maintain their privileged status. Privileged subjects within a
group enjoy a disproportionate amount of power and agency in the group
and are, therefore, better positioned to manipulate the family resemblances
that matter for familial membership. These subjects will make salient those
similarities and differences that best serve their purposes for including and
excluding people in groups and for maintaining relations of subordination
within and across groups. Privileged subjectivities have a vested interest in

creating a *center* and a *periphery* within identity groups so that there are fixed prototypes of identity that can signify the position or status of subjects within these groups. The perpetuation of privilege requires the manipulation of the networks of similarities and differences that sustain familial identities so as to create the illusion of *essentialism*, that is, of there being essential similarities and differences that can keep people in and out of groups or in particular subordinate positions within groups. This essentializing strategy tries to domesticate and contain the fluidity and heterogeneity of identity by reifying and universalizing similarities and differences so that they become fixed and homogeneous. The struggle against marginalization, exclusion, and oppression requires the neutralization and critical contestation of this essentializing strategy. This is why it is so important, in order to resist essentialism and the relations of privilege and subordination it sustains, that we call attention to the heterogeneous pluralism of identity that my familial view underscores. Similarities and differences that are claimed to be stereotypical and essential need to be constantly subject to critical contestation. My familial analysis of the internal structure of identity categories can be used to develop strategies of political contestation that can subvert the normative structure of identity categories. But it is important to keep in mind that the familial analysis can also be used to develop political strategies for maintaining privilege and subordination and for creating divisions within and across groups.

We must exercise caution in our deployments of the familial metaphor, for there are indeed philosophical and political dangers in the use of this metaphor. In order to determine whether it is helpful to think of different aspects of identity in familial terms, I propose to focus on the following two questions: How does one become a member of these families? and How are these families related to one another? It does not seem implausible to suggest that the capacity of the familial view to give good answers to these questions will be tantamount to its capacity to shed light on gender, sexuality, race, and ethnicity. It is also my belief that the familial view of identity can have political benefits as well as analytical ones, for a better understanding of identity categories can facilitate the development of political formations for the liberation of identity.

How does one become a member of those "families" designated by identity categories such as "woman," "lesbian," "Hispanic . . ."? A first step toward a Wittgensteinian answer to this question is to point out that membership in these categories is not *determined* by facts. This is not to say that facts are irrelevant to the question of membership. There are indeed facts of many kinds (biological, historical, social, biographical, etc.) that bear on this question. The point is that these facts do not speak for themselves; we speak for them. And we can only do so in discursive *contexts*, by means of discursive *practices*, and according to discursive *norms*. This claim, that familial identity is shaped in and through normatively structured and situated practices (or "language games"), already contains the three crucial ingredients of my Wittgensteinian view: *contextuality*, *performativity*, and *normativity*. Only in specific contexts, through chains of performances, and through the norms constantly reenacted in them, can the membership of particular things in particular families be decided. As Wittgenstein argues, if we abstract from contexts, practices, and norms, the question of membership becomes indeterminate and cannot be answered: on an absolute perspective, everything is similar to everything else and also different from everything else in an indefinite number of respects, and familial identity appears as utterly arbitrary. But the question of membership is not indeterminate and arbitrary when it is properly conceptualized as something context dependent, action based, and normatively regulated. As we saw, familial identity is sustained by interrelated networks of similarities and differences; and these networks become alive through practices (or "language games") in which certain things are treated as similar and others as different. These practices do not take place in a vacuum, but in concrete contexts in which things are identified and grouped together; and these contexts are structured by tacit norms (or normative expectations) that are exhibited in the behavior of the participants. By being trained into these practices one develops an eye for similarities and differences (which, as we saw, involves both sight and blindness). One's grasp of familial identities is thus domesticated.

What are the mechanisms that shape our sight and blindness with respect to similarities and differences? More specifically, we want to know the particular mechanisms at play when we are not simply grouping things into families, but we are being identified and identifying ourselves as members of certain families. There are two obvious candidates that seem to go along with the perception of similarities and differences respectively: *identification* and *counteridentification*. We can ascribe a familial identity to someone (or to ourselves) by identifying this person with the members of that family, that is, by construing her identity through her participation in the network of similarities that tie the members of that family together: thus we can see someone as a woman by stressing her similarities with other women. But one can also acquire a familial identity in opposition to the members of other families, by having one's identity being looked at through the network of differences that separates one family from others: thus we can see someone as a woman by stressing her differences with men. Both the perception of similarity involved in identification and the perception of difference involved in counteridentification are crucially dependent on a corresponding *blindness*. We are certainly different from those we identify with in many ways; and we are certainly similar to those we counteridentify with in many ways. But we are blind to these differences and similarities in the contexts of, and for the purposes of, identification and counteridentification. If the blindness of these mechanisms of identity formation was absolute and irreparable, we would fall neatly into identity categories; and our "families" or identity groups would be completely rigid and monolithic, with clear-cut relations of inclusion and exclusion at their foundations. But our familial identities are far messier than that, often involving relations of inclusion and exclusion at the same time, and sometimes falling into the cracks between identification and counteridentification. Who hasn't had the experience of not fitting completely into a preestablished mold of identity, of feeling left out while being included?

There is identity trouble everywhere. There are all kinds of identity trouble that afflict our "families." The most radical kind of trouble is that of those whose identity is systematically excluded from all families, those invisible orphans whose identity is not recognized at all. But the members of identity groups are not free from trouble. The sources of these troubles are as varied as the troubles themselves. Identity trouble can be caused by a failure to identify (counteridentifying with the members of one's family would be an example). It can also be due to a failure to counteridentify (not seeing one's oppressor as different from or in opposition to oneself is a trouble of this kind). But identity trouble persists even when processes of identification and counteridentification are in place and working at their best. The kind of identity trouble that I'm interested in for the purpose of my argument here is that which is rooted in the *blindness* to similarities and differences that accompanies familial identity and the relations of exclusion and inclusion on which it is built. This blindness hides the structural messiness that is inscribed in the very core of familial identity, a messiness that consists in the heterogeneous and fluctuating character of the interlocking networks of similarities and differences that sustain identity. This messiness can come to the surface at any given time and often does. When it does, we feel ill at ease with the members of our family, we feel that we don't quite belong. This occurs when our sight is restored and we are no longer blind to our differences with our family members and our similarities to members of other families. This is what feminist theorists and queer theorists have termed *disidentification.* Judith Butler describes it as the "experience of *misrecognition,* this uneasy sense of standing under a sign to which one does and does not belong"(1993, p. 219).

Disidentification could be described as a particularly lucid kind of identification or counteridentification; that is, as a way of identifying with the members of a family without losing sight of one's differences from them, or a way of counteridentifying with the members of other families while seeing one's similarities with them. However, it would be wrong to construe disidentification as a mere special case of identification and counteridentification. This construal would miss what is most characteristic about the relation of disidentification, namely, that it brings both similarities and differences simultaneously to bear on one's identity. Disidentificatory relations highlight the messiness of the process of identity formation, which is not reducible to simple relations of identification and counteridentification. The mechanism of disidentification messes things up and creates trouble for the established networks of similarities and differences that sustain familial identities. As José Muñoz (1999) puts it, "to disidentify is to read oneself and one's own life narrative in a moment, object, or subject that is not culturally coded to 'connect' with the disidentifying subject" (p. 12). Muñoz is quick to point out that this is not simply "to pick and choose what one takes out of an identification" (or of a counteridentification), but it involves a much deeper transformation of one's identity and one's identity relations with others. For example, in his analysis of different instances of disidentification in performance art, Muñoz examines ways in which gay Latinos disidentify with cultural images of Hispanic masculinity and how their subversive rearticulations of these images can contribute to the transformation of cultural paradigms of identity.

Butler has characterized the subversive potential of disidentification better than anybody else. On her view, disidentification contributes to the destabilization of the signifiers of identity and triggers a process of resignification. As Butler puts it, "to be constituted" by a signifier of identity is "to be compelled to cite or repeat or mime" the signifier itself, whose future depends on a "citational chain," that is, a chain of signification that operates through an insistent citing of the signifier. But this performative iterability of the signifiers of identity involves *resignification*, that is, "a repetition that fails to repeat loyally, a reciting of the signifier that must commit a disloyalty against identity—a catechresis—in order to secure its future" (1993, p. 220). For Butler, disidentification is the source of resistance to the sedimentation of signifiers; and as "a site of rearticulations," it offers a "discursive occasion for hope" (p. 219). In her exploration of "the possibilities of politicizing *dis*identification," Butler emphasizes the importance of being "critically queer" (p. 219 and pp. 223ff). The political vindication of disidentification is the critical affirmation of queerness within an identity group: "the point of departure for a more democratizing affirmation of internal difference" (p. 219). Repeated disidentification can progressively open up an identity group to difference and diversity. But it is important to note that the work of disidentification always remains unfinished, for "there can be no final or complete inclusivity" (p. 221).

From the standpoint of the familial view I'm developing in this section, the transformative potential of disidentification is of crucial importance. Disidentification messes up the relations within and across families, inviting the rearticulation of the networks of similarities and differences that sustain familial identities. In this way disidentification is an occasion for subversion,[28] for disrupting established relations of similarity and difference and the unifications and divisions they create. In order to illustrate how disidentification can transform the articulation of an identity category and the community organized around it, let's consider the development of the category *woman* in Anglo-American feminism.

As Norma Alarcón (1990) has argued, the first stages of the Anglo-American feminist movement were characterized by the logic of identification and counteridentification. In a first stage, feminist liberation presupposed the identification with men: women tried to appropriate the idea of "an autonomous, self-making, self-determining subject," thus claiming for themselves something that had traditionally been the prerogative of men. A second stage was dominated by the logic of counteridentification: women defined themselves in opposition to men, developing different aspects of their identity oppositionally by contrasting "women's ways" with "men's ways." It was soon objected that this form of oppositional thinking sustained the very binary logic that feminism was supposed to subvert. The logics of identification and counteridentification forced the feminist movement either to assimilate or to oppositionally resist assimilation to male-dominated configurations of identity, thus forcing the movement to remain parasitic on a masculinist ideology. Feminist debates repeatedly expressed the need to develop a new discourse for the unified subjectivity or shared consciousness of women. Different "common denominators" that unite women were proposed and challenged. But, more importantly, this very idea of *unity* through gender was problematized by radical feminists of color who argued that the search for the unitary subject of feminist theory was misguided. In *This Bridge Called My Back* (1981), among other works, these feminist thinkers claimed that by subsuming all women under a unitary category without thematizing racial, ethnic, sexual, and class differences, the subject posited by feminist theory had been, by default, the middle-class straight white woman. And they went on to argue that gender identity cannot be understood independently of racial, ethnic, sexual, and class identity. Until this fact is recognized, they claimed, it will be impossible to overcome the deep divisions that exist within the feminist movement, for: "'one becomes a woman' in ways that are much more complex than in a simple opposition to men. In cultures in which 'asymmetric race and class relations are a central organizing principle of society,' one may also 'become a woman' in opposition to other women"(Alarcón 1990, p. 360).

As Alarcón (1990) puts it, the challenges raised by feminists of color in *This Bridge* derived from "a process of *disidentification* with prevalent formulations of the (. . .) theoretical subject of feminism" (p. 366; my emphasis). Writing nine years later, Alarcón argues that these challenges have not yet been met, mainly because the standard strategy in feminist theory for dealing with internal differences has been to acknowledge them only to set them aside: "The difference is handed over with one hand and taken away with the other" (p. 364). An example of this strategy can be found in Teresa de Lauretis (1986) who, after stressing that "an identity [is] made up of heterogeneous and heteronomous representations of gender, race, and class," still insists on unity through gender by saying that "the female subject is always constructed and defined in gender, starting from gender" (pp. 9 and p. 14). But a free-standing account of gender won't do. By treating racial, ethnic, sexual, and class differences as secondary and analytically detachable from gender identity, feminists are imposing an artificial unity on all women.[29] Unity, far from being demanded by *solidarity* (as traditionally assumed), actually becomes an obstacle for it. The kind of solidarity that is required has to be based on diversity, not on unity. The disidentifications of women of color with the unitary subject postulated by feminist theory call for a new form of solidarity and a transformed community. As Alarcón (1990, p. 366) puts it, the challenges raised by radical feminists show that we are dealing with a "struggle of multiple antagonisms" and that the battles against "antagonistic relations between races, classes, and gender(s)" cannot be fought independently. These challenges cannot be met by the unitary logics of identification and counteridentification. They require a *pluralistic* logic of disidentification which can effect the diversification and pluralistic transformation of identity groups. The diversity and plurality disclosed by disidentification need to be accommodated not only in the structure of those communities that are built for this "struggle of multiple antagonisms," but also in the very identities of those who participate in these communities. This pluralistic view of the self can be found in the writings of feminists of color such as Gloria Anzaldúa (1987, 1999) and María Lugones (1989, 1991, and 2003).

In *Borderlands/La Frontera: The New Mestiza* Anzaldúa talks about the self as a plurality, as a site of multiple voices that give expression to multiple registers of existence. The pluralistic nature of the self is apparent in the multi-voiced subjectivity of those who live at the borders between two cultures. But this internal multiplicity of our identity is hindered and handicapped by an implacable profiling that imposes homogenized categories. Current political practices in the US subject our identity to rigid categorizations and silence the voices of those whose identity is extended over different cultural domains (those who belong to different families). This is the situation that Anzaldúa aims to transform by placing the emphasis on multiplicity. The writings of María Lugones also aim at a similar subversion. She calls our attention to the fact that it is everywhere demanded of us that we be *one*, that all the different aspects of our personality be integrated in a unified center. This general anxiety about being one induces in us the fear of duplicity or plurality, which are depicted as a loss of self or as fractures of the self. Lugones proposes ambiguity as "a creative strategy of resistance" against this unified picture of the self (cf. 1991, p. 43). Her view suggests a pluralistic logic for identity categories, emphasizing the fluidity of identity and the relationality between one's selves and those of others.[30]

From the insights and challenges developed by feminists of color we can learn as much about the complex nature of (familial) identity as we can learn about the complex relations between identity groups or families. Indeed their complaints about how the feminist family has failed so far to accommodate internal differences are complaints about how this family has failed to take into account its relations with other families or identity groups.

There are clear dangers in compartmentalizing the lives of families. Minimally, construing the life of one family as independent of the life of another breeds mutual indifference between the members of these families. But the situation is typically worse, for it is often the case that compartmentalization not only blocks paths of identification but also builds on relations of counteridentification; and, therefore, compartmentalized groups are often not just separated from each other, but placed in opposition to one another, which establishes and consolidates antagonistic relations. So, when familial groups become compartmentalized, the relations among them are either ignored or construed oppositionally; and as a result, there is either indifference or animosity. This situation cries out for change, and the change requires the subversion of the strategy of compartmentalization (which weakens familial groups and keeps them in check, contributing to their domestication). Disidentification is one of the tools that can be used for such subversion. For example, the artificial separation of Hispanic identity from Asian and African identities is resisted in various ways by the disidentifications of Hispanic Filippino/as and Afro-Caribbeans.

The mechanism of disidentification diversifies a group and strengthens the relations between groups. This mechanism has the capacity to bridge the gulf between families and to bring to the fore the internal diversity of each family. The basis of this capacity can be found in three aspects of the process of disidentification. In the first place, disidentification underscores the interrelations between the networks of similarities and differences that constitute familial identities, making it difficult to sever the ties between families or to construe these ties in purely oppositional terms (as it is done through counteridentification). In the second place, disidentification reminds us that the similarities and differences that unite and separate families are subject to fluctuations; and indeed disidentification itself is an occasion for the rearticulation of these similarities and differences. In the third place, our uneasy feeling that we do and do not belong to a family reveals that our identity is never exhausted by membership in one family, that there is always an excess in us, a surplus of identity that comprises parts of ourselves that participate in other familial associations as well as orphan aspects of our identity. The multifaceted character of identity indeed requires simultaneous membership in multiple families.

In order to understand properly this fundamental phenomenon of multiple familial associations, it is important to issue a warning against a possible misconception that can result from a dangerous simplification of the familial metaphor. The danger is to use this metaphor to construe identity as composed of *discrete* elements that can be individually explained in terms of familial associations added on to one another. This would suggest that one's identity could be sorted out, as it were, by looking for membership cards in one's wallet. But this simplification hides the fact that the different aspects of one's identity are fused together. It belies the messiness of identity and the inseparability of one's ties to different families. That one's memberships in different families are inextricably intertwined with each other can be shown through a cursory look at the three features of the formation of familial identity emphasized above: contextuality, performativity, and normativity.

In the first place, our families or identity groups do not occupy different territories. They are not like clubs that have their own spaces. There may be specific contexts that are of particular importance for our gender identity, or have special significance for our ethnicity. There are indeed contexts in which one aspect of our identity is brought to the fore and other aspects are relegated to the background. But by and large the different aspects of our identity are formed and developed simultaneously in a whole range of situations that cannot be neatly classified into gender contexts, racial contexts, class contexts, or the like.[31] In the second place, there are no discrete practices that contribute individually to the formation of different aspects of our identity. It's not as if we developed our identity by doing a bit of gender, and then a bit of race, and so on. The performativity of identity is multifaceted and does not admit divisions of this kind. Our gender performance is not separable from the performances of race, ethnicity, or sexuality; and any separation here would be artificial. Finally, the normativity of identity also seems to leave little room for compartmentalization. The norms or normative expectations that pertain to different aspects of our identity overlap and intersect one another in complex ways (not always consistently); and they are typically blended together in an undistillable mix. The things expected of a middle-class straight white woman or of a working-class gay Latino man are thrown at them in amorphous piles of expectations (not piece by piece in manageable bits) across different contexts and activities.

The normative frameworks that shape the different aspects of our identity interpenetrate each other, forming a normative blend that regulates our practices and structures the contexts in which they take place. It has been emphasized in the literature on gender and sexuality that gender normativity and sexual normativity are indistinguishable, for gender and sexual norms work together in the domestication of identity. It has also been argued that racial norms have to be added to the mix. Racist, masculinist, and heterosexist ideologies pervade the normative expectations that shape our identities. And the more one's identity deviates from this blend of normative frameworks, the more (normatively) disempowered one is. It is therefore understandable that, initially, the different movements within identity politics tried to liberate one difference at a time, considering it impossible (or suicidal) to fight too many battles at once. It is indeed no accident that certain groups were given a privileged position within these movemens: middle-class straight white women in the feminist movement, or middle-class white gay men in the queer movement, for example; for, in virtue of their (relatively) minimal deviations from established normative frameworks, they appeared as (more) valid interlocutors with the rest of society. In contemporary political contexts we still hear today these considerations voiced as pragmatic arguments to elevate people to positions of leadership within identity politics. I hope I have said enough to show that these arguments are suspect because they buy into a dangerous strategy of compartmentalization—a strategy that involves complicity with an exclusionary logic of domination and makes identity groups internally oppressive.[32] But in order to strengthen this point and neutralize conservative strategies of political activism, let me briefly consider the important warning issued by O'Connor (2005) in her critical response to my view.

O'Connor has warned that the political strategies of contestation suggested by my view can be easily monopolized by the most conservative portion of the oppressed group. According to O'Connor, the familial framework I provide runs the risk of privileging those nonconforming identities who can best *resemble* mainstream subjects, that is, those who—although deviant in some respect—are nonetheless closer to the standard subjectivities that have become privileged, for those subjects are the ones who have a best shot at claiming "We are like you." This conservative activism takes care first of those marginal subjects who are closest to the mainstream and therefore least marginal, without ever getting to the oppression of the most peripheral subjects—which is presumably the most severe oppression and the one in most need of urgent attention. And thus the political demands of truly dissimilar subjects who cannot draw on their similarities with the privileged classes become displaced. This conservative activism is unacceptable. It involves an unacceptable alliance with privileged classes and an implicit complicity with oppression. In the hands of conservative activists, the fight against oppression, instead of being a struggle for equality, becomes a struggle for *sharing privilege*.[33] I am in complete agreement with O'Connor on this point and it is for this reason that I reject "strategic essentialism"[34] and any kind of political strategy of contestation that works exclusively through similarities, basing political claims and demands on an identity claim of the form "We are like you." I take it that O'Connor's argument is a critique of philosophical conceptions of identity (such as Spivak's) that emphasize similarities over differences (if only for strategic purposes), but not a critique of my view, for one of the central tenets of my view is that similarities and differences are not mutually exclusive but bound up together, so that the critical task of contesting marginalization, exclusion, and oppression must pay attention to differences as well as to similarities. Justice and equality will not be attained by our political activism if the reconfiguration of the relations among identity groups and within them is produced through identity claims that are based on similarities with those in privileged positions. To think that oppressed subjects in order to liberate themselves must assimilate to what society takes to be mainstream is already to abandon the fight against oppression, to give up on the ideals of justice and equality of identity politics, to capitulate. In this struggle of liberation we must begin by critically examining and contesting the relation of domination between groups and what has become the privileged center or core of identity categories. And it is important to keep in mind that the struggles against oppression fought in identity politics are not "merely cultural"[35]: these struggles have to address issues of socioeconomic power and status; the cultural critique must be accompanied by the transformation of material conditions and the redistribution of resources.

There is a vast and rich body of feminist literature on intersectionality, the multiple fronts of oppression, and the formation of alliances and coalitions which is invaluable in order to improve the activist practices in movements of liberation.[36] Times have changed (a little bit at least); and the movements of identity politics have entered a new stage: a stage in which they can mutually support each other in "a struggle of multiple antagonisms," a stage in which embracing internal differences does not endanger but actually strengthens solidarity.

It seems fair to conclude that the familial view of identity developed in this section has a story to tell about how we become members of a family and how different families are related to one another, thus answering the two questions I posed. So this view can shed some light on different aspects of our identity, their interrelations, and the communities built around them. According to my Wittgensteinian familial view, identity is always and unavoidably bound up with differences. This thoroughgoing pluralism underscores the heterogeneity and instability of identity. All identity categories contain internal differences that can be disruptive; and, therefore, they keep within themselves the source of their own instability, always having a process of destabilization up their sleeve, no matter how rigidly fixed they become. On the dialogical view I have developed in this chapter, this dialectic of internal differences is conceived as a conversation of voices. Both our identities and the "families" or communities that support them involve a conversation of multiple and heterogeneous voices. The polyphony that is constitutive of our identity (cf. previous section) entails a polyphonic dialogue internal to the communities or identity groups to which we belong.[37]

So the polyphony proposed by my view is a *radical polyphony* that resists unification or orchestration. It is not a choral polyphony, the qualified version of polyphony we saw in Mead, which is subordinated to an ideal of unity. On my polyphonic view, individuals and their communities are not subject to the requirement of unification. For particular purposes and in particular contexts unified identities and unified communities may be desirable, but the point is that unification is not a universal demand that can be grounded in over-riding psychological and/or political reasons. And besides, as I have shown, even the most coherent identity and even the most cohesive and unified com-munity contain heterogeneous elements and inner diversity. My polyphonic contextualism emphasizes that homogeneity is impossible: there are always differences; there is always an *elsewhere* where our identity and our commu-nity might go. Butler explains the constitutive relation between identity and difference, and how this relation makes the process of identity formation an open-ended and always unfinished task: "Difference is the *condition of pos-sibility* of identity or, rather, its *constitutive limit*: what makes its articulation possible is at the same time *what makes any final or closed articulation impos-sible*" (1997, p. 269; my emphasis).

In the final section of this chapter I will elucidate one more aspect of this polyphonic view of identity: the constraining and oppressive elements that shape our voices. Through Bourdieu's account of the role of power and domination in the process of identity formation I will try to show that voices, far from being free and unconstrained, are domesticated and internally consti-tuted by mechanisms of censorship. With Bourdieu, I will argue that symbolic oppression is at the very core of identity; and yet the discursive agency of our voices can find paths of liberation. This brief discussion of internalized domi-nation and the possibility of liberation will introduce the central themes that will be discussed in the next two chapters.

2.2. The Flourishing of Voices and Their Domestication

The most fundamental notion of the interactional and familial view of identity I have developed in the previous sections is the notion of a *voice*. What is given primacy in my view of identity are not the subject, the ego, or the self, but *the voices*—in the plural—in which one speaks: the multiple voices that appear and develop in the conversations in which we engage with ourselves and with oth-ers. It is through a plurality of voices that one articulates her identity. Although I have made use of the notions of the self and the subject—especially in my discussion of Mead, following his terminology—my account has privileged the conceptualization of identity in terms of a multiplicity of voices. But why should a philosophical account of identity shift the emphasis to voices? What is gained by giving primacy to voices rather than to selves, or to some other configuration of subjectivity? Here too we can learn something from feminist theory, in which the subject of sexual difference has been conceptualized in terms of voices. A good example can be found in Adriana Cavarero (2000).

As Perpich (2003) puts it, Cavarero argues for the primacy of the notion of voice in our understanding of language: "before and beyond consisting in a system of signification and communication, spoken language consists of voice" (p. 402). By calling attention to the voice, Cavarero brings to the fore three crucial aspects of identity: its embodiment, its singularity, and its relationality. In the voice we find expressive materiality, concrete physical articulation. The sound of the voice is always something unique, a concrete particular. But the material particularity of a voice, its concreteness and uniqueness, can only be produced and recognized in relation to other voices. In other words, the peculiar embodied singularity of a voice can only be achieved relationally. As Perpich puts it, "voices are inherently plural and relational," for to speak is to address another, and therefore, it "presupposes the other (and still other others) by virtue of the plurivocity of language" (p. 404). This plurivocity of language is contained and maintained in each particular voice, in which the voices of past and future speakers resonate: "In speaking, I speak a language that was already given to me by others, a language that contains already a plurality of voices and a consequent plurality of shades of meaning" (p.404). A voice always echoes other voices; and with this reverberation through chains of voices, each voice becomes performatively entangled in a network of voices. We already saw this phenomenon of reverberation in the previous chapter as the *echoing* that keeps meanings alive, being both the source of semantic stability and the source of semantic innovation. Now the same echoing phenomenon appears as a crucial mechanism for the development and maintenance of identity, as that which binds voices together and defines their singularity relationally.[38] As Butler (1997) puts it, combining the performative views of Austin and Althusser, the voice of an 'I' is always conventional and therefore relational: "it is an inherited set of voices, *an echo of others* who speaks as the 'I'" (p. 25; my emphasis).

The pluralistic view of voices we find in Cavarero and other feminists[39] is very congenial to the polyphonic account of identity I have developed. This view gives an answer to the question of why we want to start with voices (rather than with selves, egos, or subjects). By developing an account of identity from the notion of voice, we are able to offer a picture in which identity appears as embodied, singular, and relational.

Embodiment, singularity, and relationality are also the features that Bourdieu's account of the identity of speakers emphasizes. His account focuses on voices and what he calls "articulatory styles," which comprise all expressive aspects of linguistic performance including word choice, intonation, pitch, gesticulation, and tone. How does our symbolic performance get stylistically marked? Bourdieu offers a sociological account of how our distinctive ways of talking and expressing ourselves are produced, socially recognized, and negotiated in social fields of action. To begin with, one's expressive style is to a large degree the result of socialization. The stylistic articulation of our performance derives from the generative capacities or productive skills we have acquired through processes of training or enculturation into social practices. But the dependence of expressive styles on socialization is crucial not only for their production but also for their reception. The recognition and classification of stylistic differences have a social existence that depends on the discriminatory capacities or recognitional skills of socialized subjects. As Bourdieu puts it, style "is a being-perceived which exists only in relation to perceiving subjects, endowed with the diacritical dispositions which enable them to make *distinctions* between different *ways of saying*, distinctive manners of speaking"; "style [. . .] exists only in relation to agents endowed with schemes of perception and appreciation that enable them to constitute it as a set of systematic differences" (1991, pp. 38–39). So the kind of identity signified by the agency of one's voice(s) will depend on how stylistic differences are recognized and classified in one's environment. According to Bourdieu's account, whether the articulatory style of a voice is perceived and classified as similar to or as different from that of other voices, depends on the aspects of articulation that we have been sensitized to, that is, those aspects that we have been trained to recognize and to attach a particular significance to.

So, on Bourdieu's view, the production and social recognition of expressive styles is the result of the productive and discriminatory capacities that agents develop through their socialization and participation in symbolic activities and practices. These capacities reside in what Bourdieu calls "the habitus." This is the most central notion of Bourdieu's social theory, which he develops in *Outline of a Theory of Practice* and in his later writings. Bourdieu describes the habitus as a practical orientation exhibited in our spontaneous reactions. He emphasizes the embodied nature of this practical sense: the habitus is a primitive form of understanding that is displayed in the stylistics of the body. This bodily understanding emerges from the agent's repeated participation in rule-governed practices and is a fundamental aspect of her participatory competence. It has a rule-like character: it incorporates the normative structure of the practices from which it derives. Bourdieu describes the habitus as "a structured structure," which brings inside the individual a normative organization that mediates her experiences and reactions; but also as "a structuring structure," which makes that internal organization productive in guiding and organizing the agency of the individual. As "a structured and structuring structure" (1984, pp. 170–71), the habitus is simultaneously a receptive and a generative capacity. A habitus is a particular *mode of generation and appreciation* inscribed in the body of the agent. It can be defined as a set of bodily dispositions[40] that make possible the articulation and interpretation of symbolic (or signifying) behavior. The habitus contains a generative principle responsible for the production of one's behavior; but it also contains a receptive principle responsible for the interpretation of behavior. It includes "a system of schemes generating classifiable practices and works" and "a system of schemes of perception and appreciation ('taste')" (1991, p. 171). The most important feature of the habitus is its *formative and generative role*: the habitus is first and foremost a system of practice-generating and judgment-forming schemes.

From her early experiences in the social world, an agent develops a habitus that is "the basis of the perception and appreciation of all subsequent experiences" (1977, p. 78; 1990, p. 54). As also suggested by Wittgenstein's discussions of initiate training (see the discussion in 1.5 above), the early experiences of initiation into a practice are pivotal for the normative structuration of one's behavior and one's taste (perception/appreciation). These experiences create anticipations; they form *normative expectations*. As Bourdieu puts it, early experiences are given a "disproportionate weight" because they are responsible for "the anticipations of the habitus" (1990, p. 54). It is on the basis of these formative experiences that certain things are "taken for granted," and a sense of familiarity, a sense of "obviousness," is formed (cf. e.g. 1990, p. 58). Given our habitus, certain things appear to us as necessary, certain actions and reactions as nonoptional (not because we cannot choose differently, but because the conditions for such a choice are not yet given for us, for the kind of social agents we are). And yet the habitus is not a rigid or fixed structure, for it is always open to variations and surprises and constantly (though unnoticeably) incorporates new forms of behavior. As Bourdieu puts it, the habitus is a "generative principle of *regulated improvisations*" (1977, p. 78; my emphasis); for it involves both a tendency to reproduce social regularities and an openness to novelty, that is, a readiness to respond to changes and to adjust to the demands of novel situations. Thus the habitus, in Bourdieu's account, exhibits the features of the *echoing* phenomenon that, as we saw, characterizes discursive agency: being at the same time the source of semantic stability and the source of semantic innovation. Our habitus is constantly echoing the old and familiar and foreshadowing the new and strange, thus containing a dynamic combination of sameness and difference. Combining freedom and constraint, necessity and spontaneity, the repetitive structure of the habitus is as much characterized by its routineness and conventionality as by its creativity and originality (more on this in the next chapter). Bourdieu emphasizes that the habitus reproduces the social training from which it originates (perpetuating the social structures from which it arises), but that it always *exceeds* this training and its surrounding conditions: "The habitus is necessity internalized and converted into a disposition that generates meaningful practices and meaning-giving perceptions; it is a general, transposable disposition which carries out a systematic, universal application—*beyond the limits of what has been directly learnt*" (1984, p. 170; my emphasis).

In the habitus we find socially produced commonalities but also differences. There is always stylistic diversification in a speech community. As

Bourdieu puts it, there is always "individual deviation from the linguistic norm" (1991, p. 38). How are these "deviations" treated? In some cases these stylistic differences may not be recognized at all, or they may be deemed purely idiosyncratic. But in other cases, they acquire a particular social significance. A distinctive way of expressing oneself then becomes the stylistic mark of a group or class; and a speech community thus becomes differentiated into subcommunities or subgroups. A distinctive style is symptomatic of one's identity as a speaker and social agent and it reveals one's memberships in social groups. This stylistic distinctiveness is what Bourdieu calls "the distinction" (which is the title of one of his seminal works). "The distinction" refers to a stylistic differentiation that has crucial social significance given the power structures and power relations inscribed in it. On Bourdieu's view, voices and their articulatory styles operate in a field of differences; but these stylistic differences do not receive equal treatment. Social distinctions of different kinds are piggied-back upon stylistic differences. One's style can be (and often is) indicative of one's economic and social power (or lack thereof), revealing one's class and social status. But more distinctively and importantly, one's style is indicative of what Bourdieu calls "symbolic power" (cf. esp. 1991), which is the power to represent or symbolize things, people, situations, and experiences, and to make one's representations or symbolizations prevail. In order to have symbolic power one's symbolic style must acquire social recognition and acceptance; it has to gain currency in "the linguistic market," in the social space of linguistic interaction. In this way styles accrue "symbolic capital." One possesses symbolic capital to the extent that one's symbolic repertoire and representational means are considered adequate in some community and in some context(s), that is, to the extent that one's style is treated as a legitimate use of language that is superior to other uses. According to Bourdieu, symbolic styles carry with them different amounts of symbolic capital, which are in turn symptomatic of one's cultural and educational capital and (more indirectly) of one's economic and social capital.

The same linguistic community can include a variety of subcommunities and a variety of "linguistic markets" or symbolic contexts in which different forms of symbolic power and capital coexist, developing dynamic dialectical relations among them (competing, collaborating, influencing, contradistinguishing, threatening each other, etc.). It is worth noting that sometimes marginal voices accumulate symbolic power; but sometimes this symbolic power does not attach (at least not exclusively) to the originating voices, but to their inflexions and modes of representations, which can then be *expropriated* and *appropriated* by others. An example of symbolic expropriation would be the hip-hop and rap styles used by white youth. Through commercialization and popularization in the media these styles have acquired symbolic power; but interestingly, this power has traveled beyond the originating black communities, and nonmarginal and nonblack subjects use them to *speak with a Black voice*, thus distinguishing themselves from mainstream white culture, (dis)identifying with marginalizaed black communities, but also appropriating their voices and their symbolic power in problematic ways.

Bourdieu emphasizes that "what circulates on the linguistic market is not 'language' as such," but stylistically marked speech or symbolic behavior (1991, p. 39). On his view, what characterizes the interaction of symbolic styles in the linguistic market is a *struggle for* symbolic power. Competing styles strive for "symbolic domination," that is, they strive to become the dominant way of speaking that can subjugate other forms of expression and control the symbolic currency in the linguistic market, keeping people's expressive behavior in check. There is typically an uneven distribution of power across the linguistic field. There is often a particular style that occupies a privileged position in the linguistic market. But even when there isn't, what we find is, typically, competition and a power struggle among styles. Divergent styles rarely coexist in peace; they typically enter into a struggle in which each style tries to acquire a dominant role, that is, it tries to acquire symbolic power so as to displace and dominate others. Thus, on Bourdieu's view, "the question of style" is, fundamentally, a question of power and domination (cf. e.g., 1991, pp. 38ff). This question has to be addressed empirically and historically, for the distribution of power in a given linguistic market is a matter of contingent historical fact. Bourdieu offers various empirical historical studies that show how a particular way of speaking becomes identified as superior to others, and in some cases even as the sole legitimate language. His most influential study concerns the evolution of "the French language." For Bourdieu, "French," like any other of the so-called natural languages, is nothing more than an abstraction, an ideological construct for the unification and homogenization of myriad ways of talking, that is, for the symbolic domination of the speech of multiple and heterogeneous groups. Bourdieu's empirical account shows how the establishment of "French" as the official language of the new republic after the French Revolution was crucial for the production of a new mentality and a new habitus: it "was an integral part of the political strategies aimed at perpetuating the gains of the Revolution through the production and the reproduction of the 'new man'" (1991, p. 47). The intellectual elite of the French Revolution recognized the crucial importance of language for social change, for indeed "to reform language, to purge it of the usages linked to the old society [. . .] was to impose a thought" (p.47). This is how Bourdieu describes what was at stake in the dispute between "the French of the revolutionary intelligentsia" and the different regional dialects and local variants: it "was a struggle for symbolic power in which what was at stake was *the formation and re-formation of mental structures*. In short, it was not only a question of communicating but of gaining recognition for a new language of authority" (p. 48; my emphasis).

According to Bourdieu, the kind of symbolic domination involved in the imposition of a language is a crucial aspect of the formation of people's habitus and, therefore, of the very production and reproduction of men and women, of the shaping of their identity as speakers and agents. What in Bourdieu's view appear as mechanisms of symbolic domination are what Althusser (2001) has famously termed "Ideological State Apparatuses" or ISAs. In his neo-Marxist analysis Althusser describes ISAs as social institutions through which the State domesticates and controls its citizens and workers by structuring their behavior and attitudes. Among these ideological apparatuses Althusser includes many different kinds of institutions, which can be either public or private: schools, churches, parties, families, newspapers, and so on. (cf. p. 97). ISAs constitute a social machinery that maintains and regenerates the system of production and the social order associated with it. The principal task of these institutions is to effect the *reproduction* of the human means of production by shaping the agents who are the source of labor. Althusser describes the task of these apparatuses as "the reproduction of labor power," which includes "not only the reproduction of its 'skills' but also the reproduction of its subjection to the ruling ideology"; for, as he puts it, "*it is in the forms and under the forms of ideological subjection that provision is made for the reproduction of the skills of labor power*" (p. 89). What is most characteristic about ISAs is that they exert and perpetuate oppression through *ideological subjection*. Similarly, for Bourdieu, symbolic domination has an essential ideological dimension: it is a form of ideological subjugation which results in the internalization of normative principles that organize and structure people's behavior and taste.

As Althusser does in his account of ISAs, Bourdieu emphasizes the decisive role that the school system plays in the ideological subjection of speakers: schools are in charge of "fashioning the similarities from which that community of consciousness which is the cement of the nation stems"; the educational system has among its functions "to devalue popular modes of expression, dismissing them as 'slang' and 'gibberish'" (p. 49). But the school system does not work by itself. Bourdieu argues that there is a "dialectical relation between the school system and the labor market" so that the educational capital and the economic and social capitals get intertwined (cf. 1991, pp. 49ff): those with economic power have better access to the educational system and have a better chance to excel in it; and only those who acquire some educational capital (those successfully domesticated by the school system) are allowed to acquire high social status and to hold economically advantageous positions. On the other hand, for the production of ideological subjection the school system recruits the help of the family and other social institutions that operate in less formal educational settings. That is, the symbolic domination of formal education counts with the cooperation of institutions run by the symbolically dominated speakers themselves who are thus *required to participate in their own ideological subjection.* In order to be successful, symbolic domination must "induce the holders of dominated linguistic competences to collaborate in the destruction of their instruments of expression, by endeavouring for example to speak 'French' to their children or requiring them to speak 'French' at home" (p. 49). Speakers are trained so as to actively participate in their own domination. The behavior of novices is subject to constant assessment and correction by the masters of the practice up to the point where the novice corrects herself without the aid or the presence of others. In other words, the goal of the training is to produce *self-corrective* behavior, which guarantees the success of symbolic subjection. As Bourdieu puts it, symbolic domination "is never more manifest than in all the corrections, whether *ad hoc* or permanent, to which dominated speakers, as they strive desperately for correctness, consciously or unconsciously subject the stigmatized aspects of their pronunciation, their diction [. . .] and their syntax, in the disarray which leaves them 'speechless,' 'tongue-tied,' 'at a loss for words,' as if they were suddenly dispossessed of their own language" (p. 52).

The most crucial mechanism of symbolic domination is the required *complicity* of the dominated subjects. This complicity is secured by the built-in structure of domination implicit in performative mechanisms of language learning and language use. Speakers are surreptitiously recruited for their own domination through training, for the habitus they develop through training has inscribed in it the reproductive structure of symbolic domination. There are two ways in which the habitus involves complicity with symbolic domination: by sustaining the "consensus of action" of a speech community and by reproducing certain normative structures of identiy. There is always a consensus of action (no matter how incipient) from which the habitus emerges and to which it reverts and contributes, a tacit orchestration of behavior that is the practical foundation of a linguistic community. This background consensus of action required by and presupposed in shared activities is constantly reinforced by the linguistic interaction of communicative partners. But one's habitus reproduces not only types of agency but also types of agents; that is, it perpetuates not only patterns of action, but also identity molds. Since I have already discussed the formation and maintenance of consensus in chapter 1 (cf. esp. 1.5. "Sustaining Agreement in Action") as well as elsewhere,[41] I will focus here on the reproduction of structures of identity in and through the habitus. In particular, I want to discuss briefly the process of identification and identity formation immanent in the spontaneous imitation that is integral to the development of the habitus.

The habitus is acquired through what Bourdieu calls "mimesis," which is not an intentional act of imitation but a spontaneous form of identification between the novice or initiate learner and the master of a practice. As Bourdieu puts it, "practical mimesis (or mimeticism) [. . .] implies an overall relation of identification and has nothing in common with an imitation that would presuppose a conscious effort to reproduce a gesture, an utterance, or an object explicitly constituted as a model" (1990, p. 73). Mimetic identification is an essential aspect of the acquisition of competence in a practice, for it brings about the practical conformity of the learner's behavior with the tacit norms that govern the practices: through mimesis the initiate learner gradually shapes her activity according to the norms that structure the behavior of practitioners. Through this mimetic process of acculturation, Bourdieu argues, "the rules of the game" are "incorporated" or "internalized" and they become "second nature"[42] (1990, p. 66). As the internalization of the normative structure of a practice, the habitus recapitulates the history of the practice; it is the performative reenactment of the normative structures cemented by the repeated behavior of practitioners. But this cultural memory incorporated in the habitus is not a conscious remembering. On the contrary, this bodily incorporation of history involves forgetting, what Bourdieu calls "genesis amnesia" (1977, p. 79): "the forgetting of history that history itself produces by incorporating the objective structures it produces in the second natures of habitus" (1977, pp. 78–79). The history of the practice is coded in the mnemonic traces that the agent's body unknowingly displays in its actions. The habitus, therefore, is an unconscious site of cultural memory, a repository of an incorporated history: "the habitus—embodied history, internalized as a second nature and so forgotten as history—is the active presence of the whole past of which it is the product" (1990, p. 56).

In the habitus the incorporated history of a practice and the internalization of its normative principles are sedimented in an *identity structure* which guides the behavior and taste of the individual. What one does under the guidance of one's elders, superiors, and peers becomes *what one is*, and this in turn guides what one is to do and how one is to react and to interpret things in subsequent situations. As Bourdieu puts it, "the power of suggestion which [. . .], instead of telling the child what he must do, tells him *what he is*, and thus leads him to become durably what he has to be, is the *condition for the effectiveness of all kinds of symbolic power* that will subsequently be able to operate on a habitus predisposed to respond to them" (p. 52; my emphasis). The identity structures formed through mimetic behavior constitute the precondition for symbolic subjection, but these structures are highly unstable. Imitation is slippery and so are the structures that result from it. No matter how demanding and inflexible a mimetic training may be, imitation cannot result in the rigid fixation of identity. Imitation always falls short of replication, which some have described as a "constitutive failure."[43] For there is never a unique and fixed path that determines how an adequate mimesis should proceed; there is always room for ambiguity and variability, which in turn leaves room for problematic identifications, and even contradictory ones (when the imitating subject is pulled in different directions by mimetic processes). It is important to note also that the contexts in which one's identity develops are often (if not typically) informal settings in which there is no *master* or clearly marked public figure or set of figures with which one is expected to identify. Moreover, given the constitutive polyphony of contexts and speaking subjects, there are always many voices, many inflexions and configurations of identity, even within the very same rule model in the very same context. And this means that the process of identification can always go in many different directions even in the most formal and rigidly structured contexts of enculturation.

There is a constant *slippage* in imitative chains, so that the transmission of identity structures from imitated subjects to imitating subjects is always problematic and pregnant with conflicts, ambiguities, and surprises. We have already seen two compelling reasons for this. The first one is given by the mechanism of *disidentification* examined in the previous section. Disidentification is unavoidable in mimesis, for imitating involves *acting as someone else* and, therefore, it invites the subject to be *and* not to be. Mimesis situates the subject in the space of ambiguity, of unexplored possibilities. Mimetic behavior typically moves away from the clear and unproblematic poles of identification and counteridentification, for mimesis opens up the door to an indefinite gallery of possible figures or characters who are in between those with whom and those against whom we are called to identify. The second reason for the instability intrinsic to imitative processes of identity formation appeared in our discussion of *echoing* above (cf. 1.5); and that is that *doing the same* always involves differences. Typically these are differences that are considered negligible and go unnoticed; but the constant presence of these minimal differences can amount to great changes, for differences accumulate. This relates to what cultural psychologists have called "cumulative cultural evolution" or "the ratchet effect" (Tomasello, Kruger, and Ratner 1993; and Tomasello 1999).[44] So mimetic repetition is a constant source of innovation. Bourdieu realizes that in imitating the symbolic behavior of others we do not passively copy, but actively reproduce in new ways. Through our symbolic mimesis old meanings are modified and new meanings are produced. There is an ongoing process of *resignification* in our mimetic symbolic performance (cf. Butler 1993). In considering the formation of identity structures through mimesis, we need to keep in mind not only that there is always the possibility of eccentric repetition, but also that *every repetition is to some extent eccentric*. So mimetic processes of identity formation breed differences and diversity and they cannot make subjects speak in one voice.

Through repeated imitation and the processes of (dis)identification at play in mimetic behavior, we come to see ourselves in particular ways. First and foremost, we come to see ourselves *as others see us*. We develop self-images or self-perceptions that involve submitting to the authority of others, for they contain a tacit acknowledgment of others' perceptions of oneself. As Mead puts it (cf. 2.1.a above), in adopting the perspective of the other as we must in symbolic interaction, we are "unconsciously seeing ourselves as others see us" and "unconsciously addressing ourselves as others address us" (MSS, p. 68). On Mead's view, as we saw, the reflexivity of symbolic interaction leads to a constitutive inner diversity in the subject: the internalized presence of others in the form of inner voices becomes an integral part of one's identity structure. Thus one's initial configuration as a speaker and agent is marked by *submission*, by the submission to the symbolic power of others, for it requires speaking to oneself in the voice of others, that is, it requires the tacit acceptance of others' conceptualizations and perceptions of oneself (even if they are later rejected or overcome). In this way Mead's notion of *reflexivity* anticipates Bourdieu's notion of the unconscious *complicity* in one's own symbolic domination. There is nothing that can better guarantee the complicity in one's own symbolic domination than having the normative presence of others inside oneself and having no option but to listen to their internalized voices. Already in Mead and more explicitly in Bourdieu we find an important reformulation of the dialectic of recognition, a reformulation that transcends the traditional cognitivist and voluntarist assumptions of the philosophy of the subject. The recognition of others and of oneself through others implicit in processes of socialization is a recognition that escapes one's knowledge and control. This is a recognition that does not happen consciously or knowingly, nor as a result of a choice. This unknowing and uncontrollable recognition is an embodied and unconscious way of acknowledging, which defies the central tenets of cognitivism and voluntarism. What results from this social process of unconscious recognition is not a self constituted by choices or volitional acts, or a self who fully knows itself and is in control of its destiny, that is, a self that is its own *master*.

At the core of Bourdieu's social theory is the idea of *the performative and unconscious formation of identity through the address of the other*. This idea has been developed by Butler's reformulation of Althusser's notion of *interpellation*. I will briefly discuss those aspects of Althusser's and Butler's views of the social constitution of identity that can shed light on Bourdieu's view. Althusser (2001) characterizes the phenomenon of interpellation as a kind of hailing that has the formative power of configuring one's identity in a particular way and of making one accept this concrete configuration as what one is. The interpellations to which individuals are subject are determined by the dominant ideology: "all ideology hails or interpellates concrete individuals as concrete subjects" (p. 117; emphasis dropped). As an illustration Althusser offers his celebrated example of an act of hailing in the street by a policeman who says "Hey, you there!" He remarks that "the hailed individual will turn around" and "by this mere one-hundred-and-eighty-degree physical conversion, he becomes a *subject*" (p. 118). By turning around the passerby responds to the address and assumes an identity projected on her; and in this way the other's recognition becomes the normative framework that defines the subjected individual. The voice of the interpellated subject is thus subordinated to the voice that interpellates her: the agency of the former is under the yoke of the latter, always taking the form of a response to the interpellating voice, which sets the terms of the interaction. As Butler (1997) puts it, in the phenomenon of interpellation "the act of recognition becomes an act of constitution: the address animates the subject into existence" (p. 25). Butler extends the Althusserian account of interpellation to elucidate the use of common nouns and names to address the subject. Developing an analysis of discrimination and hate speech, she is especially interested in terms that have a pejorative and denigrating use such as "faggot," "spic," or "nigger." According to Butler's account, the names one is called are coined forms of address which interpellate the individual in particular ways; they have the capacity to "animate the subject into existence" and to configure different aspects of her identity such as gender, sexuality, race, and ethnicity. Names constitute one socially, but Butler emphasizes that "one's social constitution takes place without one's knowing" (p. 31). This insight leads Butler to develop an important revision of Althusser's view of subjection, which requires the subject's explicit acknowledgment and appropriation of the interpellation in order to make it effective and constitutive of the subject's identity. Arguing against this cognitivist remnant of the dialectic of recognition inherited from the philosophy of the subject, she writes: "The subject need not always turn around in order to be constituted as a subject" (p. 31); "interpellation can function without the 'turning around,' without anyone ever saying, 'Here I am'" (p. 33). This is how Butler formulates the efficacy of interpellation in noncognitivist terms:

> One need not know about or register a way of being constituted for that constitution to work in an efficacious way. For the measure of that constitution is not to be found in a reflexive appropriation of that constitution, but, rather, in a chain of signification that exceeds the circuit of self-knowledge. (Butler 1997, p. 31)

According to Butler, interpellation can be efficacious and identityconstituting even when there is no responsiveness on the part of interpellated subjects. Moreover, interpellation may sometimes encounter resistance and not mere lack of response; that is, it may be answered with a repudiation or disavowal, with a refusal to accept the address in its own terms: "That is not me, you must be mistaken!" And yet, as Butler points out, it is easy to "imagine that the name continues to force itself upon you, to delineate the space you occupy, to construct a social positionality. Indifferent to your protests, the force of interpellation continues to work." (p. 33) But although the social constitution of identity through interpellation does not require the conscious and explicit acknowledgment of the subject, it still depends on the subject's *complicity*. This is of course not an explicit complicity, a chosen and self-aware form of collaboration; it is, rather, an unconscious form of complicity that is established *prior* to the explicit interpellations that require explicit responses. Prior to the acts of interpellation to which the individual is subjected and as a condition for their efficacy, we find in her a predisposition, that is, a "certain readiness to be compelled by the authoritative interpellation" (p. 32). For a hailing to be an identity-constituting interpellation, the interpellated individual must have already been subjected; that is, she must have already yielded to the authority of the interpellating voice and have thus become ready to succumb to its call. This is not to say that identity structures preexist interpellations, as if to interpellate were simply to refer to an already existing configuration of identity. Interpellations are essentially performative. As Butler explains it, the act of interpellation is not descriptive but "inaugurative": "It seeks to introduce a reality rather than report on an existing one; it accomplishes this introduction through a citation of existing convention" (p. 33). But Butler's point in her revision of the Althusserian account is that interpellation presupposes a process of subjection that has already begun before the act of hailing occurs. On Butler's view, interpellation is only efficacious as part of an ongoing subjugation, not by itself, and not as the first step in this process of symbolic domination either.

Butler's critique of Althusser tries to broaden the notion of interpellation. She criticizes Althusser for restricting "the notion of interpellation to the action of a voice" (1997, p. 32), arguing that interpellation is a mechanism whose efficacy is irreducible to the moment of enunciation. In this critique Butler warns us against overestimating the performative power of voices for the social construction of identity. She emphasizes that this power is neither absolute nor exclusive. On the one hand, Butler criticizes Althusser for assimilating social interpellation to "the divine performative" (that is, to the unbound creative power of God himself), presenting the authority of the voice of ideology as absolute. But, she insists, the voice of interpellation is not, by itself, "impossible to refuse" (p. 31). The intimidating power of the interpellating voice depends on prior conditions of subjection which are responsible for the subject's submission and incapacity to refuse. On the other hand, Butler emphasizes that social interpellation goes beyond voices: "the discourse that inaugurates the subject need not take the form of a voice at all" (p. 31); "the interpellative name may arrive without a speaker—on bureaucratic forms, the census, adoption papers, employment applications" (p. 34). In part, Butler's impetus to go beyond voices is to acknowledge that the social constitution of identity is the result of a complicated network of linguistic and nonlinguistic practices, practices that involve different forms of agency that are not always verbal and that may or may not involve enunciation. Although my account of identity in this chapter has placed heavy emphasis on voices, following Mead and Bourdieu, I agree with Butler that there is a variety of forms of agency that support one's identity. My contextualist account has acknowledged this from the beginning by emphasizing the primacy of action in the formation of meaning and identity. Voices and their articulatory styles are especially important for my contextualist analysis because they are constitutive and expressive of our identity; but they have to be put in a broader context, namely, in the context of a complicated network of social practices many of which are nonverbal. The broadening of the notion of social interpellation beyond voices and even beyond the verbal realm is crucial for Butler's analysis of hate speech. She argues that racist speech, for example, "neither begins nor ends with the subject who speaks or with the specific name that is used" (p. 34). Linguistic forms of agency piggy-back on nonlinguistic ones. According to Butler's account, symbolic domination is parasitic on other (nonverbal) forms of domination: nonverbal violence is mimicked by our discursive agency and continued in the symbolic domain; that is, it is symbolically reproduced through performative chains that *cite* (or *echo*)—and thus recreate—the violence in question. A name can be used to denigrate because it is linked to a social injury and a traumatic experience, so that its iterability is a repetition of the injury and the trauma. As Butler puts it, hate speech involves "the restaging of injury through signs" (p. 36). Injurious names are those that involve a traumatic citationality or performative iterability, that is, those in which a trauma is not simply remembered, but relived (cf. pp. 36–37).

What Butler identifies as the readiness to symbolic domination or subjugation is precisely the kind of complicity that Bourdieu sees inscribed in the habitus. The submission to symbolic power prefigured in the habitus is not established through interpellations, but through *suggestions* or *insinuations* (glances, tones, postures, etc.), which are a more subtle and powerful form of *intimidation* than the one present in hailing or interpellation, as well as prior to it. Bourdieu describes "the power of suggestion" that produces our unconscious sensitivity and predisposition to be responsive to certain interpellations as follows:

> There is every reason to think that the factors which are most influential in the formation of the habitus are transmitted without passing through language and consciousness, but through *suggestions inscribed in the most apparently insignificant aspects* of the things, situations and practices of everyday life. Thus the modalities of practices, the ways of looking, sitting, standing, keeping silent, or even of speaking ("reproachful looks" or "tones," "disapproving glances" and so on) are *full of injunctions* that are powerful and hard to resist precisely because they are *silent and insidious, insistent and insinuating*. (1991, p. 51; my emphasis)

The suggestions or insinuations that produce the sensitivity and readiness to respond to symbolic power are typically issued and received unconsciously;

they escape the knowledge and control of speakers. Bourdieu describes them as "insidious," as "silent" and "invisible," for, unlike the explicit address or name calling of interpellation, these "suggestions" do not involve any explicit statement or representation, and they take place without the appeal to convention and without the citation of coined terms. These sensitivity-shaping and readiness-forming "suggestions" are "all the more absolute and undisputed for not having to be stated" (1991, p. 52). These formative insinuations involve an "invisible, silent violence." This insidious violence exerted by symbolic power is very hard to avoid and resist because it is unrecognized, or rather, as Bourdieu puts it, *misrecognized*: symbolic power is a silent and invisible power that is *misrecognized* as such and thus tacitly and unconsciously *recognized* as legitimate. Bourdieu uses the terms "recognition" ("reconnaissance") and "misrecognition" ("méconnaissance") to convey that the exercise of power through symbolic interaction involves the sedimentation of background conceptualizations and beliefs. These conceptualizations and beliefs are embodied and unconscious symbolic formations that come alive in and through our symbolic performance. While avoiding the cognitivism and voluntarism of the philosophy of the subject, Bourdieu's account of symbolic domination through symbolic interaction still rests on a dialectic of recognition. But this dialectic proceeds through unknowing and uncontrollable forms of recognition that are inscribed in the unconscious dispositions of the body. This is a dialectic of recognition that is full of misrecognitions: of oneself, of one's peers, and of the powers that structure our symbolic interactions. One's misrecognitions of symbolic power work in spite of one's own interests and situate one's agency in a field of conflict and contradiction. There is a constant conflict between (mis)recognitions that work at cross-purposes; and there are pervasive contradictions between the symbolic powers one performatively acknowledges and those to which one consciously yields.

On Bourdieu's view, the most important feature of the imposition of symbolic power is its *elusiveness*. The infliction of symbolic violence is insidious and elusive because it involves a very peculiar kind of *intimidation*, an intimidation that takes place *without an act of intimidation*. About this form of intimidation Bourdieu observes: "a symbolic violence which is not aware of what it is (to the extent that it implies no *act of intimidation*) can only be exerted on a person predisposed (in his habitus) to feel it, whereas others will ignore it" (1991, p. 51). This insidious intimidation is invisible not only to the agents who endure it, but also to the philosophers and intellectuals who analyze it. Bourdieu remarks that what makes it impossible to see that intimidation is our tendency to search for isolatable causes and responsibilities. Our philosophical models of agency are hampered by a false dichotomy between mechanical necessity and free and autonomous agency. Given this dichotomy, the mechanical model of agency seeks to isolate causes that trigger automatic responses, while the autonomous model of agency strives to identify choices or volitional acts from which behavior flows. However, the performative consequences of the symbolic subjection of individuals are neither the result of choice nor the product of isolatable mechanical automatisms. Symbolic subjugation is neither chosen nor passively and mechanically imposed; it involves the *active complicity* of the individuals subjected to it. Speakers are not simply the passive recipients of symbolic domination; but neither do they choose to participate in their own subjection. The active complicity of speakers in symbolic domination points to new directions for the philosophical discussion of agency, and it underscores the need to develop a new model of agency. This is the challenge I take up in the next chapter. As a conclusion to this chapter and an introduction to the next, I sketch the central questions that Bourdieu's analysis of symbolic domination poses for a philosophical account of agency.

On Bourdieu's view, the active complicity in symbolic domination inscribed in the habitus consists in an unconscious readiness to be interpellated, to be responsive to the voices of others, which resides in bodily dispositions. Symbolic domination takes place with the cooperation of the dominated subjects, but this cooperation involves a very peculiar kind of agency. This is how Bourdieu describes this agency:

> All symbolic domination presupposes, on the part of those who submit to it, a form of *complicity* which is neither passive submission to external constraint nor a free adherence to values. The *recognition* of the legitimacy of the official language has nothing in common with an explicitly professed, deliberate and revocable belief, or with an intentional act of accepting a 'norm.' It is *inscribed, in a practical state, in dispositions* which are impalpably inculcated, through a long and slow process of acquisition, by the sanctions of the linguistic market. (1991, pp. 50–51; my emphasis)

I want to highlight two implicit challenges raised by Bourdieu's account of the agency involved in the phenomenon of complicity in symbolic domination. In the first place, we find here a kind of agency that cannot be reduced either to strict determination and automatism or to spontaneity and freedom. As Bourdieu puts it: "The distinctiveness of symbolic domination lies precisely in the fact that it assumes, of those who submit to it, *an attitude which challenges the usual dichotomy of freedom and constraint*" (1991, p. 51; my emphasis). So the challenge is to develop an account of discursive agency that can avoid the Scylla of voluntarism and the Charybdis of determinism and automatism. That is our task. And it is also part of this task to reformulate the notion of *responsibility*. Although complicity in symbolic domination is not a matter of free choice, it is not exempted from responsibility either. The forced compliance of the dominated in their own domination is more than a purely mechanical effect; it involves active participation, for which speakers, as accomplices, must assume some (qualified) responsibility. As Butler (1997) argues, the responsibility of speakers is typically misconstrued because it is conceived in an absolute sense as deriving from an autonomous volitional source that chooses its own acts of enunciation. In the case of hate speech, for example, the person who uses injurious language is often viewed as the sole "culpable agent, as if the speaker were at the origin of such speech" (p. 39). Of course, an individual speaker is not the originator of symbolic domination and of the performative chains through which this domination is sustained; but she is an active participant in the ongoing process of symbolic subjugation and she contributes to these chains of performative iterations through which this subjection is maintained and reproduced. Therefore, speakers must assume responsibility for their contributions to the perpetuation of symbolic violence and symbolic domination. As Butler explains it: "The speaker assumes responsibility precisely through the citational character of speech. The speaker renews the linguistic tokens of a community, reissuing and reinvigorating such speech. *Responsibility is thus linked with speech as repetition, not as origination*" (p. 39; my emphasis).

Symbolic domination can undergo change; its course is not set in stone; it can take many different turns. The performative reiteration of symbolic violence can be disrupted and even subverted. Symbolic domination can be resisted. And this brings us to our second challenge, namely, carving out a space for *critique and subversion* in our account of discursive agency. We need an account of discursive agency that is critical and subversive, an account that acknowledges the inescapability of symbolic domination and yet makes room for critical and subversive processes of liberation through symbolic interaction. The paths of symbolic domination are not predetermined but performatively developed through the symbolic interaction of speakers; they depend on our agency, and we have in principle the power to change them, although this is a very limited and constrained power. Indeed, symbolic domination cannot be brought under the complete subjective control of individuals; for symbolic power by its very nature exceeds the discursive agency of individuals and, therefore, symbolic domination can always surprise us and catch us off guard. As my discussion of censorship in the next chapter will make clear, there is no such thing as absolute liberation: we cannot escape all forms of symbolic domination. But any given form of symbolic domination can in principle be resisted and could eventually be escaped or overcome. My view from *elsewhere* will show that there is always a place for resistance, critique, and subversion, no matter how strict and thorough the subjugation of speakers may become. The subversive potential of *eccentric* discursive agency—of *speaking from elsewhere*—will be explored in the final chapter through a discussion of how silences can be broken, how communities can be disrupted, and how new communities can be anticipated.

Chapter 3

Contextualizing Agency

> "Voluntarily" and "involuntarily," then, are not opposed in the
> obvious sort of way that they are made to be in philosophy or
> jurisprudence. A belief in *opposites and dichotomies* encourages,
> among other things, a *blindness* to the combinations and disso-
> ciations of adverbs that are possible, even to such obvious facts
> that *we can act at once on impulse and intentionally.*
>
> —Austin, 1979, p. 191 and p. 195; my emphasis.

WHAT KIND OF AGENCY do we have as speakers? To what extent is it vol-
untary and intentional and to what extent habitual and automatic? Do we
own our speech acts? Can we control them? Or are they out of control and
unownable? There are well-entrenched assumptions in philosophy that polar-
ize the answers to these questions. It is extremely difficult to answer these
questions without being trapped into philosophical dichotomies, in particular the dichotomy between voluntarism and automatism. In this chapter I
will try to uncover and criticize the assumptions that support these dichotomies and force us to choose between the horns of a dilemma. The goal of
this diagnostic and therapeutic task is to enable us to approach philosophical
questions about agency with fresh eyes. I will draw on Wittgenstein's later
philosophy for my diagnosis and critical examination of the misguided and
distorting assumptions about agency that haunt the philosophical literature.
After getting rid of these assumptions, I will develop a new philosophical
elucidation of discursive agency that tries to transcend the standard polarized
positions that have been in dispute. This positive proposal (though inspired by

Wittgenstein's later philosophy) will be elaborated with the help of Austin's, Butler's, and Felman's discussions of linguistic performativity.

The contextualist account of discursive agency that I develop in this chapter follows directly from the accounts of meaning and identity I have offered in previous chapters. A corollary of the contextualist view of speaker's identity developed in chapter 2 is that the agency of one's voice is neither determined from the outside (i.e. by the linguistic community) nor from the inside (i.e., by the speaker's subjectivity, as if it were the product of unconstrained volitional acts). Arguing that discursive agency can be reduced neither to strict determination and automatism nor to spontaneity and freedom, this chapter takes up the challenge of developing an account of discursive agency that can avoid the Scylla of voluntarism and the Charybdis of determinism. In the next section (3.1) I offer a diagnosis of common misconceptions about linguistic performativity that create the false dichotomy between voluntarism and automatism. I will then articulate a contextualist view of agency that transcends this dichotomy (3.2). Finally, I will conclude with a discussion of the normative aspects of our capacity to produce speech acts, especially in relation to issues concerning linguistic stability and instability (3.3).

3.1. Fighting Philosophical Myths about Discursive Agency

In the debate in speech act theory during the twentieth century two main philosophical models of agency were in competition: an intentionalistic, subject-centered model and a sociological, community-centered model. The individualistic subject-centered model was defended, among others, by Grice and by Searle in his early writings. This model explained linguistic performance in terms of the communicative intentions of the speaker. On this model, the powers of intentionality of individual speakers were considered the primary motor of communication; and everything else, all the other aspects of communication (intersubjectivity, consensus, linguistic conventions, etc.), were considered secondary and derivative, thus becoming subordinated to the individualistic and intentional domain. This model construed speaker's intentionality[1] as the source of agency, that is, as that which makes our verbal acts meaningful and subject to normative assessments. Accordingly, the semantic and normative dimensions of speech acts were claimed to be explicable, ultimately, in individualistic and intentional terms. The principal competing model of performativity put the emphasis not on the individual's powers of intentionality, but on the social milieu and the linguistic conventions of the community. It is only by virtue of some sort of social consensus, of agreed-upon norms and conventions—some argued—that our speech acts acquire meaning, that our utterances and silences can be deemed intelligible or unintelligible. Some people read Austin and the later Wittgenstein as proposing this sociological account of performativity. Austin does indeed emphasize the crucial significance of linguistic conventions and standardized procedures and rituals for maintaining the illocutionary force of our speech acts. But it is not at all clear that he erects the conventional aspects of language as the ultimate arbiter of meaning and communication, as many have claimed. Some interpreters of Austin such as Cavell (1976 and 1979) and Felman (2002) have challenged the standard sociological reading. And indeed, the quote from Austin that opened this chapter casts doubt on the adequacy of any one-sided, single-factor account of agency, as will the discussion of his views in this chapter. Similarly, Wittgenstein insists that communication is made possible thanks to a background agreement in action and forms of life. But this is a far cry from claiming that what the community decides is the new foundation of language, the be-all and end-all of meaning and communication. However, this is precisely what Kripke's reading of Wittgenstein claims by ascribing to him a community view of meaning and rule following. And it is worth noting that the Kripkean reading of Wittgenstein has been very influential although it has also come under heavy attack in recent years. My interpretation of Wittgenstein in previous chapters as well as the discussion of his views in this chapter and the next call into question the central claims of the Kripkean reading. Perhaps the clearest and least problematic example of the sociological model of performativity can be found in the behavioral approach to the study of language in sociology,[2] social psychology, linguistics, and philosophy of language. We find an unqualified version of the sociological model of discursive agency in the Skinnerian account of verbal behavior[3] and in its philosophical counterpart in Quine.[4]

Although they are hard to find in pure form, the intentionalistic and sociological models of discursive agency have polarized the philosophical discussion of performativity. These models have retained the polarized conceptualizations of action proposed and promoted by the traditional views of agency: intentionalism allying itself with voluntarism and sociologism with automatism. It is no accident that contemporary philosophy of language is infested with voluntaristic and automatistic descriptions of speech acts. The preferred description of our speech acts is determined by whether these acts are thought to be under the control of the individual speaker or under the control of the linguistic community. What controls our agency in language? What exerts primary control over our discursive practices? Whether we choose a voluntaristic or an automatistic inflection for our descriptions of speech acts depends on our construal of discursive control, that is, on whether discursive control is said to lie in the intentional capacities of an individual's mind and will, or in the impersonal mechanisms and structures of society.

Voluntaristic and automatistic conceptualizations of discursive agency are pervasive in contemporary philosophy of language and they affect all camps.

For example, even within the single camp of Wittgensteinian philosophers we find both voluntaristic and automatistic descriptions of verbal behavior, depending on whether these philosophers put the emphasis on the individual or the community in their discussions of speech acts, thus leaning toward an intentionalistic or a sociological model of performativity. Among Wittgenstenians it is not difficult to find voluntaristic descriptions in which speakers are depicted as "taking" positions or perspectives, as "putting themselves" in a position of speechlessness or positioning themselves in the domain of intelligibility (Crary 2001). Speakers are also described as "having good reasons" to conform to the rules of the language game or to depart from them and create alternatives (O'Connor 2002). Voluntarism is also what inspires Wittgenstenians to describe creative agency leading to linguistic innovations as "the deliberate construction of new ways of talking" (Braaten 2002). But this is not how speakers typically behave when they act or refrain from action in discursive practices: the positions or perspectives they occupy are typically not chosen; their attitudes toward norms and their linguistic conformity or nonconformity are typically not the result of a reasoned position. This lack of choice and rational control is particularly clear when we find speakers in terribly uncomfortable positions: these positions are not chosen, and neither is the discomfort they produce, nor the disruptive moves that may result from them, for these are more spontaneous reactions (jerking, twisting and turning, so to speak) than deliberate attempts at subversion planned by balancing reasons— although of course the latter do occur as well in specific contexts. As we will see, there is always a level of unknowingness in discursive agency, even when there is deliberation and planning behind our speech acts. This is precisely what is obscured and implicitly denied in voluntaristic descriptions, which lure us into the illusion that discursive agency falls fully under the control of the speaker. This illusion is what I will call the "Myth of Self-Possession."

The critics of voluntarism and its associated Myth often go to another extreme: *automatism*. This is a fatalist view that depicts speakers as automata reacting to one another in mechanical ways. This automatism can be seen in the social behaviorism still defended by very influential figures in philosophy of language such as Quine (1990). This view can also be found among Wittgenstenians. On this view a language game becomes a puppet theater in which players are at the mercy of an invisible puppeteer (i.e., the Game itself, its Rules, or some Force within it such as Custom). In the Wittgenstein literature this is the view that we can find in the most radical versions of the community view of rule following such as the one defended by Kripke (1982). Automatism also involves an illusion, which is the mirror image of the Myth of Self-Possession. The illusion here is that nothing falls under the speaker's control, that there is something else, something external to the speaker, that pulls the strings and is responsible for her actions. I will term this illusion the

"Myth of Subjective Dispossession," since it portrays speakers and their speech acts as deprived of all subjectivity and spontaneity. These extreme positions and their associated myths provide the central challenge for any philosophical account of discursive agency. The challenge is to successfully navigate between the Scylla of voluntarism and the Charybdis of automatism, carefully steering one's way between the Myth of Self-Possession and the Myth of Subjective Dispossession. In order to accomplish this feat, we need a bit of diagnostic work to prepare ourselves for the journey.

In order to be able to avoid voluntarism and automatism, we need to find out the specific dangers and attractions of these views, that is, we need to know what exactly is wrong with them and what makes them so appealing. The central task of my diagnosis of these views is to identify the assumption(s) on which they rest and the distortion(s) they involve. It is my contention that voluntarism and automatism have a common root: there is a common assumption that gives rise to both views. This is the idea that there must be *a control system*, whether inside or outside the speaker, which governs our speech acts, the idea that discursive agency must spring from a particular source that dictates its direction. The only disagreement between voluntarism and autom-atism is about what this control system is, that is, about what occupies the high commanding office in the production of speech acts. The voluntaristic candidate is the speaker's will, or intellect, or some other internal faculty in the speaker's subjectivity; the automatistic candidate is something or other in the speaker's milieu, that is, outside the speaker's subjectivity (e.g. social institutions, structures, rules, customs, etc.). These are different versions of the same assumption, namely: that we must be able to locate the seat of agency somewhere. But in postulating an ultimate source of agency, voluntarism and automatism are appealing to a *deus ex machina*. And whence this need for divine intervention? What are the problems that these different *dei* (the will, the social milieu, etc.) are supposed to solve? The crucial set of problems at stake seems to involve issues of imputability and responsibility. Viewed in this light, voluntarism is an *inculpatory* model of discursive agency. This is a model that proclaims complete autonomy for our speech behavior and inculpates the speaking subject in a radical way, disavowing all external influences. In this way the inculpatory model indulges in the Myth of Self-Possession. This myth is expressed in radical formulations of the thesis of first-person author-ity, according to which nothing but the speaking subject herself can claim control over and can be held responsible for her speech acts. On the other hand, automatism involves an *exculpatory* model of discursive agency that argues for the absolute heteronomy of speech behavior and disavows any kind of individual responsibility. This model dismisses the very notion of responsi-bility or transfers it to something other than speaking subjects, thus indulging in the Myth of Subjective Dispossession.

In the debates between voluntarism and automatism there is a constant oscillating movement between the Myth of Self-Possession and the Myth of Subjective Dispossession. This hypnotic oscillation involves a dangerous dialectic between inculpation and exculpation, which in turn relies on an untenable inner/outer dichotomy. In order to find a way out of this dialectic and to undo its hypnotic effect, we need to show that it is impossible to neatly sort out the multicausal processes that go into the production of speech acts according to an inner/outer dichotomy. When it comes to issues of imputability and responsibility, the inner/outer dichotomy is thought to correspond to the subject/object dichotomy. One way to understand the debate between voluntarism and automatism is as a dispute concerning *whether speakers are subjects or objects*. But this subject/object dilemma rests on important misconceptions. We cannot separate out the subjective and objective aspects of our speech behavior and their production in the way suggested by voluntarism and automatism. We have to keep in mind that there is traffic between what is *subjective* and what is *objective*, as well as between what is *internal* and what is *external*. It is important to appreciate that these terms do not designate fixed positions, but fluid and relational ones. It is not accurate to say that things *just are* inner-subjective or outer-objective, as if we could classify all things and phenomena into one of these poles once and for all. Things *become* inner and subjective, outer and objective;[5] that is, they are internalized and externalized, they are subjectified and objectified.[6]

In developmental psychology the Vygotskian tradition has underscored the importance of processes of *internalization* through which things that are initially objective ingredients of the social milieu become reflected in the child's behavior and later internalized in her mental states and attitudes. Thus, resulting from the internalization of processes of enculturation, we can find internal and subjective counterparts of public symbols in inner speech, and of social values in the normative attitudes of individual subjects.[7] More recently, the paradigm of cultural psychology within the Vygotskian tradition has also emphasized the importance of processes of *externalization* as a source of linguisitic and cultural innovation and social change.[8] Through externalization processes subjective elements that are initially idiosyncratic and pertain to the inner workings of individual minds become reflected in speech and behavior. And thus, by finding public expressions, these subjective elements (novel reactions, ideas, beliefs, goals, plans, etc.) become objectified and externalized; and their objective and external counterparts can make important contributions to our social practices, enriching, modifying, and sometimes even radically transforming the social milieu. The existence of processes of internalization and externalization calls into question traditional notions of interiority and exteriority, creating a traffic that makes it impossible to maintain a sharp distinction between what qualifies as inner-subjective and as outer-objective.

The very fact of speakers' *embodiment* also problematizes the distinction between what is "inside" and what is "outside" the speaking subject. In this respect, feminist theorists such as Butler (1993, 1997) and Felman (2002) have called our attention to the corporeal dimension of performativity: it is not an inner subjectivity, but a body that speaks. And this corporeal dimension of speech affects crucially our discursive agency: which body speaks (a male or female body, a racial body, an ethnic body, etc.) has a tremendous impact on the illocutionary—that is, on the kind of speech act it is and the force attached to it; on the perlocutionary—that is, on the effects or consequences of the speech act; and on the semantic and interpretative—that is, on the content of the speech act as a whole and the meanings ascribed to its components.

More importantly, we cannot neatly divide the ingredients of discursive agency into *subjective* and *objective* simply because these are not mutually exclusive categories. Speakers can simultaneously occupy subject and object positions; and their agency often exhibits both subjective and objective aspects. Indeed there are discursive processes of subjectification and objectification that go in different directions and are at odds with one another; and it is important to note that they can coexist even when they contradict each other.[9] "Are we subjects or objects of discourse?" We are both and we are neither. However, voluntarism answers the question in one way and automatism in another. The mistake, though, is to accept the question as a legitimate one in the first place. The antidote to this question is to reverse the relation between agency and the subject/object positions. Rather than treating agency as the *explanandum* and the subject/object positions as the *explanans*, we should try to shed light on the latter through the former, for it is agency that is primary and should come first in the order of explanation. We should replace fixed subject/object positions with transactional and fluid forms of agency, so that we no longer talk about *being* a subject or an object, but rather, about *becoming* and *acting as* a subject or an object. This conceptualization puts the emphasis on performative processes of subjectification and objectification, rather than on their products. On this performative model, the subject/object positions are not a given, but the result of agency; and even the most rigid subject and object positions are thought to be produced and maintained by particular forms of agency. According to this model, discursive agents are neither subjects nor objects in an absolute sense, as voluntarism and automatism would have us believe. We should assess this performative and dynamic model vis-à-vis the reified and static model underlying the subject/object dilemma in terms of what they can do for us. When we treat the subject/object positions as fixed and mutually exclusive unexplained explainers, some of the most interesting and fundamental questions about discursive agency cannot even be formulated; and the questions that are raised suffer systematic distortions.

The subject/object dilemma systematically distorts issues of imputability and responsibility by formulating them in overly simplistic terms. One such oversimplified formulation is offered by the *proprietary model* that translates the question "Who/What is responsible for this action?" into the question "Who/What *owns* this action?" When couched in these terms, voluntarism depicts speakers as possessors while automatism depicts them as being (dis)possessed. But these two views share the assumption that there is something to be possessed in discursive agency, that a speech act is the kind of thing that can have an owner, whether this owner is the speaker or someone/something else. That is, the common assumption underlying both views is the *commodification of discursive agency*. Wittgenstein's critique of the proprietary subject can be used as an argument against this assumption. Although the target of this critique is the commodification of experiential contents, the critique can be generalized to apply to the analogous commodification of actions. For if the subject's relationship to her experiences can be construed on the model of ownership, so can her relationship to her actions (including her speech acts). This critique is summarized in section 398 of the *Philosophical Investigations*. Talking about visual sensations Wittgenstein writes:

> "At any rate only *I* have got THIS." What are these words for? They serve no purpose. Can one not add: "There is no question of a 'seeing'—and therefore none of a 'having'—nor of a subject, nor therefore of 'I' either"? Might I not ask: In what sense have you *got* what you are talking about and saying that you only have got it? *Do you possess it?*
>
> [. . .] you are talking (if, for example, you are sitting in a room) of the "visual room." The "visual room" is the one that has no owner. I can as little own it as I can walk about it, or look at it, or point to it. Inasmuch as it cannot be any one else's it is not mine either. [. . .] the visual room *cannot* have any owner. "For"—one might say—"it has no master, outside or in." (PI §398; emphasis preserved and added)

Wittgenstein emphasizes that the logic of ownership applies to public objects that can be manipulated at will by their proprietors. When experiential subjects are conceived as owners, the contents of their experience become commodities that are fully under their control or mastery. Thus when applied to the allegedly private, inner domain of subjectivity, the logic of ownership results in untenable subjective reifications. And the alleged privacy and interiority of these subjective commodities ultimately undermines the logic of ownership, which requires public and in principle transferable and sharable objects. Moreover, the attempt to reproduce this logic at the level of the subjective is not only self-defeating and vain but also dangerous. For when we construe the relationship between the subject and her experiential contents in terms of ownership and mastery, we structure subjectivity according to the model of total subordination and submission to a sovereign power with full control over oneself. As Smith (2002) has argued, the proprietary model of subjective ownership or self-mastery is only apparently empowering, for whether the owner/master to whom we submit is outside or inside, this model involves a kind of harsh disciplining of subjective life that is heavily constraining and demanding. The postulation of an inner "master/owner" entails a submissive attitude and the internalization of relations of subordination: "such an internalized 'master' needs to be challenged [. . .] because it is [. . .] likely to demand the kind of harsh, unbending, uncritical submission to authority that produces abuse" (p. 356). Smith urges us to repudiate the idea of an internal master/owner and to abandon the model of proprietorship. She proposes instead an action-based view of "masterless subjectivities" as more adequate to a progressive agenda in social and political philosophy.

It is not uncommon to find in feminist theory, queer theory, and critical race theory descriptions of oppressed minorities that rely on the language of ownership: members of oppressed groups are depicted as being *dispossessed* of their subjectivity, as being *expropriated* of their experiences, their actions, and their meanings.[10] (I have myself used this language above in my analysis and discussion of Bourdieu.) The metaphorical description of oppressed subjects as "have-nots" is illuminating and fruitful insofar as it calls attention to economic exploitation in the most literal sense and it relates different forms of alienation to this fundamental one. However, when it comes to discursive agency (i.e., to speech acts and their meaning), it is misleading to talk about *dispossession* and *expropriation* because the language of ownership obscures the specific form of alienation that operates here, which is not property based. The alienation of discursive agency cannot be overcome by acquiring discursive property or capital. It is an illusion to think that there is such thing (as if the products of discursive agency could be inherited, purchased, or donated as gifts). It is misleading to say that subjects can be expropriated of the products of their discursive agency because this agency does not yield products that can be had, it does not produce *a capital* that can be possessed. In this respect I take exception to Bourdieu's notion of "linguistic capital" (see esp. his 1991), which applies the economic model of possession and expropriation to language and promotes the commodification of discursive agency. It is clear that Bourdieu wants to apply the notion of "capital" to language in order to call our attention to the interplay of power relations in discursive practices and to how power accrues in some discursive styles and habitus. However, although we should indeed pay attention to the unequal distribution of power in our discursive practices, the economic model is not particularly helpful; in fact, it is distorting, for it obscures precisely what—as we shall see—is the most specific feature of the discursive life of power: what characterizes the power dynamics of discursive practices is precisely its diffuse and uncontrollable nature, its *unownability*.

The language of possession and ownership is ineffective in the fight against certain forms of oppression, especially those that have been internalized and go to the very core of subjectivity. The most problematic kind of oppression we find in our discursive practices is the discursive oppression or marginalization that gets internalized and becomes constitutive of (i.e., part of the normative structure of) the subjectivity of certain speakers. Speaking subjects internalize the normative structures of the practices in which they have been acculturated and in which they are competent participants. We have to pay attention to how subject positions are construed in these practices, that is, how speakers' identities are shaped and domesticated when they are inserted in the grid of power relations that organize and structure those practices. Power relations are established in our discursive practices through our everyday activity of playing language games in the *same* way, which in fact means conducting these activities in similar enough ways in certain respects in our day-to-day routines; and if these power positions and relations are to be sustained across generations, they have to be sedimented by means of their transmission through processes of enculturation that bring new generations into the discursive practices. These enculturation processes try to guarantee (insofar as it is possible) that our practices will be conducted in similar ways in the future (similar enough so as to preserve the current power structure and normative apparatus of these practices). There is always a grid of power relations in our language games and these power relations (although always unstable and open to change, as we shall see) shape and domesticate discursive positions and speakers' identities. Precisely because of this performative production and maintenance of discursive subordination and oppression, the reified language of ownership is distorting and unhelpful. Far from facilitating liberation, this language is complacent with performative dynamics of power relations and facilitates relations of subjugation by preserving the idea of a master or owner in relation to something uncontrollable that admits no master or owner, for discursive agency cannot be owned or dominated. As Smith (2002) argues, in our attempts to liberate oppressed subjectivities, the language of ownership is counterproductive because it produces an internal counterpart of subjugation[11] since "dispossession invites repossession and reclaiming" (p. 357). Subordination and subjugation are not the best model for interpersonal relations. And if it is wrong to relate to others as owners relate to their property, it is also wrong to relate to oneself in those terms for the same reasons. The ownership model is wrong both at the interpersonal and at the personal level; and we are better off without it in fighting against oppressed subjectivities. As Smith (2002) puts it, "in order to emerge from oppressive situations, it may be not needed, not useful, and contrary to our ideals to take the model of the external master into our personal, so-called private, experience" (p. 351).

The metaphorical descriptions of oppressed subjectivities as being dispossessed invokes the dangerous rhetoric of commodification and invites voluntarism and automatism to come to the rescue. Both voluntarism and automatism claim to have liberating power. Their stories of empowerment are narratives that rely on the assumption of an ultimate source of agency with full control over speakers and agents—narratives often couched in the language of possession and dispossession. Voluntarism tries to achieve the empowerment of the individual by emphasizing her first-person authority and disavowing the influence of external forces on her discursive agency. This retreat to the individual is a crucial part of the Myth of Self-Possession that is behind liberal individualism. Automatism criticizes this myth as a conservative illusion that distracts us from those forces that actually determine our behavior. But this view of discursive agency goes to the other extreme, arguing for the unavoidable determinations of discursive agency and denying any kind of spontaneity on the part of the speaker. According to automatism, self-empowerment can only come from the recognition of these determinations, of one's predicament as a dispossessed subject—an idea that has been fully elaborated in the Stoic tradition. To these views, we should reply, with Wittgenstein, "No master, outside or in." In calling for total submission to a sovereign source of control and authority (wherever this source happens to be located), both of these views impose an *impossible rigidity* on discursive agency that can be grotesque. How can it be a condition of possibility of speech acts that they be *owned* by the speaker or that they be *commanded* by some external (ventriloqual or puppeteering) force? As Scheman has suggested,[12] a good parody of the voluntaristic model can be found in those cartoon characters that run over the edge of cliffs and only fall when they notice that there is no longer any ground underneath their feet. But outside cartoons we fall whether we notice or not. Hence the absurdity of thinking that a signifying act can only happen when it is brought under the speaker's control and authority, when it enjoys the consent of its rightful owner. Equally absurd is to think that the signifying actions of human beings are automatic effects of impersonal forces and that subjectivities are not implicated in them at all. A caricature of this mechanistic view of subjectivity as pure passivity can be found in the numerous jokes circulating in academia after the demise of behaviorism: jokes about agents patiently waiting for conditioning processes to kick in, or jokes about incarcerating institutions or the grandparents or the oldest members of a criminal's family as an appropriate response to a crime.

Wittgenstein's critique of the proprietary subject helps us to identify the implausible implications and dangers of voluntarism and automatism. But we can draw more than negative conclusions from Wittgenstein's critique. Building on this critique, I will offer an alternative account of discursive agency in the remainder of this chapter. The first positive conclusion that derives directly

from Wittgenstein's critique is the *unownability* of speech acts. This feature is
the centerpiece of my contextualist account of discursive agency. But someone
might reply that I'm going too fast. That is, one might argue that actions are
unlike experiential contents and that the logic of ownership can be applied to
them. Aren't speech acts (and their meanings) public and sharable? So why
can't they be owned? We need further argumentation to establish the intrinsic
unownability of discursive agency. To begin to see why speech acts (and their
meanings) can have no owner, we can reflect on Toni Morrison's parable of the
blind woman discussed by Butler in *Excitable Speech*. In Morrison's parable the
experienced speaker/writer is analogized to a blind woman whose interlocutors are a group of children who ask her to guess whether the bird they have in
their hands is dead or alive. She replies: "I don't know . . . but what I do know
is that it is in your hands. It is in your hands." As Butler (1997) puts it, this
parable emphasizes that all speaking and writing is *blind* in the sense that "it
cannot know the hands into which it will fall" (p. 8). According to the parable,
a speaker (or writer) does not own her language; her speech acts are always at
the mercy of others. Moreover, no particular other can lay claim to the meaning of one's utterance or silence, at least not in an exclusive sense, because the
same reasoning would apply to this interpreter as well: the meaning of the
speech act in question is not "in the hands" of this speaker/writer either, but
"in the hands" of others.

   But while fighting against individualistic versions of the ownership model
of discursive agency, this parable is still quite sympathetic to collectivistic versions of this model. In fact, the parable invites a proprietary claim, inducing
us to think that while the meaning or interpretation of a speech act is not
in the hands of anyone in particular, it is in the hands of all speakers/writ-
ers taken collectively, that is, in the hands of the linguistic community. This is
precisely the proprietary claim defended by *a consensus view of meaning* such as
Kripke's community interpretation of Wittgenstein on meaning and rule-following, or by its transcendental counterpart, which we can find in Habermas's
account of communicative action or in Peirce's semiotics.[13] In order to over-
throw the ownership model, we need to take the parable a step further and say
that speech acts are not the kind of thing that can be held in hands; that is,
they are not the kind of thing that can be subject to the control of a sovereign
power, whether this alleged power is held by an individual speaker or by a linguistic community (actual or possible). The move to the social does not help
the ownership model. And it doesn't help because the lack of control over a
speech act does not result only from the intersubjectivity of language, but also
from a bedrock level of *underdetermination* that cannot be eliminated.[14] (I will
elaborate on this point in the next section with my contextualist analysis of
what it means to have a voice, and with the discussion of the different levels of
the underdetermination and uncontrollability of our voices.)

As Butler (1997) notes, Morrison's parable depicts language "as a living thing over which one has control," "as agency—as an act with consequences" (p. 6). We have to go further and qualify this depiction in the following way: the use of language is indeed "an act with consequences," but an act with *unforesee-able* consequences; language is "a living thing" indeed, but a living thing that cannot be brought under the control of a sovereign power. As Butler suggests in her performative analysis of hate speech, it is the *perlocutionary* (the effects achieved through our locutions) that shapes and gives force to the *illocutionary* (the types of locutions recognized in our practices and the peculiar strength and significance they have): nothing is hate speech in itself, but only in virtue of its consequences, in virtue of the possible injuries that it can produce to others given the contingent history of our practices, given the historical emergence of discursive positions that render certain subjects vulnerable to harm, to be wounded by certain words in certain contexts. It is this contingent history of effects which is sustained in our everyday practices that can transform words into weapons. And, of course, the perlocutionary effects of our speech acts (including possible injuries) are not under anyone's control. The kind of speech act an utterance (or silence) constitutes and the force it has are not things that indivuals or even entire communities can decide. This point can be generalized to all kinds of speech acts and their illocutionary forces. "I pronounce you husband and wife" as uttered by certain speakers under certain conditions constitutes an act of marriage, the very performative production of the act, given the history of our legal, social, cultural, and religious practices which have endowed that performative ritual (in the different recognized and accepted forms of the ceremony) with its consequences (legal incidents as well as personal, social, and cultural effects). The link between the speech act and its consequences is established and maintained by a vast system of interrelated language games which are backed up by a legal apparatus as well as by a complicated network of social practices that support the institution of marriage. And the same can be said of "I promise . . . ," "I apologize . . . ," "I assert . . . ," and all the other performatives that Austin (1975) recognized (which in the end include all possible utterances since they all have a performative dimension insofar as they constitute the production of a linguistic act with normative force and normative consequences).[15]

The general point is that it is by virtue of their repeated consequences in our discursive practices that certain speech acts acquire a particular significance and a particular force is attached to them. The force of these locutions is certainly not determined by anybody's will. It is not a matter of decision at all. I cannot decide what kind of speech act I produce because I cannot control its consequences. The illocutionary force of my speech acts is not up to me; it escapes my control; it will be determined, over time, by the perlocutionary effects of those acts. But it is important to note that the illocutionary force of our speech acts is not up to the linguistic community either; it also escapes community control. Linguistic conventions can acquire more or less force in our discursive practices depending on their use; but no matter how powerful agreed-upon conventions become, they never strictly determine the force and significance of our speech acts; they cannot fix illocutionary forces and semantic contents once and for all. As we saw in chapter 1, semantic contents are contextually determinate but always remain intrinsically unstable and open. We now see that what goes for meanings also holds, for similar reasons, for the illocutionary forces of our speech acts. For example, what counts as a successful performative act of marriage? Should a same-sex marriage ceremony qualify as a felicitous performance if the people originally invested with authority to perform marriage ceremonies decide to include same-sex couples in this institution? Or if the local authorities so decide (e.g., the major's office, as in San Francisco in 2004)? Or do we have to wait for higher authorities beyond particular individuals or local authorities to settle the issue? And if so, which authorities? The State Supreme Court (as in MA)? The U.S. Supreme Court? A referendum? What is important to note is that when questions of this sort are brought up (no matter before what authority) there is *always room for social negotiation*. (The interesting case of the critical interrogation of the scope and limits of the institution of marriage through *eccentric* practices—that is, through chains of nonstandard performances—will be explored later in 3.3.) The *instability of illocutionary forces* is of crucial importance: to say that these forces are unstable is to say that the parameters they establish are also unstable; and these are the parameters for how our locutions can circulate in the linguistic market (as a promise, an apology, an assertion, an act of marriage, etc.), and therefore the parameters within which our communicative interactions are interpreted. This instability of the performative underscores the central point of my analysis: once again, speech acts cannot be *owned*.

What I call the "unownability" of discursive agency is not only a point about the interpretation of speech acts being an intersubjective enterprise. This unownable character has to do with the fact that others have a say in shaping the meaning of my speech acts, but also with the fact that this meaning is essentially underdetermined and always remains *unfinished and open*—unfinished and open for individual speakers as well as for speech communities (even if these are indefinitely extended and idealized à la Peirce or à la Habermas); forever unfinished and open however we construe the relevant performative chains of utterances in which words are used. Unownability, therefore, means *uncontrollability as a matter of principle*; that is, it means that here (in the discursive) control and ownership constitute an illusion. As Butler (1997) puts it, linguistic competence is to be "distinguished from forms of control or mastery," for when it comes to language use, "'agency' is not the same as 'control'" (p. 8). Speech acts are uncontrollable: they are neither in the speaker's hands nor in someone else's hands; they are in no one's hands, they are not the kind of thing that can be held in hands. Given this uncontrollability, we must give a negative answer to Cavell's question "Must we mean what we say?"[16] In an important sense we cannot mean what we say because we cannot know what we mean. No one can. This *unknowingness* is intrinsic to language use. This constitutive unknowingness is the epistemic dimension of the unownability or uncontrollability of discursive agency. I want to distinguish between two different dimensions of this unownability or uncontrollability: an *epistemic* dimension, in which we find the *unknowingness* of speaking subjects; and a *structural or praxiological* dimension, in which we find the inescapable *openness* of our discursive practices.

At the epistemic level, the fact that our speech acts cannot be anyone's property and cannot be brought under anyone's control means that these acts cannot ever be fully known and predictable. Uncontrollability and unownability yield unknowability and unpredictability. As Wittgenstein puts it: "You must bear in mind that the language-game is so to say something *unpredictable*. I mean: it is not based on grounds. It is not reasonable (or unreasonable). *It is there—like our life*" (1969 [OC] §559; my emphasis). And this existential unknowingness of linguistic actions is not only an epistemic feature of individual speakers, but also an epistemic feature of the entire speech community. Speech is indeed a living thing and it is as unpredictable as our own life or the life of our community. The communal life of speech is as opaque to the community as the life of my utterances (including their force and consequences) is to myself as a speaker. This inescapable unknowingness is always present in communication both at the interpersonal and at the personal level of speech production and reception. It is not only that my speech is unpredictable when it is out of my hands because it is continued by the speech of others and shaped and reshaped by their interpretations; even my own speech and my own interpretations are unpredictable: they contain a level of ineludible unknowingness insofar as they are not under my sovereign control or under the control of any sovereign power. But this uncontrollability has also another dimension, a structural or praxiological dimension, which goes beyond the epistemic.

It would be a mistake to think that the lack of control or ownership over speech is due only to unconscious elements of our discursive agency which can in principle be repaired as more and more aspects of this agency are brought to consciousness and become known. The misleading thought here is that if we could recover everything there is to know about our discursive agency—everything that has thus far remained unconscious for individual speakers and linguistic communities—our speech acts would no longer be uncontrollable and unownable. In other words, the idea is that the apparent uncontrollability and unownability of speech is only the product of our cognitive limitations, so that if these limitations were removed, such appearance would disappear: from an omniscient perspective, discursive agency is perfectly controllable and ownable. The uncontrollability and unownability of speech acts is a *structural* feature of our agency that is independent of our cognitive limitations. This feature would remain unaffected even if we could extend our cognitive powers indefinitely. It does not help to say "If we only knew!" for there is nothing there to know! There is nothing there to know that could possibly eliminate the uncontrollability and unownability of speech. There is no factor or set of factors which, unbeknownst to us, could determine the pragmatic and semantic life of our speech. Its uncontrollability or unownability is constitutive; it is grounded in a structural feature of discursive agency: its *radical openness*.

Discursive agency is radically open because it is *indefinite* in Kant's sense, that is, because it cannot be synthesized. Kant argued that a series of worldly events is neither finite nor infinite, but indefinite because it is never given once and for all and, therefore, it cannot be synthesized in a complete and final way. The same can be said about a series of speech acts: the series is never given (*gegeben*) but only proposed (*aufgegeben*), because its synthesis is always deferred. Any attempt to synthesize a performative chain of speech acts with a final statement is in vain because this statement is itself a speech act that is integrated in the performative chain. An utterance cannot be a final synthesis of a discursive series because it is destined to become part of the series, to be synthesized by the next utterance. Thus the series of discursive acts remains indefinite, that is, indefinitely open. These Kantian reflections are at the core of Wittgenstein's indeterminacy arguments in the *Philosophical Investigations* (see the rule-following discussion in PI §§143ff).[17] Butler (1997) also implicitly refers to this Kantian indefiniteness or openness as a constitutive aspect of discursive agency when she characterizes performative chains as being constituted by "a failure to achieve a totalized form in any of its given instances" (p. 3). Explaining the relation between the items in a performative chain as a relation of *citation* or invocation, Butler characterizes openness in terms of *excess*: any speech act in a performative chain has "a condensed historicity: it exceeds itself in past and future directions, an effect of prior and future invocations that constitute the instance of utterance" (p. 3). Butler's account of citationality shows that performative chains are inherently unstable. This points to possibilities of insurrection and subversion in discursive practices which I will explore in the next chapter.[18] In the next section I will elaborate on the Butlerian view through an exploration of the excessive character of voices and their uncontrollability from a polyphonic perspective.

Its constitutive lack of fixity, its inherent instability, makes discursive agency radically uncontrollable and open. On my view, the radical uncontrollability and openness of discursive agency relates directly to (and can be explained in terms of) the indomitability of language games discussed above in relation to their polyphonic nature. It is because of the ever present possibility of unexpected voices that a language-game and our agency in it cannot be controlled or subsumed under a closed semiotic system with fixed rules. Through an elucidation of the indomitable polyphony of language games I will offer an account of what is involved in having a voice and the kind of responsibility imputable to it. What is the speaker's responsibility for her speech acts? And what is the responsibility of the linguistic community? Drawing on the accounts of performativity developed in feminist theory by Butler (1997) and Felman (2002), in what follows I will articulate my polyphonic view of discursive agency through a discussion of the individual and collective aspects of responsibility underlying our speech acts.

3.2. On Having a Voice: Uncontrollability, Polyphony, and a Hybrid View of Agency and Responsibility

As my diagnostic discussion in the previous section argued, one-factor accounts of performativity result in one-sided and distorted views of speech acts; and these polarized views of discursive agency promote neurotic or obsessive attitudes toward the responsibility for one's words. Voluntarism suggests an inculpatory model that assigns full responsibility to speakers as authors of their speech acts. By contrast, automatism puts forward an exculpatory model that relieves speakers of responsibility and assigns it instead to some impersonal control system or source of agency such as linguistic conventions, institutions, communities, or traditions. We are thus left with a choice between two equally unsatisfactory models of discursive responsibility, either inculpation or exculpation. My contextualism suggests a way out of this false dichotomy. The alternative that my contextualist perspective proposes is a hybrid view of agency and responsibility that contains heterogeneous elements: subjective and objective, individual and collective. This hybrid view contrasts sharply with the pure and homogeneous views of voluntarism and automatism. The heart of the contrast is that my hybrid view does not construe agency in terms of control and responsibility, in terms of an autonomous, self-governing control system (inside or outside the speaker) that can claim authorship of and take credit or blame for speech acts. The core difference with traditional views is that my contextualism proposes a *kaleidoscopic or polyphonic perspective* in which agency is fractured or splintered in performative chains and, accordingly, discursive responsibility is diffused across the links of these chains.

We still have agency and responsibility after we give up the illusory philosophical notions of complete authorship and full control—let's not throw away the baby with the bathwater. The notion of responsibility has been traditionally tied to the notions of sovereign subjectivity and authorship. But by severing this tie we do not do away with the notion of responsibility; on the contrary, this notion acquires a new force and its applicability is revitalized because we can now look at it with fresh eyes, not through the lenses of the philosophical requirements of one-sided theories. Far from marking the demise of agency and responsibility, the rejection of the traditional notions of authorship and sovereignty constitutes the starting point of notions of discursive agency and discursive responsibility that remain close to our actual practices and are directly relevant to ordinary contexts and readily applicable in them, thus being also socially and politically useful. Focusing on hate speech, Butler (1997) has argued for a conception of discursive agency and discursive responsibility that transcends traditional conceptions of sovereign subjectivity. She sets the agenda for such a conception in the following way:

> Untethering the speech act from the sovereign subject founds an *alternative notion of agency and, ultimately, of responsibility*, one that more fully acknowledges the way in which the subject is constituted in language, how what it creates is also what it derives *from elsewhere*. Whereas some critics mistake the critique of sovereignty for the demolition of agency, I propose that agency begins where sovereignty wanes. The one who acts (who is not the same as the sovereign subject) acts precisely to the extent that he or she is constituted as an actor and, hence, operating within a linguistic field of enabling constraints from the outset. (Butler 1997, pp. 15–16; my emphasis)

As Butler suggests, the lack of autonomy and control of our speech acts has to do with the fact that our agency is conditioned by constraints that lie elsewhere and the products of our agency also point elsewhere: as she says, they are derived from elsewhere and, as she goes on to explain (though not in these terms), they will also be taken up elsewhere. The uncontrollability/unownability thesis I defended in the previous section relates to the elsewhere-orientation that, as we saw in chapter 1, is consubstantial to language games and to our agency in them. The elsewhere-consitution of our agency is responsible for its uncontrollability and unownability. As explained above, the elsewhere-orientation of our language games refers to their *indomitable polyphony*, that is, to their being constituted by an irreducible multiplicity of voices (actual and possible) that cannot be restricted in any principled way. But this wild multiplicity characterizes not only the games we play, but also our very identities as players of these games: it is not only the language game or discursive practice as a whole that exhibit a polyphonic structure; our very agency in it as speakers is also polyphonic, our own voice is plural or choral. In what follows I explain the elsewhere-consitution of discursive agency in polyphonic terms, and I try to show that it is the indomitable polyphony of our agency that is responsible for its uncontrollability and unownability. It is precisely because of its polyphonic nature that discursive agency is not something that can be controlled and owned. The internal and constitutive relation between polyphony and uncontrollability/unownability can be expressed in the thesis that *it is not possible to speak in a single voice*, that the very possibility of speaking at all presupposes a chorus of voices. Neither individuals nor communities (or institutions, traditions, cultures, conventions, etc.) can speak in a single voice. For a voice is *intrinsically relational*: it is defined vis-à-vis other voices; it acquires specificity and a distinctive existence only in a field of voices (actual and possible) in relation to which it is positioned; and this *positionality* is dynamically and dialectically altered as the choral field of voices changes. The relationality of voices has two distinct dimension: a *social* dimension and a *temporal or historical* dimension. According to these two dimensions of their relationality, I now provide a two-fold elucidation of the polyphony that belongs to the internal constitution of voices.

In the first place, the relational character of voices derives from the social dynamics in which they are produced and in which they operate. A sociogenetic account of the relationality of voices rich in empirical specificity is provided by Bourdieu in *Language and Symbolic Power*. Bourdieu (1991) offers a sociological account of how voices distinguish themselves from one another in specific sociohistorical contexts and practices. The core of this account is how voices become stylistically marked vis-à-vis other voices (whether actual or possible). The stylistic dimension of a voice is crucial—in fact, constitutive (a voice cannot exist without it); and herein lies its relational character. For Bourdieu, having a voice consists in a highly situated, embodied capacity or "practical sense" (*sens pratique*) that cannot be reduced to an abstract set of generative rules or algorithmic recipes for sign manipulation. To have a voice is to have a particular way of speaking and listening, a linguistic *habitus* that is exhibited in the actual and situated performances of embodied speech. The speaker's habitus contains stable forms of sensitivity and generativity that have been laboriously manufactured through repeated performance. A particular style exists only in relation to other styles. Styles are ways of producing and interpreting speech that define themselves in relation to one another, and typically against each other. A style is something shared with some people and not with others; and the more rare the style, the more valuable it becomes. A style, therefore, involves a community of stylistically marked voices which is maintained through relations of inclusion and exclusion, that is, by allowing some people in and keeping other people out. A voice presupposes a collection of voices that speak in *similar* ways (voices that precede, currently concur, and will later follow one's voice) as well as a diverse collection of heterogeneous voices that speak *differently*. Bourdieu's sociogenetic analysis makes this very clear by showing how the habitus is a historically produced style, a generative and receptive capacity that has become stylistically marked through a history of habituation. Bourdie emphasizes how important it is to recognize the sociohistorical production of a habitus which is typically neglected and forgotten. And this forgetfulness of the habitus (this *genesis amnesia*)[19] is of course no accident: the sociohistorical processes of its generation cover over its socio-genesis in order to sediment it all the more forcefully by protecting it against any possible questioning in the light of alternatives. The habitus misrecognizes itself and this misrecognition (*meconnaisance*) of its genesis leaves unrecognized the power struggles that have gone into the production of our forms of speech and the ones that are still ongoing, that is, the power struggles that sustain our habitus. Stylistically marked voices typically misrecognize themselves because they fail to recognize their relational nature, that is, their polyphonic character, the fact that there are other voices on which they depend for their own existence. Indeed this pervasive misrecognition of one's voice takes place when the similar voices that support one's own as well as all those other (actual and possible) voices that differ from it are not acknowledged in their constitutive relations to one's own stylistically marked speech.

In the second place, as my foregoing discussion of the social dynamics in which voices enter has already indicated, the relationality of voices has another crucial dimension; namely, the *temporality or historicity* of discursive agency. Our voices are the product of a history and they participate in and contribute to this history as links in (open-ended) performative chains of voices. These performative chains of voices that speak to one another are described by Butler's notion of *citationality* and by my notion of *echoing* (see chapter 1). Voices acquire force and distinctiveness only insofar as they echo one another. Singular[20] voices can only develop and operate in a social field of voices and perspectives (both harmonious and dissonant ones). When a voice speaks, it unavoidably echoes other voices: past and future voices; concrete voices as well as abstract and impersonal ones—for we echo particular others, but we also echo conventions, institutions, and traditions. Whether we speak as individuals or as communities, in the singular or in the plural, there is always a chorus of voices involved: when I speak as an individual, as an 'I,' my voice presupposes dissonant voices from which it has become differentiated as well as similar voices with which it bonds; and when I speak as the representative of a group or community, I echo the other members of that community—those who have actually been part of it as well as possible participants, those *included* but indirectly also—by contradistinction—those *excluded*.

This echoing of voices was already suggested by Austin's analysis of the conventionality of speech acts. As Butler remarks, "the Austinian subject speaks *conventionally*, that is, it speaks in a voice that is *never fully singular*" (1997, p. 25; emphasis preserved and added). Austin's speech-act theory suggests that, insofar as our discursive agency has a conventional aspect, the "singularity" of our voices explodes into a chorus of voices. This becomes particularly clear when we examine the ritualistic dimension of speech acts in which performative formulas (such as "I pronounce you husband and wife") are invoked. The performative force of these formulaic expressions clearly derives from their repeated use in our practices; and this force has to be renewed and sustained over time by the linguistic community, an extended community that reaches us from the past and projects itself into the future. As Butler (1997) puts it: "The ritual dimension of convention implies that the moment of utterance is informed by the prior and, indeed, future moments that are occluded by the moment itself" (p. 25). The maintenance and transmission of performative force thus involve the *accumulation of voices* in performative chains in which there is a repeated citation of formulas and procedures. So when the authorized speaker performs the ritual, when she exerts the power with which she has been invested, what's the voice with which she speaks? How should we understand this voice? "Who speaks when convention speaks? In what time does convention speak? In some sense, it is *an inherited set of voices, an echo of others* who speak as the 'I'" (p. 25; my emphasis).

Against traditional accounts of speech acts (including the traditional reading of Austin's own theory), Butler argues that there is no such thing as "a totalized speech situation," that is, a final and self-contained discursive context that envelops the speech act and makes it explicable in its own terms without having to appeal to other contexts, without pointing elsewhere. As suggested by Butler's analysis, this conception of discursive contexts is illusory; there cannot be such a thing as "a totalized speech situation": it is rendered impossible by the peculiar temporality or historicity of speech. And note than nothing short of "a totalized speech situation" can support traditional notions of authorship and autonomy: such a self-contained and final totalized context is needed in order to proclaim oneself the absolute originator of speech acts—without implicitly citing previous usage, without implicitly echoing other voices—and in order to claim full control over and full responsibility for one's speech acts. These traditional notions of authorship and autonomy are challenged by the polyphonic character of performativity, by the echoing of a diverse multiplicity of voices. The interconnectedness of voices overlapping and criss-crossing is made necessary by the temporality or historicity of our discursive agency, for our speech always is and remains open to encounters with other voices that influence, modify, and shape our own; that is, our speech acts are necessarily extended into past and future directions in which they are taken up by indefinitely many other voices that echo one another and thus become dependent on one another, owing their force to each other. These interdependences between voices are captured by the Butlerian notion of *condensed and excessive historicity* that I alluded to at the end of the previous section: speech has "a condensed historicity: it exceeds itself in past and future directions, an effect of prior and future invocations that constitute the instance of utterance" (p. 3). Butler explains the excessive character of the historicity of speech and how it undermines (or at least strongly qualifies) the autonomy of the speaking subject in the following way: "Autonomy in speech, to the extent that it exists, is conditioned by a radical and originary dependency on a language whose historicity exceeds in all directions the historicity of the speaking subject" (p. 28). This is because the very constitution of a subject as a speaker is temporally structured by this *excessive historicity*: "the subject has its own 'existence' implicated in a language that precedes and exceeds the subject, a language whose historicity includes a past and future that exceeds that of the subject who speaks. And yet, this 'excess' is what makes possible the speech of the subject" (p. 28).

The socially and historically grounded polyphony of our agency goes against traditional conceptions of linguistic agents as having their performative powers within themselves. The two agents of discourse that have been traditionally considered as plausible candidates for the source of discursive agency are institutions and individual speakers. Whether impersonal or personal, these agents have been conceived as holding an autonomous or sovereign power over language. But in fact these agents are intrinsically polyphonic, and the heterogeneous plurality of voices that goes into their very constitution renders their autonomy and sovereignty impossible. It is very clear that institutions such as the French or the Spanish Royal Academy of Language contain a plurality of voices among its members, which are in turn affected by a wild variety of heterogeneous voices that speak to them from the living practices of language use. It is no wonder then that the linguistic conventions these institutions codify and enforce contain all kinds of tensions (implicit and explicit) that reveal the indomitable polyphony of language, that is, the uncontrollable dialogues and struggles among voices that maintain the language alive and resist any final systematization, unification, or homogeneization. As Benhabib (2002) and Narayan (1997)—among others, including myself[21]—have argued, cultures do not speak in one voice; and neither do cultural products and agencies such as linguistic conventions, social institutions, or cultural traditions. But, as I have suggested, even individual subjects are polyphonic and derive their discursive powers from a collection of inherited voices, echoing voices. One cannot have a voice unless one is situated within a network of overlapping and criss-crossing voices. Speaking subjects never speak in a voice that is fully singular; and as a result, their autonomy or sovereignty as speakers is always compromised and never absolute. The very constitution of a subject as a speaker involves a fundamental lack of autonomy and the impossibility of being an absolute author or originator of speech acts. As the Althusserian account of the genesis of subjectivity through communicative interaction shows (see 2.2 above), the speaking subject is constituted through interpellation, that is, through the address of the other—in fact, multiple others. A speaker is always interpellated by contemporaneous voices as well as by voices that speak from the past and from the future. These voices address the speaker in particular ways (for example, as a woman, as a lesbian, as black, as an intellectual, as immature, etcetera); and they also address her speech by assessing it, continuing it, and sanctioning it in particular ways (as sound, or irreverent, or injurious, or comforting, or as the case may be). Speakers always remain vulnerable to such an address since interpellation is part of their constitution as speakers.

Bringing together the Austinian account of the conventionality of language and the Althusserian account of the formation of the speaking subject through the address of the other, Butler emphasizes that being a speaker involves both *vulnerability and agency*: "To bridge the Austinian and Althusserian views, one would need to offer an account of how the subject constituted through the address of the Other becomes then a subject capable of addressing others" (1997, pp. 25–26). Having a voice or occupying a discursive position in a language game involves being linguistically vulnerable, that is, vulnerable to the address of other voices. And this vulnerability is never overcome (no matter how many defense mechanisms are erected to protect it). For it is the other side of agential power. Agency and vulnerability go together necessarily. This is a crucial aspect of the hybrid character of our discursive agency: we are always and at the same time subjects and objects of discourse, agents who can address others and be addressed by others. As speakers, we participate both actively and passively in performative chains that exceed our agency and nonetheless are sustained by it. This dual, hybrid character of our agency is there from the beginning, brewing in the formation of our agential powers, unfolding in the gradual constitution of our identity as speakers through processes in which we are both objectified and subjectified at the same time. The interpellative processes of subject formation treat subjects as objects by assigning to them particular discursive positions in our language games that constrain their moves within those games. But these constraining factors are at the same time enabling factors. Through the very address that inaugurates our existence as speaking subjects, we are also endowed with *responsive powers*. And this responsiveness can be the path to our self-liberation as speakers, for it can be used to play an active role in the construction of our identity as speakers, that is, in the modulation of our own voice. A speaking subject is *neither fully autonomous nor fully heteronomous*: it is not controlled from the inside but it is not determined from the outside either. Our voice is not only vulnerable to the address of other voices, but also responsive to it. Since linguistic vulnerability is never fully overcome, we cannot find such things as complete autonomy and total emancipation in our discursive agency. But for this very reason, as Butler argues, critique and the emancipatory and liberatory activities it can unleash become all the more necessary: "a critical perspective on the kinds of language that govern the regulation and constitution of subjects becomes all the more imperative once we realize how inevitable is our dependency on the ways we are addressed in order to exercise any agency at all" (1997, p. 27). The emancipation and autonomy of speakers can never be taken as a given; if and when we find some degree of emancipation and autonomy, it is always an achievement, and a fragile and partial one at that, one that needs to be constantly sustained and renewed.

The core idea of my hybrid conception is that speaker's agency is neither fully autonomous nor completely heteronomous. This hybrid view of agency marks the demise of the traditional notion of responsibility tied to unqualified notions of authorship, autonomy, and sovereignty. But at the same time it inaugurates a new notion of responsibility. The speaker assumes responsibility for her speech acts *not as originator, but as contributor* to a chain of linguistic performances that echo one another. As we have seen, the meaning and force of our speech acts are maintained by performative chains that exceed particular speakers and communities, chains to which new contributions can always be added. Accordingly, the responsibility of speakers concerns how to contribute to these performative sequences, how to continue or discontinue them, how to echo voices and their performances in and through these chains. As Butler puts it, discursive responsibility concerns *citation*, that is, it concerns how to repeat or cite in performative chains of speech acts: "The speaker assumes responsibility precisely through the citational character of speech. The speaker renews the linguistic tokens of a community, reissuing and reinvigorating such speech. Responsibility is thus linked with speech *as repetition, not as origination*" (1997, p. 39; my emphasis). This is what I call "echoing responsibility": the responsibility we have to take as discursive agents for echoing voices and their speech acts (including utterances and silences). Echoing responsibility is a more robust notion than it may seem at first sight, for it concerns crucial normative issues and the mobilization of our discursive powers to tackle these issues. The issues we are confronted with as speakers are whether a legacy of use is worth maintaining and in what way, whether the received use should be modified and how. In any performative chain in which we participate we should ask ourselves, What are the transformations that are needed in this chain, if any? and How can they be produced? These normative questions involved in the echoing responsibility of speakers reveal that although our discursive agency is not absolute or autonomous, it contains nonetheless tremendous transformative powers that often go unrecognized and unexploited. My notion of echoing responsibility thus agrees with Butler's citational account of speech: "the citationality of discourse can work to enhance and intensify our sense of responsibility for it. [. . .] The responsibility of the speaker does not consist of remaking language ex nihilo, but rather of *negotiating the legacies of usage* that constrain and enable the speaker's speech" (p. 27; my emphasis).

Our echoing responsibility refers to the negotiations that are constantly taking place in our communicative exchanges and discursive responsiveness to one another. Although we are typically not aware of these ongoing discursive negotiations, our speech acts are nonetheless situated in them; and given the position our speech acts come to occupy in performative sequences, they make particular contributions to the implicit negotiations that animate the performative chains. Our discursive agency should be conceived first and foremost as a process of negotiation. When we speak we are *implicitly negotiating* legacies of use with our interlocutors as well as with possible communication partners from the past and from the future. The negotiation processes through which the meaning and force of our speech acts are manufactured and reproduced, made and remade, are processes of *resignification*. Whether they result in the maintenance of a legacy of use or in its transformation, our speech acts always resignify. Since, as argued above, given the polyphonic contextuality of speech, signifying in the *same* way is not and cannot be fixed once and for all, *sub specie aeternitatis*, we are doomed to resignify in *similar and dissimilar* ways. In any performative chain there is always a continuum of cases of possible resignification ranging from the closest fidelity available to us (which always involves differences in the speech situation that are regarded as negligible) to radical reversals of meaning and force. As Butler puts it: "There is no possibility of *not* repeating. The only question that remains is: How will that repetition occur, at what site, juridical or nonjuridical, and with what pain and promise?" (1997, p. 102). In other words, we are doomed to repeat, but how we repeat is up to us. My notion of echoing tries to broaden this notion of repetition or citation by including silences among the speech acts that resignify in performative chains (without explicitly repeating or citing). With the proper support of the discursive context in which speakers find themselves, a legacy of use can be echoed in a silence and critical demands can be imposed on this legacy by silent speakers. When properly contextualized, certain silences can be construed as the refusal to repeat, as a kind of *negative echoing*; and therefore, they constitute critical interventions in our performative chains. In our speech acts we can repeat words with fidelity, with a difference (whether a major or a minor twist), and in certain cases we can refuse to repeat at all. The general point is that all these forms of echoing are ways of resignifying. As Butler has recognized, the specific power of our discursive agency lies in the power of resignification. Accordingly, echoing responsibility is responsibility for resignification.

The notion of echoing responsibility is a robust notion, but it is *not* a *pure or unconditional* notion (as the unqualified responsibility of the author or absolute originator of speech was supposed to be). As Butler puts it, this is a "sense of responsibility [. . .] afflicted with *impurity*" (p. 28; my emphasis). The impurity of our discursive responsibility is directly related to the hybridity of our agency. We only have a mixed, partial, and impure responsibility for our speech acts because our discursive agency is always *precarious, codependent*, and *open-ended*. These three features summarize the hybrid view of agency my contextualism proposes. On this view, our speech acts are always precarious and fragile: they are never solidly fixed, but crucially dependent on all kinds of contingencies that make them frail and unstable. In the second place, our speech acts are constitutively interdependent: our discursive agency relies on interdependencies that spread across performative chains; for indeed, as we have seen, our speech acts are not self-contained, self-governing, or autonomous, but intrinsically interdependent. And in the third place, our speech acts are always radically open: they remain always unfinished and never completed because they can always be continued in new ways. These three features of the hybridity of our agency underscores the fact that our speech acts are *beyond themselves*: they contain an unavoidable *excess* that cannot be tamed or controlled (which I have explained in terms of the *indomitable polyphony* of linguistic performance). And this excessive character of our speech acts makes clear that the processes of negotiation and resignification that take place in and through them are *never final*. As Butler puts it, in our performative chains "no final adjudication of conflicting positions can emerge"; and it is important to note, with Butler, that this "*lack of finality* [. . .] suspends the need for final judgment in favor of an affirmation of a certain linguistic *vulnerability to reappropriation*" (1997, p. 92; my emphasis). Resignification never achieves total closure. And this interpretive vulnerability, this openness to resignification, is consubstantial to the echoing that defines our discursive agency. This renders the responsibility of speakers an unavoidable burden, but also a burden that is always conditioned and limited; that is, it makes our discursive responsibility fundamental and inescapable, and at the same time fraught with impurities that are constitutive. These impurities cannot be eliminated because the hybridity of our agency cannot be overcome or transcended: our speech acts always retain their precariousness and fragility, their constitutive interdependencies, and their inevitable openness.

The lack of finality of performative chains defines the predicament of our agency and responsibility as individual speakers and as linguistic communities. Our individual and collective responsibility in discursive practices concerns our participation in endless process of negotiation and resignification. The open-ended nature of our performative engagements underscores the unlimited plurality of voices and perspectives to which our discursive practices must be open and ready to accommodate. In this sense what is most characteristic of the polyphonic contextualism defended in this book is its *thoroughgoing pluralism*. This brings to the fore the political dimension of my hybrid notions of agency and responsibility. These notions recommend a thoroughgoing pluralism that is very similar to the one at the core of the political paradigm of *radical democracy* proposed and defended by social and political theorists such as Chantal Mouffe.[22] Indeed the hybrid and impure notions of agency and responsibility I have offered are consonant with the political frameworks of pluralistic democracies in which processes of negotiation and deliberation always remain open. By contrast, these notions undermine absolutists conceptions of political power that rest on traditional notions of complete autonomy and sovereignty. The radically pluralistic and radically democratic organization of our discursive practices cannot be transcendentally justified by the structure of communication à la Habermas; but it can be recommended as the best way to deal with the radical openness of our agency. This openness is reflected in the interpretative vulnerability and openness to resignification of performative chains, which affects any of their component parts, that is, any speech act. This is how, as Butler puts it, "a *postsovereign democratic demand* makes itself felt in the contemporary scene of the utterance" (1997, p. 92; my emphasis).

The radically pluralistic structure of our discursive agency that my polyphonic view reveals has important normative implications, which I will explore in the next section. As an introduction to these implications, I want to note here two general consequences of my radical pluralism. In the first place, the pluralistic character of performativity leads to *normative instability*, for there cannot be fixed, absolute and unquestionable discursive norms that control our practices: the norms that underlie and regulate discursive practices do not and cannot speak in one voice and are, therefore, intrinsically unstable. But at the same time this pluralism underscores the implicit *normative richness* of our discursive practices, for these practices contain a wild plurality of normative standpoints that can make distinctive contributions to the normative regulation or deregulation of performance. Our discursive norms have unpredictable lives, since their existence depends upon our polyphonic uses of language in an open plurality of heterogeneous contexts. This can be taken as bad news if one was hoping for the rigidification of normativity and expecting us to reach, eventually, fixed and absolute norms. But the fluidity and flexibility of the normative structure of our practices can be taken as good news insofar as these features of discursive normativity maintain always open the possibility of learning and progressing in these practices in unforeseeable ways. There are of course no guarantees that learning and progress will take place just because we are open to their possibility. Given the precariousness and fragility of our discursive agency—its dependence on all sorts of contingencies—it goes without saying that our discursive practices can also become epistemically unproductive (even counterproductive) and regressive. We have to keep in mind that our discursive norms can always be extended, expanded, and enriched in new and interesting ways; but we have to keep in mind that they can also be narrowed down, rigidified, and impoverished. The risky and dangerous life of our discursive norms is not an obstacle for our discursive responsibility; far from it: it actually intensifies the responsibility for our contributions to performative chains in which, through our echoing, norms are continued, transformed, and discontinued.

3.3. The *Scandal* of Our Agency: Agency without Sovereignty and the Possibility of Transgression

In the previous section I articulated hybrid notions of agency and responsibility. I argued that although the speaker is not the free and autonomous source of her own agency, she is an active participant in the production of speech, contributing to the chains of performances through which linguistic practices are maintained and reproduced. I concluded that speakers must assume echoing responsibility, that is, responsibility for their echoing of other voices, for their contributions (or lack thereof) to the maintenance and perpetuation of discursive practices. Following Butler, I argued that the core of these hybrid notions of agency and responsibility is captured by the concept of *resignification*. I now want to look at this concept from the perspective of the normative relations between contexts of communication. For indeed the issue of how to resignify is the issue of how to travel across communicative contexts and how to create normative connections between them. How are the paths for inter-contextuality (to which I have been alluding since chapter 1) established? The issue of resignification thus becomes the issue of *recontextualization*: we resignify in new ways because we echo the meanings and forces of previous speech acts in new communicative contexts. The inescapable and always unfinished task of resignifying is at the same time the task of *reworking the normative structure* of our discursive practices. This always ongoing normative restructuring is accomplished through the processes of negotiation and resignification that are always underway. The normativity of speech is, therefore, a normativity in the making, a normativity that comes alive in and through the performative practices of resignification that take place in our actual linguistic activities.

What is the normative weight of prior contexts of use, including the "originating contexts" in which new meanings are first used and new illocutionary forces first exercised? One answer is that "originating contexts" establish linguistic conventions that are later further consolidated in subsequent contexts that are continuous and congruous with the original ones. This view is often ascribed to Austin. On the standard reading of Austin's view of the performative, discursive norms are thought of as established and sedimented in continuous contexts of use; and our speech acts are said to acquire normative force from their compliance with norm-consolidating contexts—a compliance that is specified typically in quite precise terms by the *felicity* conditions of these acts. This view of contextualization depicts our speech acts as constrained by linguistic conventions, that is, by the norms sedimented by use in prior contexts. On this view, departing from the received norms of past uses makes our speech acts lose their force and fail, becoming *infelicitous*—mere misfires or failed attempts at doing something with words. Derrida (1982) has been among the most fierce critics of this view. In "Signature, Event, Context", he develops a critique of Austin and proposes an alternative account of the normative relation between communicative contexts. With his notion of *rein-scription* Derrida (1982) argues that the use of language in new communicative contexts, far from relying on a process of contextualization that ties the new use to prior usage, consists, in fact, in a process of *decontextualization* that always involves a departure from previous contexts. Derrida contends that the performative force of a speech acts is derived from its *break* with prior contexts. Accordingly, he refers to the force of the performative as "breaking force" (*force de rupture*). Derrida's view accentuates the relative autonomy of speech acts with respects to their contexts of use. This *contextual freedom* is based on the model of written language. Derrida's account assimilates all language use, all speech acts, to the paradigm of decontextualization that is allegedly found in the written language. As Butler (1997) puts it, for Derrida, "performative utterances operate according to the same logic as written marks [. . .] which, as signs, carry 'a force that breaks with its context [and this] breaking force (*force de rupture*) is not an accidental predicate but the very structure of the written text" (p. 148). Derrida calls our attention to the gaps or intervals between instances of use and argues that they are a constitutive feature of the iterability of signs: as iterable structures, signs are marks cut off from their putative originating contexts. Against the Austinian emphasis on the continuity between contexts of use Derrida underscores the *discontinuity* between contexts. And against the Austinian emphasis on the conventionality of signs and ritualized contexts, Derrida underscores their *arbitrariness*: "the arbitrary nature of the sign" and the irregular and broken contexts in which they are used (see Derrida 1982, p. 323). As Butler (1997) has pointed out, this dispute between the Austinian model and the Derridian model "raises the question of whether the function of the sign is essentially related to the sedimentation of its usages, or essentially free of its historicity" (p. 148).

Are our speech acts cut off from prior usage or tethered to it? Things are far more complicated than this debate between polarized positions on performativity makes it seem. These polarized views make us think about performativity and contextuality in distorted and unhelpful terms, keeping us entangled in ill-posed questions: If we want to do things with words, do we have to contextualize or decontextualize these words? Do they acquire force by complying with norms or by breaking them, by being faithful to previous contexts of use or by departing from them? The polarized dichotomy between rigid contextualization and unconstrained decontextualization is a false dilemma and both of its horns should be rejected. On the one hand, the strict conventionalism ascribed to Austin involves a rigidified contextualization that can only be obtained if discursive contexts are glued together by absolutely fixed and stable norms or conventions. But it is illusory to think that there is an absolute continuity between contexts of use, as if they cascaded with a perfect flow in an unrelenting succession of congruous slices. On the other hand, the Derridian paradigm of decontextualization proposes an illusory freedom from historical contexts. This contextual freedom is illusory because, as argued above, historical contexts of communication do indeed constrain—even if they do not determine—the range of acts that can be successfully performed at any given time and their domain of significance. There are no radical breaks or absolute gaps between discursive contexts and, therefore, it is misleading (at best) to characterize language use as the capricious decontextualization of signs. Radical continuity and discontinuity are impossible ideals or illusions that do not capture at all the normative relations that exist between actual contexts of communication. My polyphonic contextualism offers an alternative view of intercontextuality which underscores the crucial normative relations of dependence between contexts that speak to each other or echo one another, while at the same time emphasizing the openness of the performative chains that can be found across contexts. On my view, communicative contexts are not insulated and sealed off from one another; they are in dialogue, and these intercontextual dialogues exhibit diverse and heterogeneous tendencies that can be exploited in many ways. There is no such thing as an absolute contextual determination or an absolute contextual freedom. Our discursive agency is hybrid: it is determined and not determined, free and not free; it is creative but limited. Our linguistic creativity, our capacity to continue performative chains in different directions, is always contextually constrained, that is, conditioned by past discursive contexts as well as by the contexts that are available to us for communicative interaction.

In order to find a way out of the false dilemma that my polyphonic contextualism tries to overcome, I want to call attention to the nonstandard reading of Austin that departs from and contrasts sharply with the caricature circulated in French philosophy—by prominent authors such as Derrida (1982) and Bourdieu (1991)—as well as in Anglo-American philosophy. This reading has been suggested by Cavell (1979, 2002), Felman (1986, 2002), and Butler (1997). This alternative reading of Austin, which deserves the title of *The New Austin*,[23] can help us recognize and dismiss two pervasive sets of misconceptions about performativity and contextuality, which sustain the false dilemma between contextualization and decontextualization and its concomitant illusions. I will follow this line of interpretation and oppose the strict conventionalism often ascribed to Austin. The first set of misconceptions present in the received reading of Austin stems from giving exclusive normative weight to past usage to which our discursive practices are said to be normatively subordinated in a complete and thorough way. The Austinian conventionalism that speech-act theorists often invoke assigns to normative contexts of communication a *fullness and definitiveness* ("the total speech situation") that is illusory and, in fact, critically questioned by Austin's own discussions. For

Austin, communicative contexts and their normative structures are indeed the products of history, but they do not have a complete and finished character, for the communication history from which they emerge is ongoing. It is a mistake to ascribe to Austin the view that a speech act context is fully structured by the conventions established in prior usage. Austin's discussions make clear that the normative force of the performative derives from prior contexts of use as well as from future ones—that is, from the *promise* of future uses that will echo one's own. It follows, then, that the derivation or establishment of performative forces is never complete but *always in progress*. In his critique of the subjectivist and intentional model of speech acts, Austin emphasizes the *open-ended intercontextual constitution* of speech acts with his famous image of the "miner's lamp." He writes:

> Although we have this notion of my idea of what I'm doing—and indeed we have as a general rule such an idea, as it were *a miner's lamp on our forehead* which illuminates always just so far ahead as we go along—it is not to be supposed that there are any precise rules about the extent and degree of the illumination it sheds. The only general rule is that the illumination is always *limited*, and that in several ways. *It will never extend indefinitely far ahead.* (Austin, 1979, p. 284; emphasis preserved and added)

We have an intrinsically limited perspective on our speech acts and on the way in which they are constituted in communicative contexts, past, present, and future. The plural limitations of our perspective that Austin alludes to fall into two kinds of unknowingness involved in our linguistic performances. The first kind of unknowingness that afflicts our limited perspective on the intercontextual constitution of our acts has to do with our cognitive predicament as finite, embodied, and temporally extended agents and speakers. The intercontextual constitution of performative forces escapes us simply because of the limitations of our *situated* perspective: our vision of the intercontextual constitution of our speech acts is always partial because we can only navigate and explore so many contexts in so many ways and there are always unexplored contexts and unexplored paths in and between these contexts. As Austin puts it, "whatever I am doing is being done [. . .] amidst a background of *circumstances* (including [. . .] activities by other agents) [. . .] Furthermore, the doing of it will involve *incidentally* all kinds of minutiae [. . .] below the level of any intention" (p. 284). But there is a more radical kind of unknowingness afflicting the intercontextual constitution of linguistic performance, an unknowingness that goes beyond the limitations of the cognitive predicament of individual speakers. This constitutive unknowingness stems from the openness and unpredictability of communicative contexts.[24] Contexts of communication are always unsaturated (to use a Fregean metaphor), for their completion is always deferred: their normative structure is projected into the

future and in need of completion by indefinitely many contexts yet to be produced. This normative dependence on contexts that have not been produced
yet creates a level of indeterminacy and unknowingness that could not possibly be eliminated by overcoming our cognitive limitations and extending our
cognitive powers, or by shifting from the perspective of individuals to that of
linguistic communities and traditions.

The deferred and unsaturated nature of communicative contexts is what
Derrida calls "the *illimitability* of contexts." This contextual illimitability is
the discursive *excess* I have discussed above as a crucial feature of speech. But
this illimitability does not have the destructive effects for the contextualization of normativity and performativity that Derrida thinks. Derrida is wrong
in thinking that illimitability leads to the collapse of the normative structure of discursive contexts. On Derrida's view, communicative contexts are
revealed to be normatively inert when they are deconstructed. In this sense
deconstruction consists in emptying communicative contexts of their apparent normative force. According to Derrida, the force of speech is not contained in particular contexts; and given its lack of containment, contextual
normativity dissipates and ultimately disappears. But it is a mistake to think
that the fact that contextual normativity cannot be bounded or self-contained
signals its demise. It is a mistake to infer from the fact this normativity cannot be located anywhere in particular, that it exists nowhere at all, that it is
illusory. As Butler has argued, from the illimitability of context we should
not infer the context-independence of our speech acts. Pace Derrida, the illi-
mitiability of discursive contexts does not call for the decontextualization of
the discursive, but for its *repeated contextualization*, an ongoing and neverending contextualization. As Butler puts it: "The 'illimitability' of contexts simply
means that any delineation of a context that one might perform is itself subject to a further contextualization, and that contexts are not given in unitary
forms. This does not mean [. . .] that one should cease any effort to delineate a context; it means only that any such delineation is subject to potentially
infinite revision" (1997, pp. 147–48).

Performative forces are not consolidated in a final and absolute way. The
openness of our communicative contexts makes it impossible to eliminate the
instability of the performative and to fix once and for all the discursive norms
to which our speech acts are subject. Our communicative contexts do not
allow for the definitive settlement of discursive norms. There is no room in
our situated discursive practices for a self-determining normativity, an autonomous and invulnerable normativity that can thoroughly control our speech
acts. The norms of our discursive practices are always extended in new contexts of interaction. And as active members of these practices and makers of
language, we contribute to these extensions: we participate in the reworking
of normative structures, in the continuation or discontinuation of discursive

norms in particular ways. For this we have to take responsibility. We are always confronted with new contexts and new possible ways of speaking and signifying; and, as argued above, our discursive agency has to take responsibility for opening or closing possibilities in our practices. This responsibility emerges with every use of language; it attaches itself to all utterances and to all silences (insofar as they are speech acts or moves in a language game). Through our agency the normative structure of our practices can always be modified in a variety of ways. We can try to keep our discursive norms as intact as possible and work hard for maintaining them stable; but we have to remember that the continuity and stability of these norms, if attained, are always performative achievements, and achievements that do not eliminate the ever present possibility of these norms being augmented or expanded, diminished, and even reversed. The openness of discursive contexts grounds the ever present possibility of revising the discursive norms underlying these contexts, of *redoing* and even *undoing* the normative structure of discursive contexts. The normative structure of our contexts can always come *undone*. And this possibility of a normative undoing brings us to the second set of misconceptions about performativity, contextuality, and their normative relation that are present in the received interpretation of Austin's views. This second set of misconceptions concerns the normative significance of the infelicities that our speech acts are subject to. The mistake that the received interpretation of Austin makes is to think of these infelicities as purely accidental occurrences, while in fact they are constitutive of the normative structure of the performative. My discussion will try to show the normative significance of the fact that our speech acts are always susceptible to misfires and abuses. I will argue that the standard reading of Austin misses the normative significance of performative failures and therefore also their critical potential. I will try to show that these failures are of paramount importance for the reworking of the normative structure of our practices. Let's start this discussion of infelicity with Austin's famous claims and definitions:

> Performing actions then, as actions, [. . .] will be subject to certain whole dimensions of unsatisfactoriness to which all actions are subject. (1975, p. 21)

> We shall call in general those infelicities [. . .] which are such that the act [. . .] is not achieved, by the name of MISFIRES; and on the other hand we may christen those infelicities where the act is achieved ABUSES. (1975, p. 16)

In order to illustrate these two kinds of infelicities, we can consider the speech act of declaring two people a married couple—one of Austin's favorite examples of performative utterance. An abuse of this performative procedure or ceremony occurs when it is performed by an impostor—that is, by someone posing as a priest in a religious wedding or as a city official in a civil marriage.

Here we have an instance of a violation of one of the felicity conditions—that
the speaker be properly invested with the authority to perform the act—which
nonetheless does not prevent the act from being achieved. By contrast, a misfire occurs when the violation of one of the established felicity conditions
does prevent the act from being achieved. We would have instances of misfire
whenever two people of the same sex are declared married in a jurisdiction
in which there is legislation prohibiting same-sex marriage. But note how
thin, shaky, and indeed movable are the lines that are supposed to separate
abuses from misfires and both cases of performative failure from successful
performances. Our example of an impostor performing a wedding illustrates
how easily an abuse can become a misfire: it all depends on whether or not
the impostor is recognized as such; it is the success of the deception that
marks the successful (even if abusive) achievement of the act. On the other
hand, the example of same-sex marriage shows how misfires can be turned
into successful performances, as indeed recently happened in San Francisco
when Mayor Gavin Newsom decided to grant marriage licenses to same-sex
couples. But the most cursory reflection on these recent events show that
matters are more complicated: some people thought that these locally sanctioned marriages were in fact abuses and the courts should correct them; and
in fact, they have been declared void by the lower courts and, thus annulled,
these ceremonies have become misfires again: acts that were never properly
achieved and therefore never happened as such, strictly speaking.[25] So the
boundary between successfully accomplished performances and failed speech
acts is not a hard and fast one. Even if there seem to be clear cases, there is
always room for negotiations.

It is important to note that the negotiations that go into the making of
speech acts and establish their felicity conditions can lead to different results
from community to community, even within the same social or political unit.
So, for example, while in most states of the U.S. same-sex marriage ceremonies
are either abuses or misfires, as of now this is not so in Massachusetts where
they are felicitous performances when properly conducted, for they have been
legalized by the legislature (which was forced to do so by the State Supreme
Court)—although the validity of these marriages will surely be challenged in
the future. The recent *eccentric* practices that try to expand the scope of the
institution of marriage underscore the room for normative transformations that
is always present in our practices and institutions, no matter how old and rigidified they appear to be at any given time. There is certainly room for different
normative attitudes in the assessment of these cases: some people deem these
same-sex marriage ceremonies misfires, others abuses, others infelicitous acts
of a regular kind, and yet others felicitous acts that are simply adventurous and
pioneer in their novel kind of felicity. But no matter how strongly we may feel
about these cases, it is clear that the relevant legal, social, and political practices

are flexible enough to allow for disagreements and reasonable disputes, leaving different courses of action open to us. Without disregarding the constraints that emerge from established practices, social institutions, and historical traditions, it is important to recognize that, within some limits, it is ultimately up to us how to carve the normative space that separates felicities from infelicities, abuses, and misfires.[26]

Our performative procedures and rituals can misfire, and they can be abused; but what is the significance of all this? Infelicities can be seen as occasions to call into question the normativity of our practices, as opportunities to critically interrogate the norms that regulate our speech acts and test their limits. These normative failures of the performative have a critical potential and can, at least in principle, be used as the path to undo and/or redo the normative structures of our discursive practices. Failing performances can implicitly or explicitly suggest that things could be done differently, even if they mustn't. Alternatively, they can simply be taken to be a way of calling our attention to the fact that things cannot (and must not) be done in this (alternative) way, even if they should. In this respect it is important to note the crucial critical potential that fictional discourses have. Insofar as standard felicity conditions are suspended in the sphere of the fictional, fictional discourses are failed performatives—and indeed Austin often talks about them in this way. Fiction can be thought of as *abusive* language or a kind of symbolic *misfiring* (abortive "language"). But this does not undermine the significance of fiction. On the contrary, this gives fictional discourses a special position in our discursive practices: they are very valuable abuses or misfires of language. Their special importance resides in their capacity to critically question the norms of our actual practices by providing alternative normative frameworks. Fictional discourses are invaluable critical tools in experimenting with the felicity conditions of our acts. By giving free rein to the imagination, we are capable of playing with felicity conditions: we can think up different (and often unexpected) ways in which felicity conditions can be violated; we can explore the consequences of these violations; and we can also invent felicity conditions that are altogether different from current ones and explore the consequences of complying with these alternative conditions as well as the consequences of violating them. But of course the distinction between the felicitous and the infelicitous is not only critically questioned through the imagination but also through our agency in real life. Social experimentation and political activism often take the shape of attempts at transforming the infelicitous into the felicitous, subverting this distinction and promoting social change.

As occasions of critical interrogation, infelicities play a crucial role in critically questioning the (movable) boundary or normative frontier between performative successes and failures. The received interpretation of Austin's view misses this crucial critical significance of infelicities or failing acts by construing them as something purely accidental and external to the normative constitution of our speech acts. On this interpretation, abuses are simply degenerative cases of speech acts, performativity gone wrong; and misfires are conceptualized as being *outside speech* altogether, that is, as nonacts, as very peculiar things that simply *look like* performative utterances: as performative *freaks* that have the misleading appearance of being linguistic acts but in fact aren't. By misplacing the emphasis on the contingency and externality of infelicities, speech-act theorists have often missed that performative failures have an *internal* and *necessary* character: they are constitutive and unavoidable.

In the first place, the unavoidable character of performative failures follows directly from the fact that speech acts do not fall under the sovereign control of subjects or institutions. It follows from the uncontrollability of discursive agency that there are *no guarantees* for performative success: speech acts can always go wrong, or simply develop in ways that had not been anticipated (by the individuals and institutions involved, or by the codified norms to which these acts are subject). Occasional performative failures are bound to occur in our discursive practices. Nothing short of a miracle could prevent their occurrence. But, in the second place, independently of their actual occurrence, performative failures are necessary in a certain sense: although their actual occurrence is indeed purely contingent, their *possibility* is necessary insofar as it is *constitutive*. Whether failures actually occur or not, they are always waiting to happen; their possibility is always there—casting a shadow on our successes—even if it is constantly avoided. Failing is constitutive of the performative insofar as the performative has a normative dimension and can, therefore, be felicitious or infelicitous. The normative dimension of performativity presupposes that things can be done right or wrong, correctly or incorrectly: an act can be achieved properly or improperly; and it can also be attempted without being achieved at all. Successful performances are achieved against the background of infelicities; and performative success depends on the maintenance of this background, that is, on pushing a whole array of possible acts out of the realm of the performative, keeping them in check as *failing* possibilities. In this sense Austin points out that *the abnormal is the precondition of the normal* (more on this later) and, therefore, infelicities are the precondition of felicity.

Whether intentionally or not, performative failures can become critical interventions in the practice in which they occur. The normative significance that attaches to an occasional failure depends on whether and how the failure is echoed and repeated in the actions of others; some failures may be repeated enough times so that it becomes a performative chain that, though initially parasitic on another chain, takes a life of its own and becomes an alternative practice or an extension (or alternative configuration) of the current practice. Performative chains are always vulnerable to failing practice or to *the practice of failure*. Repeated failures, or the practice of failure, can become ways of resisting the established normative order that regulates the practice. The critical potential of the practice of performative failures cannot be overemphasize: the normative failures of the performative can reconfigure normative contexts of communication and reshape our norms. The practice of failure or the practice of infelicity can have the effect of weakening and eventually relaxing the felicity conditions of an act, allowing for new kinds of performative success. It calls our attention to borderline cases and cases that are arbitrarily excluded from the realm of the performative. The practice of failure or infelicity can also suggest a more radical possibility, namely, that *the infelicities of today could become the felicities or performative successes of tomorrow*. This is indeed the hope of gay and lesbian activists who are trying to obtain legal recognition for same-sex marriages. As Butler (1990, 1993, 1997) has shown, this is also the goal of *parodic performances* that practice infelicity and exploit failing possibilities in order to expose the arbitrary bounds of the felicitous and the normal—that is, the "normal" conditions on which preformative successes are supposed to rest. As Butler puts it, when we examine our discursive practices and their normative consequences we have to ask, "Is there a possibility of disrupting and subverting the effects produced by such speech, a faultline exposed that leads to the undoing of this process of discursive constitution?" (1997, p. 19). Following Austin, Butler argues that the possibility of performative failure is always there and it constitutes the condition of a critical response and resistance, for example, through parodic performance. This omnipresent possibility of failure (which opens up the possibility of critique and transformation in every context) was emphasized by Austin.[27] But this is something that the received interpretation of Austin has missed[28] and has, therefore, failed to realize that Austin's account of the performative already contains the theoretical elements required to explain how and why our discursive structures can "suffer destructuration through being reiterated, repeated, and rearticulated." (1997, p. 19)

The Austinian account of performativity suggests that the critical elucidation of our discursive practices and their normative structures requires *the critical reconstruction of felicity*; that is, the critical undoing and redoing of felicity, of the felicity conditions and the concomitant infelicity conditions of our speech acts. This critical reconstruction of felicity entails the reconstruction of *normalcy*, for the felicity and infelicity of acts depend on what are considered to be normal and abnormal conditions. Austin recognizes this when he poignantly remarks: "To examine excuses is to examine cases where there has been some abnormality or failure: and as so often, *the abnormal will throw light on the normal, will help us to penetrate the blinding veil of ease and obviousness that hides the mechanisms of the natural successful act*" (1979, pp. 179–80; emphasis preserved and added). There is a taken-for-granted normative background that supports our actions and practices, a background of assumptions and expectations ("the mechanisms of the natural successful act") that we are *blind* to. This blindness to what counts as normal is the blindness to the tacit norms of our practices. This normative blindness has also been underscored, as we saw, by Wittgenstein's discussion of rule following and by Bourdieu's discussion of "misrecognition" in his account of the speakers' recognition of each other's voices and habitus. In sociology the normative blindness of agent and speakers has also been studied by ethnomethodology: through a variety of *breaching* experiments, Garfinkel and his followers studied how the normative assumptions and expectations that structure people's actions and reactions in particular practices can be revealed and made explicit when they are violated.[29]

The critical reconstruction of normalcy requires the inspection of those tacit norms that we are typically blind to. We have to uncover the conditions of normalcy that are assumed and taken for granted. While unreconstructed, these normative conditions remain protected from critical questioning precisely because they have been hidden in the background and have become invisible to us. The reconstruction of normalcy, therefore, involves undoing the normative blindness to which all speakers are subject; that is, it involves piercing "the blinding veil of ease and obviousness." In order to overcome our blindness to the norms that shape our actions and judgments in the games we play, we have to step outside of what comes "natural," of what is obvious and taken for granted. Hence the importance of disruptive moments which, by violating normative assumptions and expectations, bring tacit norms to the foreground and render them visible. In this sense, the practice of failure or infelicity can afford us *normative lucidity*; that is, it can restore our sight with respect to the norms that our own behavior embodies and responds to. Through the practice of failure or infelicity we can repair our blindness and gain normative sight piecemeal, context by context. This normative lucidity contextually achieved through failures or infelicities can be further analyzed by reflecting on what Felman calls the *scandalous* nature of our linguistic performances, which cannot help but violate normative expectations. Felman's discussions of "the *scandal* of the speaking body" can help us better understand the critical task of undoing and reconstructing normalcy.

Felman (2002) finds inspiration in Austin for her account of the scandalous moments of speech in which normalcy breaks down: "When Austin [. . .] refers to the normal/abnormal opposition [. . .] it is not in order to leave this opposition intact nor to promote the criterion of 'normality,' but rather—like Freud—in order to analyze the abnormal insofar as it is *constitutive of the normal*, that is, in order to undo or to explode the very criterion of 'normality'" (p. 102). As Felman emphasizes, Austin calls our attention to the innumerable ways in which a speech act can go wrong and thus underscores the ever-present possibility of felicity and normality exploding before our very eyes. This makes manifest the fragility of our discursive norms; these norms are contingent through and through and to some extent arbitrary. The contingency and arbitrariness of these norms are revealed in their violation, which becomes something scandalous. That in language things can be done otherwise, and often are, is scandalous because it is assumed that they shouldn't be; and when things are in fact done differently, our speech acts are considered an *outrage*, an inadmissible way of "outraging speech," to use Austin's phrase. In *How to Do Things with Words* Austin argues that speaking is giving one's word and characterizes linguistic agents as *promising* animals. The scandal, according to Felman, is that the promise of the performative cannot be maintained, at least not all the time, at least not completely, for speakers are also promise-breaking animals. To illustrate this scandalous nature of our failing discursive agency Felman examines the literary figure of Don Juan. This rhetorical figure represents the compulsive promise maker and promise breaker: the agent who can't help but commit himself while at the same time cannot help but fail to fulfill his commitments and follow through with his promises.

Felman's analysis suggests that Don Juan's predicament is revealing because it is in fact a radicalized (or pathological) version of the predicament of every speaker: as Austin indicated, to be a speaker is to be committed. But constrained by our commitments as we are, we are never able to maintain them perfectly and all the time; we are always in some respect failing as normative agents or promise keepers. This constitutive failing of the performative constitutes the basis of the scandalous nature of speech, which stems directly from what I have called the "unownability" of discursive agency. That is, the scandal derives from promising what one does not have and cannot own: one's words and their meanings. As Felman (2002) puts it: "The scandal, according to Austin, thus arises from the performative logic of 'giving what you don't have' [. . .]. The scandal, in other words, is always in a certain way the scandal of the promise of love, the scandal of the *untenable*, that is, still and always, the scandal—Donjuanian in the extreme—of the promising animal, incapable of keeping his promise, incapable of not making it, powerless both to fulfill the commitment and to avoid *committing* himself" (p. 111). Pace Felman,[30] this "scandal" does not undermine completely the normative force of our speech acts and discursive commitments, but it does underscore its fragility and its dependence on all sorts of social and historical contingencies. It is precisely the fragility of our normative capacity of word giving—not its denial—that is the central lesson to learn from Austin's account of the performative.

The normativity of speech is dominated by the *logic of scandal*. This logic exceeds the logic of contradiction (which is predicated on a narrow logic of fixed categories). As Austin puts it, "this is the sort of thing [. . .] we overlook: *there are more ways of outraging speech than contradiction merely*" (1975, p. 48). Indeed there are "'statements' which, though not false exactly nor yet 'contradictory,' are yet *outrageous*" (1975, p. 20). Classic examples (which Austin goes on to examine) are those assertions that are infelicitous because they contain referential failures: for example, "The present king of France is bald." But there is an indefinite class of cases here. The logic of scandal is necessarily an *open-ended* logic because there is an indefinite number of ways in which speech can be outraged. Performative failures or infelicities cannot be fully systematized because they derive from an *indomitable excess* of the performative. As Felman puts it, in her interpretation of Austin, "the act of failing [. . .] leads, para-doxically, to an excess of utterance: [. . .] the Austinian 'force of utterance' is constantly in excess over the *meaning* of the theoretical statement" (2002; p. 80). Given the *excessive* nature of performativity—its uncontrollability and unownability (see previous section)—there cannot be a final systematization of the logic of scandal; we can only take a piecemeal approach in our elucida-tions of this logic. Note that even when Austin appeals to the notions of "the total speech act" and "the total speech situation," he nonetheless emphasizes this piecemeal approach: "We must consider the total situation . . . the total speech act. . . . So the *total speech act* in the total speech situation is *emerging from logic piecemeal*" (1975, p. 52). This shows that Austin's appeals to totality are meant to underscore the holistic nature of speech, rather than its com-plete or self-contained character. In fact, the emphasis on the holistic nature of speech grounds its openness and gives support to the claim that the logic of the performative (including "the logic of scandal") has to be reconstructed piecemeal from context to context and can never be finished or completed once and for all.

There is no exhaustive account of the scandalous nature of the performa-tive, but we can recognize some of its crucial features. I want to call attention to two of these features. It is important to note that the scandal of the performa-tive has a *corporeal* and *sensuous* dimension: it involves the body that speaks and its desire and erotic relations. The embodied and erotic aspects of speech have been thematized in Felman's account of scandalous speech. In the first place, according to Felman, the scandalous nature of speech derives directly from its *corporeal* dimension, which involves unknowingness and failing. For Felman, embodiment is "the blindspot of speech," the point at which speaking neces-sarily fails to recognize itself and what it does: "the scandal lies less in sex than in language, insofar as language is inhabited by the *act of failing* through which the body is lacking to itself: the act of failing through which the body's *doing* always fails to speak itself, whereas the *speaking* never fails to *do*" (p. 78). On Felman's view, the scandal that structures our discursive agency consists in the fact that a speaking body and its speech are always incongruously related. This incongruous relation between speech and the body is a scandalous one: "a rela-tion consisting at once of incongruity and of inseparability [. . .] The scandal consists in the fact that the act cannot know what it is doing" (p. 96). Speakers are *blind* because their speaking bodies are always unknowing about what they

perform and always say something they do not intend. Following Felman, Butler (1997) explains this blindness or unknowingness of the speaking body as
follows: "the body is the blindspot of speech, that which acts in excess of what
is said, but which also acts in and through what is said" (p. 11).

In the second place, the scandal of the performative also involves *pleasure*. The scandalous nature of speech has a pleasurable dimension that is tied
to desire, but goes beyond the purely erotic and relates to the desire to fail
and to produce failures, individually and collectively. This is made very clear in
Felman's performative analysis of humor, which she sees as a subtle and often
missed performative dimension of Austin's own expositions: "There exists, in
fact, in Austin, something like a *pleasure in scandal*" (p. 80); "Austin's invitation to laughter is [. . .] an invitation to the *pleasure of scandal* [. . .]. The
laughter provoked by a joke turns the reader into an accomplice precisely in
scandal" (p. 81). Humor requires actively recruiting others as accomplices in
the performative production of failures or infelicities. A joke typically involves
a performative way of sharing or partaking in a collective discharge of performative excess. The performative excess that is always present in infelicities is
explicitly thematized and manipulated in humor. As Felman puts it: "Humor
indeed is preeminently not a 'saying' but a 'doing': a 'making (someone) laugh.'
[. . .] the supreme performance of the body's failing itself is that of making
jokes" (pp. 80–81).

But what is most important is the critical and transformative impact that
humor can have in our discursive practices. Precisely because humor plays with
failures and infelicities it has an *unsettling effect*; and this unsettling effect, this
disruption, can have critical consequences. Felman describes as follows the
critical and subversive power of the shared pleasure we take in failures: "Trip-
ping someone [. . .] is much more than a 'pastime': it is not simply a *pleasurable* act, it is also, and especially, a *subversive* act. In fact, humor in Austin
intervenes very often only to subvert knowledge, to call it into question, to
cast doubt upon it" (p. 86). The critical power of humor has both an epistemic
and a political dimension. As Felman puts it, "humor constitutes not only an
assault on knowledge but also an assault on power, on repression in every sense
of the word—political and analytical" (p. 87). The critical and transformative
potential of the playfulness of humor has been missed by Austin's followers in
Speech Act Theory. Felman criticizes Austin's "heirs" for missing completely
the Austinian blurring of the "serious" and the "unserious"—the felicitous and
the infelicitous—and for undertaking the task of "establishing a series of 'rules'
or safeguards in order to exclude anomaly and to eliminate the *scandal of infelicity*" (p. 96). A good example of this unAustinian attempt to purify speech
of its scandalous nature trying to eliminate possible infelicities can be found
in H. P. Grice's "logic of conversation" with its "cooperative principle" and the
different maxims that are supposed to regulate communicative exchanges. As

Felman puts it, "Grice's theory constitutes, in a way, an enterprise aimed at *'correcting'* the possible *unhappiness* of the performative, an effort to eliminate the scandal of the act of failing inherent in the performative. [. . .] Hence Grice's effort to correct the abnormal by his own attempt to *normalize* the acts of language—or of the speaking body. By improving the manual—which he takes at face value—Grice, it seems, thinks he has really understood *'how to do things with words'*" (p. 97).

The lesson to learn from Felman's discussion of the scandalous nature of performativity—a lesson that was already implicit in Austin—is that the success of linguistic performance cannot be legislated, and possible performative failures cannot be ruled out by decree. In other words, our agency cannot contain itself: it is not susceptible to being constricted by a normative straitjacket of rigid rules; it does not admit a foolproof normative confinement: we cannot confine the normativity of discursive practices in a set of absolute rules that protect felicities from infelicities and can determine what is admissible and what is inadmissible once and for all. There is no normative framework that can rule out all performative failures in an absolute way and guarantee the exclusion of misfires and abuses in our performances. All discursive norms involve normative exclusions, that is, the exclusion of certain ways of speaking, of certain things that cannot be said legitimately and intelligibly. But these exclusions are precarious and they bring the excluded into the very core of the normative framework, so that there cannot be *pure inclusions*, that is, there cannot be an uncontaminated repertoire of discursive elements that can be protected from differences and alien elements. The *scandal* is that, in the precarious normative exclusions that shape our practices, differences are *internal* to the norms themselves: while legislating certain things as unsayable, we are invited to say them in order to exclude them; while deeming certain things (or forms of expression) unthinkable, we are required to think them in order to push them out of the realm of our thoughts. Discursive norms thus contain within themselves the source of their own instability, for the possibility of their violation is *constitutive*: it is a crucial aspect of any normative structure that tries to regulate what can and can*not* be done. The possibility of systematic violation and normative failure is always a present and vivid menace, an imminent threat, which can destabilize the normative structure of a discursive practice at any time. Therefore, the possibility of scandal, of stepping out of the normative bounds of the discursive practice, is always there. The scandal of the performative is inevitable; it is a necessary, unavoidable part of the normative structure of any linguistic performance because it situates itself within the very discursive norms that regulate our linguistic exchanges. Our discursive norms themselves have a scandalous nature because they contain the possibility of their own violation, and thus their exclusionary nature is always on the verge of being exposed as arbitrary.

The scandalous nature of discursive normativity is what Butler (1997) describes as "the *alterity* within the norm," which marks the constitutive *ambivalence* of the normative, an ambivalence between what can and cannot be done, between what is meaningful and what is nonsensical, admissible and inadmissible, in our discursive practices. Any norm is ambivalent: it includes and excludes at the same time. And what is most interesting and important about these ambivalent relations of inclusion and exclusion is their contingent and unstable character. Like Butler's, my performative account of discursive norms underscores the instability of the boundary that separates what is included in the norm and what is excluded by it. The actual inclusions and exclusions effected by discursive norms ultimately depend on the ways in which the norms are actually used in particular practices and particular contexts, on the ways in which rules are followed, enacted and reenacted, in our actual, concrete and situated performances. The ambivalence of discursive norms can be tamed, but never fully eliminated. Whether something is admissible or inadmissible is indeed settled in actual discursive contexts through the negotiations of participants; and thus what is included and excluded in our actual discursive practices becomes heavily constrained, but never fully determined and fixed once and for all. As Butler recognizes, the alterity and constitutive ambivalence of discursive norms opens up the always present possibility of performative critique and transformation of our practices. This is what Butler (1997) calls "the promising ambivalence of the norm." As she puts it:

> Speaking is not a simple assimilation to an existing norm [. . .]. Speaking and exposing the alterity within the norm (the alterity without which the norm would not "know itself") exposes the failure of the norm to effect the universal reach for which it stands, exposes what we might underscore as *the promising ambivalence of the norm.* (p. 91)

I will conclude this chapter with a discussion of the anxieties and compulsive attitudes that the constitutive ambivalence and scandalous nature of discursive norms can provoke. This discussion tries to accomplish two things: first, to drive the last nail into the coffin of the false dilemmas that plague the literature on discursive agency; and second, to make clear how my own account of recontextualization through the notion of *echoing* can overcome the false dichotomy between contextualization and decontextualization. These final reflections on the scandal of our agency will also serve as a bridge to the next and final chapter, which focuses on the critical task of reconstructing the normativity of our discursive practices. The scandalous aspect of our agency can make a great contribution to this critical task, for, as I have argued above, normative frameworks can be critically interrogated, destabilized, and (in some cases) even subverted through the *practice of failure or infelicity.* By practicing infelicity in a critical way we can redraw the normative boundaries between what is included and excluded, admissible and inadmissible, in our discursive practices. Our discursive agency has to be reminded that there are different ways of *echoing* performative successes and failures (ironic and parodic performance, for example) which have the capacity to resignify in critical and transformative ways. In order to exploit the critical and transformative potential of performative mechanisms, critique has to become performative, that is, our agency has to critically engage with the constitutive ambivalence and scandalous nature of discursive norms and linguistic performativity.

As we have seen, the indomitable polyphony of discursive practices entails that our agency in language is not only radically uncontrollable and open, but also scandalous. We can distinguish between two senses in which our discursive agency is scandalous. First, we can talk about specific *moments of scandal* that destabilize our discursive practices, moments in which there is a revelation of misconduct, an exposure of wrongdoing, where we thought that no misconduct or wrongdoing was possible. These scandalous moments can be characterized as moments of dereification or denaturalization: for any discursive norm that we reinforce with our actions, the scandal happens when we catch ourselves making it up. In these scandalous moments there is always some sort of unmasking or exposé. But, more importantly, there is always an *ongoing scandal* taking place in our discursive practices, whether we notice it or not. This continuous scandal is due to the fact that our discursive agency cannot help itself, it cannot contain itself, and it is always on the verge of radical misconduct, that is, of transgressing the normative structure of our practices in a way that destabilizes their normative economy. This point is underscored by Dollimore's (1991) reading of Augustine and Lacan, according to which "language is [. . .] always potentially perverse" (p. 282). As Dollimore puts it, in Lacanian terms, every speech act is *"under an inner necessity to err"* (p. 282). This potential perversity cannot be isolated and contained in specific speech acts that we can set apart from others: any speech act can be deemed a disgraceful or discreditable action; any performance is in principle liable to fall into public disgrace and to be revealed as radical misconduct, as falling outside the normative framework of our discursive practices. The omnipresent possibility of normative failure is immanent in all our linguistic performances; the potential perversity of language underlies all our speech acts. And we do not need an explicit exposé to feel (albeit unconsciously) the scandalous nature of discursive agency and to permit (albeit unknowingly) that the possibility of a scandal structures our speech acts. This is made clear in Felman's account of the structural scandal of speech. As Felman (2002) emphasizes, the inherent scandal of our discursive agency results from our embodiment as speaking voices and from the unknowingness of our speaking bodies.

It is important to note that there is no such thing as a scandal without a prudish mentality. There is no scandal (no embarrassment, no discredit, no shame) if we are indifferent to normative expectations, if we are not moved by normative considerations. But the prudishness that constitutes the precondition of our scandalous agency does not derive from any particular morality or any particular normative structuration of language but, rather, from the fact that a discursive practice involves discipline, that a language game requires rules of some sort (i.e., normative expectations and constraints), no matter how vague and implicit they happen to be. The normative structure of the language game regulates the relation of our speech act to previous ones. This regulation creates certain forms of anxieties in the speakers or players—anxieties that are thematized in philosophical accounts and turned into polarized philosophical theories of discursive agency and meaning. One form of anxiety is reflected in the attitude of those speakers who are obsessed with being faithful to previous uses. This literalism or obsessive concern with fidelity generates what we can call a "Fidelity Anxiety," which involves the ideal of being absolutely faithful to the meanings we have inherited from previous speech acts. This ideal fidelity requires a fixed and exclusive relation among the speech acts that constitute a performative chain. This obsessive fidelity creates the illusion of an originating context of use that determines meaning, that is, an original first use of a term that fixes what counts as the correct employment and as the correct interpretation of the term in subsequent use. When this illusion is abandoned, the ideal of absolute fidelity has to be deemed impossible. It is impossible for our speech to be faithful to prior usage in an absolute sense because the relation of a speech act to previous items in the performative chain is constructed as we go and it can never be established once and for all, since it depends on future instances in the performative chain that have not been produced yet. But the impossibility of absolute fidelity can create an anxious attitude that goes in the opposite direction, namely, an attitude obsessed with being unfaithful, with departing from previous uses. We can refer to this obsessive flight from fidelity as "Promiscuity Anxiety." This obsessive attitude involves a pathological fear of commitment, of being tied down to any particular context. If the ideal of compulsive fidelity underlying the former anxiety rested on a fixed and exclusive relation with the past, the ideal of compulsive promiscuity behind the latter anxiety requires the denial of any relation with the past that can constrain one's agency. This anxious linguistic promiscuity involves an escapist attitude that tries to sever all ties to previous speech acts and disavow all commitments to future ones. But being unfaithful in an absolute sense is also impossible: if there is nothing whatsoever that ties my utterance or silence to previous ones or future ones, then my speech act is not part of a performative chain and, therefore, it is not part of any language game or discursive practice. Another way to put the point against the obsessions and illusions involved in Fidelity and Promiscuity Anxieties is to say that discursive agency cannot be completely disciplined or undisciplined, absolutely controlled or absolutely unruly.

It is these pathological forms of anxiety about fidelity and promiscuity that constitute the source of the obsessive attitudes with respect to the contextual character of our agency that we discussed above. On the one hand, the Fidelity Anxiety motivates a rigid view of contextualization that wants to firmly tie each speech act to past usage, establishing an inflexible continuity between any given communicative context and prior contexts of use. As we saw, we find this rigid view of the contextualization of linguisitic performance in the received interpretation of Austin, *the Old Austin*, which I criticized above. On the other hand, the Promiscuity Anxiety animates another extreme view, namely, a radical view of decontextualization that depicts each linguistic performance as breaking from history and prior contexts of use. What characterizes this view is a pathological escapism, that is, an untenable escapist attitude that involves an illusory denial of any contextual constraint and an absolute affirmation of discursive freedom. As we saw, this unqualified celebration of "breakage" or "rupture" can be found in Derridian deconstruction (at least in some early texts by Derrida in which he criticizes the Austinian view).

In sharp contrast to these extreme views, my contextualism focuses on the interrelations between contextual constraints and discursive freedom. The dialectical relation between freedom and constraint is what is at the core of my hybrid notion of agency. The promise of my hybrid view of agency is that it can overcome the pathological anxieties concerning fidelity and promiscuity and the obsessive attitudes that go with them. Without giving exclusive normative weight to the past, my contextualist perspective acknowledges the constraints that derive from the histories of use embedded in our discursive practices. And without falling into a naïve and illusory escapism that denies all constraints, my contextualism also acknowledges the lack of contextual determination and the space for departures from historical contexts in our discursive practices. My account of recontextualization in terms of *echoing* shows how any given linguistic performance situates itself in a historical chain of speech acts, drawing relations (often precarious and unstable) with past and future contexts, weaving together different historical paths, negotiating and combining constraints from the past and openness into the future. Historicity is not something that simply happens as the product of blind determination, as it were; rather, it is something that we make—though always precariously—through our agency, through the *echoing* of our speech acts, which (taken collectively) forges historical paths for our discursive practices. These paths need to be constantly renewed by and sustained through performative chains of speech acts and remain always precarious. This precarious historicity in the making that results from our agency—unconsciously more often than consciously, blindly more often than lucidly—is something for which we have to take responsibility, individually and collectively. Thus intercontextual relations are forged performatively through the *echoing* of our speech acts, which signify by invoking, implicitly or explicitly, other contexts—past, future, and contemporaneous contexts, both actual and possible or imaginary ones. The notion of intercontextuality captures well how past, present, and future contexts interpenetrate each other and become tied together in a nondeterministic way through our performances and ongoing negotiations. While rigid views of contextualization and decontextualization depict the bond of our words as either too tight or too loose, my account of re-contextualization and echoing gets it *just right*, thus becoming the *Goldie Locks* of performativity. Not surprisingly, my eccentric contextualism emerges as the heroine of my story about discursive agency, the Goldie Locks of speech-act theory. But it is important to note that my contextualist position in performativity theory is a therapeutic Goldie Locks, that is, a view that tries to avoid and transcend polarized positions that become one-sided and distorting by focusing exclusively on one factor. In this way my view from *elsewhere* aims to overcome anxieties and obsessions concerning our agency in language.

The obsessive attitudes with respect to discursive fidelity and promiscuity that we find both in academia and in lay discourses are related to inflated aspirations concerning censorship and disclosure in language. If the Fidelity Anxiety can be associated with a puritanical mentality that tries to censor speech as much as possible, the Promiscuity Anxiety should be associated with an exhibitionist mentality that tries to disclose in speech as much as possible. But neither absolute censorship nor total disclosure is possible. There are always things that can and things that cannot be said in our discursive practices. Censorship and disclosure are bound up with each other. And since we cannot have one without the other, we cannot achieve a total disclosure that overcomes all discursive constraints, or an absolute censorship that keeps in check all utterances and silences and all nonconforming voices. The ideals of total disclosure and absolute censorship are not achievable in our discursive practices. These are opposing illusions that obscure the tight dialectical relation between censorship and disclosure in our discursive agency, which makes it impossible for speakers to show everything or to show nothing in their speech. A "show everything" attitude is illusory because it disregards that things get said at a price, that is, at the expense of other things not being said. There is always a background of things unsaid that supports the foreground of what is said. But a "show nothing" attitude is equally illusory. For "show nothing" is a prohibition that is impossible to obey. Even if you try to relegate everything (in a given semantic domain) to the background of things unsaid there is always something in the foreground (even if it is pure silence) that can be symbolically linked to what is in the background. In fact, the more we stress the prohibition "show nothing," the more we call attention to what is not said and to the symbolic connection between what is said and what is left unsaid, turning whatever happens to be in the explicit foreground into a coverup for what is hidden in the background. I will provide two different illustrations of the failures and paradoxical consequences of censorship—one concerns explicit censorship, the other tacit censorship; one is from real life, the other from literature (although the traffic between literature and life is certainly dense and difficult to direct).

Take as an example of explicit censorship the U.S. congressional statute passed in October 1994 that put into law the "Don't Ask, Don't Tell" policy on homosexual self-declaration in the military. It is an interesting consequence of this policy that over the years it has led to an enormous increase in public self-declarations of homosexual identity as well as in the official investigations of the sexual orientation of military personnel suspected of being homosexual. The policy has also given rise to the proliferation of a complex network of discourses concerning homosexuality in the military. It is as if "Don't Ask, Don't Tell" actually promoted the asking and telling of people's sexual orientation, as if the prohibition actually invited people to ask and tell, as if it excited speech and provoked in speakers an obsessive attitude toward the forbidden. Butler has argued that the statute has in fact contributed to the proliferation of references to homosexuality "not only in its supporting documentation but also in the public debates fostered on the issue" (1998, p. 250). The proliferation in the use of a term triggered by explicit censorship is what Butler calls the phenomenon of "redoubling" (a special kind of *echoing*, I would say): "Regulation of the term 'homosexual' is thus no simple act of censorship or silencing; on the contrary, the statute redoubles the term it seeks to constrain and can only effect this constraint through this paradoxical redoubling" (p. 250). Explicit censorship is "compelled to repeat what it seeks to constrain, and so invariably reproduces and restages the very text that it seeks to silence" (p. 249). Explicit censorship has a special kind of vulnerability that derives from the fact that, in order to declare something outside the boundaries of admissible speech, that something must be cited. An explicit prohibition cannot take place without a conjuring of the very act prohibited; and a verbal prohibition must cite the very term that is being banned from language; and thus, as Butler puts it, "the effort to constrain the term culminates in its proliferation": explicit prohibitions require "rehearsing and proliferating the very terms that they seek to bar from discourse" (p. 250).

Another example of the failures and paradoxical consequences of censorship is provided by Enterline's analysis of female voices in Shakespearean plays. According to Enterline (1999), in the early modern period the cultural desideratum that women remain silent about sexual matters becomes an absolute prohibition that "seems to solicit its own violation," a prohibition that is "at risk at the moment a woman opens her mouth" (p. 33). Thus the ideal of female chastity implodes from the inside by requiring an impossible silence, a silence that cannot be kept because any discursive move (any utterance or silence) of a female voice can be given a sexual meaning. The obsessive policing of this expected silence creates an anxious expectation about breaking it, an obsessive suspicion about hidden sexual meanings. The absolute prohibition thus becomes at the same time an invitation to speak or to intimate, an incitement to double talk, making women's speech always *scandalous*. Everything said by a female voice becomes suspect; hence the phenomenon of "the repeated misfiring of a woman's speech" (Enterline 1999, p. 34). In this way the discursive agency of female voices becomes subject to contradictory cultural expectations: women are expected to remain silent about sexuality; and at the same time they are expected to speak of nothing other than sexuality; and even their silences can be interpreted as intimating a sexual meaning.

On the one hand, as Butler (1998) has argued, *the censoring of speech is never complete*. Speech can never be fully constrained by censorship because the censoring powers can never anticipate all the meanings that can possibly be contained in it or read into it. This uncontrollable polysemy of language is the *excessive* dimension of speech. In some sense speech always escapes censorship, for there is always something in the speech being censored that exceeds the reach of the censor. There are kinds of censorship that are more complete than others, but there is no censorship that can be absolutely complete, foolproof, and final. But, on the other hand, *the liberation of speech is also never complete*. As Butler argues, "no text can remain a text—that is, remain readable—without first being subjected to some kind of censorship"; every text is "produced through a process of selection that rules out certain possibilities, and realizes others" (p. 248). And, of course, Butler's point applies not only to written texts but to the use of language and symbols more generally, that is, to our speech acts or symbolic performance. The process of selection underlying our symbolic performance often appears to be under the control of the decisions made by the author of the speech act. But this appearance of control is illusory, for, as Butler points out, "the author does not create the rules according to which selection is made" (p. 248). In order to become intelligible, a speech act must be subject to a structural kind of censorship that is inescapable.[31] One cannot lift this form of censorship completely, for "to oppose censorship fully is to oppose the conditions of intelligibility" (p. 253).

So how can we oppose censorship at all? How can we fight all these different forms of censorship, explicit and implicit, that constrain our speech and shape us as subjects within language? Butler emphasizes the "political salience of impossible speech," that is, of silences and of apparently nonsensical forms of expressions, because they can be indicative of symbolic oppression: they may indicate ways of being in language that could be liberated and expressed if certain censorships were lifted. Like Butler's own view, my *eccentric* contextualism—my view from *elsewhere*—offers an account that acknowledges the inescapability of censorship and yet makes room for critical and subversive processes of liberation in our symbolic performance. Symbolic domination can undergo change—its course is not set in stone; it can take many different turns. The performative reiteration of symbolic domination can be disrupted and even subverted. The paths of symbolic domination are not predetermined, but performatively deployed through the symbolic interaction of speakers; they depend on our agency and we have in principle the power to change them, although this is a very limited and constrained power. For censoring and uncensoring language are not phenomena that can be brought under the complete control of anybody or anything, of any individual or any institution. As Butler's discussion of censorship makes clear, there is no such thing as absolute liberation: we cannot escape all forms of symbolic domination. But any given form of symbolic domination can in principle be resisted and could eventually be escaped or overcome.

Just as "show nothing" is a futile prudish illusion because censoring is always incomplete, "show everything" is an unattainable exhibitionist dream because uncensoring is also always incomplete. Discursive disclosure constantly fails because there is a constitutive and unavoidable form of censorship built into the normative structure of our language games. At the same time, the censoring of speech is always failing too because there are always inevitable forms of unexpected disclosure through silences and oblique speech, that is, because our discursive agency resists containment. The dialectical relation between censorship and disclosure will be explored further in the next chapter through a discussion of silence. My account of the discursive disempowerment of agents and the silencing of their voices will be based on the contextualist account of discursive agency developed in this chapter. Building on the critique of the ownership model, my analysis has identified three crucial interrelated features of discursive agency: its uncontrollability, its radical openness, and its scandalous nature. These features are proposed as the pillars of an alternative model of agency that avoids the Scylla of voluntarism and the Charybdis of automatism. This contextualist model, which I have characterized as a view from *elsewhere*, is a close ally of Butler's performativity view. My Wittgensteinian contextualism and Butler's performativity view complement each other, and together they can offer an account of discursive agency that successfully transcends traditional conceptions of sovereign subjectivity.

According to the hybrid view of agency suggested by my contextualism and by Butler's performativity theory, *agency begins where sovereignty wanes*. As Butler (1997) puts it, there is an "unofficial censorship or primary restriction" that "constitutes the possibility of agency in speech"; "this view suggests that agency is derived from limitations in language, and that limitation is not fully negative in its implications" (p. 41). The goal of my eccentric contextualism is precisely to show how we can critically exploit discursive limitations, how we can make limits productive. My contextualist view underscores *the critical productivity of discursive limits* and gives center stage to those who speak at the limits or on the margins of our discursive practices. It is for this reason that I will conclude the book with a discussion of *marginal discourses* in the final chapter. My view from *elsewhere* calls attention to the critical and transformative potential of the eccentric speech of those who have a frontier identity and speak on the border of what is deemed unsayable and nonsensical, troubling the always contingent boundary historically erected between the sayable and the unsayable. These marginal discourses that speak on the borders or at the limits constitute a risky speech that has a dangerous and precarious life and is always stuttering, always perilously starting to speak while being erased or silenced, always fighting the extinction of its precarious presence in the horizon of the discursive. Trying to speak at the limits or on the margins of discursive practices is always perceived as a menace, for this risky speech threatens with shaking our practices at their roots insofar as it threatens the very normative identity of what counts as legitimate speech. As Butler puts it: "The kind of speaking that takes place on the border of the unsayable promises to expose the vacillating boundaries of legitimacy in speech" (1997, p. 41).

The vacillation of our agency between discursive freedom and contextual constraints is precisely what polarized views of performativity neglect and ultimately render incomprehensible (even impossible), thus remaining entangled in false dichotomies and spurious dilemmas. On my view, discursive agency involves a process of constant recontextualization or echoing, in which our discursive acts are constantly being oriented by histories of use and at the same time they are constantly reorienting these histories as well. Discursive orientations and reorientation are intertwined in an always ongoing and neverending process of performative negotiations. My historical and dialectical view of performativity as *echoing* action thus converges with Butler's view of performativity as *renewable* action. These views underscore the hybridity of discursive agency and call attention to the interrelations and unavoidable dialectics between "fidelity" to and "breakage" from contexts. Butler draws explicitly the political implications of a hybrid view of agency in the following brilliant passage:

> Understanding performativity as a *renewable action without clear origin or end* suggests that speech is finally constrained neither by its specific speaker nor by its originating context. Not only defined by social context, such speech is also marked by its capacity to break with context. Thus, performativity has its own social temporality in which it remains enabled precisely by the contexts from which it breaks. This ambivalent structure at the heart of performativity implies that, within political discourse, the very terms of resistance and insurgency are spawned in part by the powers they oppose (which is not to say that the latter are reducible to the former or always already coopted by them in advance). (1997, p. 40; my emphasis)

This hybrid view of agency emphasizes the crucial importance of opening up discursive spaces for critique and transformation, for *radical resignification or echoing*. My contextualism recommends an experimentalist attitude that always tries to make room for echoing in new ways. We should always try to prepare ourselves for hearing new echoes in our discursive practices. The experimentalism of our resignifying or echoing agency has to be facilitated and encouraged, rather than constrained and dejected. We have to take responsibility for continuing or discontinuing available discursive contexts in particular ways through our agency, but also for opening up *new contexts*, contexts that by definition have not yet been legitimated by any normative framework. Whether we know it or not, and whether we like it or not, our discursive agency is always burdened with this responsibility (a crucial part of what I call "echoing responsibility"): in our speech acts we are always engaged in the reorientation of performative chains and the rearticulation of historical paths of use. We are always confronted with the critical task of reconstructing the normative frameworks underlying our practices; in our everyday discursive activities, we face the challenge of critically examining and rearticulating the expectations of normalcy that derive from these normative frameworks. This critical process of reconstruction and rearticulation is an endless task that is never fully completed in our discursive practices; and this lack of finality is crucial, for it reminds us that this critical task always constitutes a pressing challenge and responsibility for the ongoing negotiations and renegotiations of our speech acts in particular practices and particular contexts. The challenges of radical critique and radical resignification or echoing are the themes that the concluding chapter will explore. A performative way of carrying out radical critique and radical echoing is what I have called "the practice of infelicity."

As argued above, it is of crucial importance to exploit the critical potential of performative failures, which can be taken as occasions for transforming the infelicitous into the felicitous and thus rethinking and redoing the norms underlying our discursive practices. Failing performatives can be used to redirect a practice, to undo and redo its normative structure by rethinking the (often assumed and taken-for-granted) conditions for felicity and infelicity. The liberating potential of the practice of infelicity—of stigmatized eccentric agency—can be appreciated even more fully when we recognize that the normative distinctions between felicity and infelicity apply not only to our discursive agency but also to our identity as speakers and agents. Let me elaborate.

It is impossible to overemphasize the crucial importance of the norms that structure our linguistic practices and shape what in them counts as a performative success and a performative failure. The norms of linguistic performativity are of crucial importance not only for the things we *do* with language but also for the things we *are* in language. Linguistic performativity has a crucial significance for different aspects of our identity, and not only for their expression, but also for their formation or constitution, as performative theories of identity have argued. As Butler (1990, 1993, 2004), Sedgwick (1990), and other feminist theorists have argued, gender is not simply something that we are, but also something that we do: gender norms are constantly being enacted and reenacted in our linguistic practices. And we can perform our gender felicitously or infelicitously, depending on whether or not our gender performances conform to the established norms of masculinity and femininity. This performative account has also been applied to other aspects of identity such as sexual orientation, race, and ethnicity.[32] We perform these different aspects of our identity through our speech acts in all kinds of ways—through diction, tone, use of specific words and expressions, particular claims and assertions, and so on; and the performance of our gender, sexuality, race, and ethnicity is deemed felicitous or infelicitous according to its conformity with standardized or normalized social expectations and accepted norms of conduct. We will come back to the complex relationship between language and identity[33] in the next chapter. But I want to propose here the following distinction concerning nonconforming performances of identity that are deemed infelicitous. We have to distinguish between the kind of infelicity that is simply *incidental* and does not affect the identity of the violator or the status or content of the norm infringed—an occasional deviation of a previously established norm that is accepted in the community and can be appealed to straightforwardly (saying, for example, "That is simply not masculine behavior," "Things are not done that way," or "One should not speak that way"); and, on the other hand, a kind of infelicity that is *constitutive*, not because it violates any law written in stone or any essential constitution of the relevant aspect of identity, but, on the contrary, precisely because it institutes what cannot be done, because it exemplifies infelicity and thus becomes an *exemplar or prototype of transgression*, a paradigm of how things should not be done, setting and reinforcing the norms and normative expectations that structure the relevant practice (doing gender, doing race, etc.). The former are *infelicitous acts* while the latter are *the acts of infelicitous subjects*. This distinction between infelicitous acts and the acts of infelicitous subjects (between incidental and constitutive infelicities) is a distinction that enables us to recognize different ways in which the normativity of a linguistic practice operates and develops: it is crucial for linguistic normativity that not only speech acts but also speakers can be infelicitous.

Infelicitous subjects are the nonconformists. They may acquire this deviant status in the practice through an original transgression or series of transgressive acts; the status of infelicitous performers may also be attributed to them quite arbitrarily without any explicit violation on their part (on the basis of a rumor, a fear, a projection, or whatever the case may be). But however they acquire their status, the important point is that deviation or transgression becomes the distinctive mark of these speakers, defining who they are as linguistic agents:

their modes of comportment, their linguistic habitus, and their ways of generating speech acts are perceived as having an inescapable deviant or transgressive
character. *Infelicity has been inscribed in their very identity*, and they have been
deemed inadequate for the performative expression of certain aspects of their
identity: everything they say and do becomes a paradigm of how *not* to signify
femininity, blackness, Hispanicity, Americanness, or whatever the case may be.
No matter what the origin of their stigmatization as linguistic agents happens
to be (their accent, their diction, any aspect of their linguistic habitus, certain
aspects of their lifestyle, or whatever), infelicitous performers play a special
role in the normative economy of a practice as living and walking *exemplars of
infelicity*, of how things should not be done, and of what can happen to you—to
anyone—if you are not careful enough to comply with the established norms
and the accepted patterns of behavior. For the normalization of our modes
of expression and the disciplining of possible violations and transgressions
(which cannot all be anticipated in explicit codes), it is of the utmost importance that infelicity can attach itself (and adhere its negative force) not only to
particular acts but also to particular identities, which can produce an indefinite
number of transgressions and thus delineate indirectly, in a piecemeal fashion, how things are to be done. Although—as Austin emphasized—there is no
complete set of rules or algorithm that can guarantee the attainment of felicity in our speech acts, prudential considerations can be derived in an indirect
and negative way from the following general rule of thumb: "Do not associate
yourself with infelicitous subjects and stay away from their distinctive ways of
producing speech acts."

Infelicitous subjects are at the normative margins of our practices. They
are *border people*,[34] the very embodiment of the normative frontiers between
felicity and infelicity which are drawn piecemeal from practice to practice and
from context to context, and are used to discipline not only our agency but
also our very identity. It is not only particular acts or even whole practices, but
also particular speakers and even entire groups of speakers and agents—entire
identities—that are deemed infelicitous. In the normative economy of our
discursive practices infelicitous subjects play the important role of *negative
exemplars*.[35] In the next chapter I will critically examine repressive processes of
silencing as processes of stigmatization and marginalization of particular types
of subjects and their voices. It is important to note that, insofar as these infelicitous subjects are negative exemplars, these silencing processes are also—
indirectly—normative processes for disciplining the linguistic performance of
all speakers.

Chapter 4

Speaking from Elsewhere:
Silence, Exclusion, and Marginality

> *Silence itself*—the things one declines to say, or is forbidden to name, the discretion that is required between different speakers—*is less the absolute limit of discourse*, the other side from which it is separated by a strict boundary, *than an element that functions alongside the things said, with them and in relation to them within over-all strategies.* There is no binary division to be made between what one says and what one does not say; we must try to determine the *different ways of not saying* such things, how those who can and those who cannot speak of them are distributed, which type of discourse is authorized, or which form of discretion is required in each case. *There is not one but many silences, and they are an integral part of the strategies that underlie and permeate discourses.*
>
> —M. Foucault, *History of Sexuality I*, p. 27; my emphasis

> In the vicinity of the closet, even what *counts* as a speech act is problematized in a perfectly routine basis. [. . .] "Closetedness" itself is a performance initiated as such by the *speech act of a silence*—not a particular silence, but a silence that accrues particularity by fits and starts, in relation to the discourse that surrounds and differentially constitutes it. The speech acts that coming out, in turn, can comprise are as strangely specific. And they may have nothing to do with the acquisition of new information.
>
> —E. Sedgwick, *Epistemology of the Closet*, p. 3; emphasis
> preserved and added

Wʜᴀᴛ ɪꜱ ᴛʜᴇ ᴍᴇᴀɴɪɴɢ of silence? As suggested by the texts quoted above, this question is ill-posed, for there are many silences and they can have many meanings. Depending on the specifics of the case, the significance of a silence may range from an obvious meaning to utter nonsensicality. Foucault and Sedgwick urge us to think of silences as situated speech acts that can be understood only in their particularity, that is, as they function in particular sociohistorical contexts and within particular discursive practices. This insight, I will argue, is elaborated in an interesting way in Wittgenstein's philosophy of language. I will use my Wittgensteinian contextualism in this chapter to make two crucial points about the intelligibility of silence. The first point is that whether a silence has meaning is a *context-specific* issue. Silences, like utterances, are not significant or nonsensical in themselves. Asking "What does silence mean?" in the abstract does not get us anywhere. But we can pointedly ask "Which silences are significant and which ones nonsensical?" in situated ways, that is, in particular language games (or clusters of them). The second point is that the intelligibility of a silence is an *achievement* that depends on, and always remains dependent upon, the *agency* of speakers. Silences, like utterances, are not born meaningful or senseless, they are *made* significant or nonsensical. This is why it is a mistake to think that intelligibility is an absolute, "all or nothing" issue. Intelligibility comes in degrees, and so does nonsensicality. When we ask about the significance of a speech act, there is more than a yes or no answer; there is an entire spectrum of different possibilities, a continuum of cases between clear, perfect sense and obvious, utter nonsense. We need to ask about the discursive processes through which utterances and silences are rendered (more or less) significant or nonsensical; and in particular, in order to elucidate how to repair unintelligible silences, we have to investigate how silences are made significant and how they are broken or overcome.

One of Wittgenstein's lifelong philosophical preoccupations was to elucidate the limits of intelligibility, to provide an account of language that could shed light on (and dissolve the mystifications around) the boundaries between what can and cannot be said. A core idea of his later philosophy (perhaps already present in the *Tractatus*) is that there are no absolute limits or boundaries that we can impose on language, that the domain of significance cannot be looked at *sub specie aeternitatis*, that there is no way to determine a priori the bounds of sense, to fix once and for all the range of all possible significant speech acts. According to Wittgenstein's view of intelligibility, whatever limits or boundaries we may find in language are drawn locally and piecemeal by diverse and heterogeneous discursive practices, and they are never final; these limits and boundaries are contingently erected by historical practices that are frequently fluctuating and always open to change. This approach to discursive practices is already implicit in the very notion of a language game, which highlights three crucial dimensions of language use: its situatedness or contextuality, its performativity, and its normativity. First, our speech acts are embedded in the situated activities that compose our "form of life"; their significance can only be understood in the context of a life praxis ("words have meaning only in the stream of life"; RPP II §687). Secondly, language and action are interwoven in such a way that we cannot separate questions about language and questions about agency: a philosophical account of language requires a philosophical elucidation of linguistic performance, of the things we do and don't do with, through, and around language, and of the place that our linguistic performances occupy in our lives. Thirdly, language use is always subject to normative expectations: the players' performance is governed by (typically tacit) norms or rules (no matter how vague, flexible, and fluctuating they may be); there are proper and improper ways of playing, correct and incorrect moves within the game. These central aspects of language use are crucial for the analysis of silence that I develop in what follows. Whether it is conceived as a move within a language game or as a way of stepping outside the language game, silence has a contextual, performative, and normative dimension: the significance of a silence can only be understood when it is properly situated, that is, when it is placed in the context of overlapping language games or discursive practices whose configurations and intersections shape our lives in particular ways. Being silent is doing or not doing something: it is a form of action or inaction, a way of engaging or a refusal to engage; and it is a linguistic move regulated by norms and subject to normative assessments.

On certain *therapeutic* readings (also called "deflationary" or "quietist"),[1] the Wittgensteinian view just sketched has the implication of unmasking a particular kind of silence as a philosophical illusion: this is the *radical silence* of complete *outsiders*, or of those within a practice who nonetheless claim to be left out. According to the therapeutic interpretation, this radical silence and its alleged significance are illusory, impossible, delusional. The pathological delusion in question is a philosophical fiction based on metaphysical assumptions that distort our linguistic practices and our relationship to them. This is the fiction of a meaning that cannot be linguistically articulated, of an experience that cannot be put into words, of a voice that cannot speak. This fiction is produced by a vain metaphysical impulse (to which both philosophers and nonphilosophers can succumb): the impulse to get outside our linguistic skins, to stand outside our language games, to adopt a "view from nowhere." We need to fight this metaphysical impulse in order to purge ourselves of the philosophical fiction of a radically elusive silence. We win this therapeutic fight when we come to the realization that an incessantly elusive silence that remains outside all language games requires a practice-transcendent perspective that cannot be had. We cannot get outside language; there is no outside, at least nor for us, linguistic beings constituted by discursive practices that permeate all the aspects of our life. As Wittgenstein puts it, "there is no outside; outside you cannot breathe"; "it is only in a language that we can mean something by something" (PI §103 and p. 18, footnote). This realization, the therapeutic view contends, should enable us to see that the effort to speak after we abandon the familiar terrain of our language games is hopeless, that the vain attempt to meaning-fully occupy a discursive position outside language, outside all our linguistic practices, amounts to nothing more than the pathetic spectacle of emitting an inarticulate noise and claiming a significance for it that is impossible to recog-nize and acknowledge. There is some truth to this analysis but also an impor-tant oversight with dangerous ramifications.

The truth in the therapeutic view is that there are no *absolute* (final, unmovable) limits to intelligibility and, therefore, there is no such thing as a symbolic space that is *necessarily* outside language and *must* remain forever elusive. In this sense, there are no absolute outsiders, that is, there are no voices that stand outside *all possible* language games. But there are those who find themselves unable to speak in the discursive practices available to them, voices whose signifying powers fall outside the language games that are their home, even if they can become refugees in other practices or games. More impor-tantly, it is (at least in principle) possible to find voices that are systematically excluded from all language games developed so far and cannot receive asylum in other practices (at least not yet). There can be voices that have nowhere to go (although they can always invent a place). These radical exclusions produce the radical silences that the therapeutic view dismisses. The therapeutic view does not do justice to these silenced voices by telling them that their radical silence is illusory or pathological; for their predicament is not (at least not always) the artifact of a philosophical fiction, but the result of very real exclusions. The therapeutic view ignores the reality of these radical exclusions and insists that there is no (meaningful) silence when we don't have the capacity to speak. On this view, the discursive discomfort of those who feel radically and systemati-cally excluded requires therapy that can cure them of (and make them aban-don) their extreme symbolic aspirations. The therapeutic view assumes that the only real basis that a forced silence can have consists in mundane difficulties and pedestrian obstructions in communication. Under the spell of metaphysi-cal impulses, we are told, these prosaic obstacles and impediments are inflated into insurmountable barriers, when in fact they can be easily overcome with our communicative efforts: we have to try harder in the articulation of mean-ings, we have to introduce *reforms* in linguistic usage, internal changes in our language games. This reformist view misses the *radical discursive exclusions* that are built into the normative structure of our practices and the *silencing processes* that are constitutive of the way in which our language games are played. The central thesis of this chapter is that radical silences can be very real and that they call for more than therapy and reform: they call for the dismantling of our

language games, for a *radical critique* that aims at deep structural transformations (and in some cases the abandonment) of our practices.

In the next section I will develop my Wittgensteinian approach to the
hermeneutics of silence while arguing against the therapeutic view. I will then
offer a contextualist analysis of the limited agency of disempowered voices that
tries to identify ways in which those marginal voices that have been excluded
and silenced can acquire more agency and critical power, if only obliquely,
through the fissures of our language games.

4.1. Contextualism and the Hermeneutics of Silence

Defending a therapeutic interpretation of Wittgenstein, Alice Crary (2001,
2002) has argued that certain views in feminist theory (as well as in queer
theory and race theory) fall victim to a pathological metaphysical impulse and
need therapy. These are the views that claim that there are meaningful experiences that cannot be linguistically articulated in our language games, that
there are voices that have things to say and yet cannot speak in our discursive
practices. These views conjure up the illusion of a nonsensical silence that is
nonetheless revealing and important, that is, a silence that hides an inexpress-
ible "meaning." This illusory silence, Crary contends, involves the philosophical
fiction of "intelligible nonsense," an inherently contradictory notion that forces
us to postulate meanings outside language. Crary criticizes this notion from
an *internalist* perspective, arguing that meaningful silences are always internal
to a discursive practice: only internal silences are interpretable, for it is only
within a language game that we can attribute a tacit meaning to a silence. As
other champions of the therapeutic view, Crary insists that there is no silence
(properly so-called) when there is nothing to say, when we do not even have
the capacity to speak. On this analysis, those who claim that they are unable
to articulate certain meanings in the language game suffer from a *delusion*
provoked by a particular mistake; namely, the mistake of taking the present
configuration of the language game for what the game is once and for all.
Those who insist on their incapacity to speak within a discursive practice do
not see that what may look to them like an impossibility is simply a difficulty
created by *contingent obstacles* that can be removed from within the practice.
Emphasizing this last point, Crary tries to turn the bad news of the therapeutic diagnosis into good news: the good news is that it is always possible for the
participants in the language game to articulate their experiences and give linguistic expression to their meanings; in principle, any voice can be heard, any
discursive perspective can find a place within the practice. According to this
view, our discursive practices are never perfect but they are always improvable;
and, therefore, we may have good reasons to complain about them but not to
despair to the point of giving up on them. Crary insists that participants can

face all kinds of obstacles in their discursive lives, but they can always introduce internal changes in the game to overcome these obstacles. People may feel unable to express themselves, but their inability to give linguistic articulation to their thoughts and experiences is contingent and can always be overcome (at least in principle) within the language games or discursive practices in which they participate.

The principal mistake of this reformist and meliorist view is to assume that we are all *participants* in the discursive practices that shape our lives, that we all have a *voice* and are endowed with (sufficient degrees of) *discursive agency* (i.e., with the capacity to perform speech acts and to act on, react to, and contend with the speech acts of others). This is a mistake because we are not always players in the language games in which we find ourselves. In many of these games our agency is significantly curtailed and in some cases even denied. If we examine actual practices in their specific social and historical contexts, it is not difficult to find in them speaking subjects who have been objectified in certain aspects of their lives and have to remain silent about them, and even voices that have been silenced completely. (Think, for instance, of the traditional exclusions of homosexuals from modern discursive practices for the expression of desire and the articulation of sexual meanings. Think also of the exclusions of racial and ethnic minorities from the mainstream political language games in which interests, needs, ideals, and aspirations are negotiated.) We cannot understand how silences are produced and how they can be overcome if we don't critically question what it means to be a participant and to have a voice or to be deprived of it in a language game.

A hermeneutics of silence needs to address critical questions concerning discursive agency: how it can be curtailed and denied; how it can be acquired and exercised, and at what expense; how normative structures are sedimented and become perpetuated through the agency of speakers; how power is transmitted and distributed through speech acts, and so on. I will try to show, pace the therapeutic view, that the reality of radical exclusions and radical silences does not force us to step *outside* language and to adopt a *practice-transcendent* perspective or a "view from nowhere." In order to make sense of these radical exclusions and silences, my contextualism draws attention to what I call the "polyphony" of language games, that is, to the fact that our discursive practices always allow for a multiplicity of voices and standpoints. This polyphonic multiplicity suggests that meanings that cannot be recognized and expressed from our situated discursive perspective could be recognizable and expressible *elsewhere*, that is, from a different perspective. In other words, my polyphonic account of discursive practices enables us to make sense of the possibility of radical exclusions and silences and even of the notion of "intelligible nonsense": what appears as nonsensical in one practice can be intelligible in another and, therefore, it should be possible to identify and criticize the discursive limitations of a practice from the standpoint of another. According to my polyphonic contextualism, the lack of discursive agency in one practice can be countered by (and compensated with) agency in alternative practices, whether these alternative practices are *actual or possible*—for in some cases such alternatives may not be available and will have to be created precisely for the purpose of fighting exclusions and silences and empowering speakers.

Wittgenstein's contextualism is misconstrued by the reformist and meliorist perspective of the therapeutic view. According to this view, all discursive contexts or symbolic spaces can be looked at as constituting a heterogeneous but nonetheless unified domain of sense. This is the *common* sphere of intelligibility shared by all speakers, the symbolic space *inside* language, the only one there is. This hegemonic realm of significance is explained and defended on the therapeutic view according to the following recipe: first, you start with the dichotomy between being inside and being outside language; then, you go on to show that there is no outside for the kind of symbolic beings we are; and finally, you conclude that we all share the same symbolic space, ending up with a nice and exclusive field of signification for all language users. This recipe is flawed from the outset. To begin with, the problem with the inside/outside dichotomy is not simply that one side of it turns out to be empty; the problem is, rather, that the dichotomy *as such* involves a distortion. The problem is not simply that there is no "outside" for our language games. For, in an important sense, there is no "inside" either: there is no such thing as a symbolic perspective common to all language users. The distortion implicit in this dichotomy is the assumption that there is a principled way of drawing the boundaries between what is inside and what is outside language, while in fact these boundaries are constantly being drawn and redrawn in different ways for different purposes and from the perspective of different discursive practices and different practitioners. These blurred and shifting boundaries are hopeless when used to ground and justify the inside/outside dichotomy. And yet this unwarranted dichotomy is used to force on us the misleading twofold classification of silences into internal and external, real and illusory. But how to locate silences within our language games is a more complicated issue than it may seem, an issue that is highly oversimplified by the therapeutic view.

What the therapeutic view tells us is that if we want to make sense by what we say or not say, if we want to have meaningful utterances and silences, then we have to stand over "here," that is, we have to occupy the *perspective of a participant*. But with this (apparently innocent) reasoning the therapeutic view ushers us to a false dilemma: "either here or nowhere." I call it the "therapeutic dilemma." This is a false dilemma because there is always a multiplicity of symbolic spaces and discursive perspectives that resist assimilation to one of its horns. Both horns of the dilemma, the "here" and the "nowhere," are highly problematic and ought to be questioned. Let's start with the second horn of the therapeutic dilemma. What is this *nowhere*? It is a construct that requires a particular conceptualization of its counterpart, the *here*, in order to make sense. This construct, the *nowhere*, is a direct result of construing the *here* as a hegemonic space: without argument, the therapeutic view construes the internal perspective of practitioners, of those invested with participatory status and endowed with discursive agency, as exhausting the domain of significance. To assume that if we don't speak "from here" we must be hopelessly trying to speak "from nowhere" is to assume that there is *nowhere else but here*. But there is always "somewhere else," even if it needs to be invented; that is, there is always the possibility of alternative discursive contexts in which new voices and perspectives can be expressed. These alternative contexts may not always be available; they may require inventing new language games or radically transforming existing practices until they acquire a new face. Indeed Wittgenstein often talks about the invention of new language games (e.g. PI §492) and of the possibility of replacing old games with new ones (e.g. PI §64). He emphasizes that language games are constantly fluctuating and that this fluctuation allows for radical changes in which our practices can be twisted, bent, and rearranged beyond recognition. It is purely arbitrary to insist that these transformations always have to be understood as internal changes or reforms of the *same* practice. This insistence is just an arbitrary imposition of a priori constraints on our conceptualizations of the evolution of linguistic practices.

It is important to note that speaking from "somewhere else" does not require that we abandon the situated perspective of a speaker. There is no reason why those who don't (or even can't) adopt the so-called perspective of the participant in a language game should be depicted as disappearing in a vacuum, rather than as defecting the game or going in hiding within the game. The defectors of a game and the resistance fighters within it occupy alternative discursive contexts. These alternative contexts may be provided by already existing practices or by fragile practices under construction (games in the making), which are sometimes gestated in the repressed and forgotten interstices of the very language game in question. For example, consider how heterosexist language games have been systematically disrupted by the proliferation of forms of expression and cultural representations that "queer" sexual meanings by twisting them in unexpected ways and applying them beyond the heterosexual semantic domain for which they were developed. These "queer" ways of talking about desire and sexuality have often remained anomalous parts of mainstream practices—subtexts or double-talks (often repressed or simply ignored by the majority); but sometimes they have developed into somewhat independent alternative practices—often marginalized language games played only by those who do not fit the heterosexual normative scheme. The "queering" of sexual meanings both from within mainstream practices and from alternative practices has been recently studied meticulously by historians and literary critics in Queer Theory.[2]

Those who abandon (or are forced to abandon) the so-called here of an established practice are not doomed to adopt a "view from nowhere"; rather, they are taking up the burden of developing *a view from elsewhere*. Speaking from elsewhere can be negatively characterized as speaking from a not-yet recognized discursive context and with a not-yet recognizable voice. But it implicitly involves a struggle for recognition; and it can be positively characterized as contributing to the creation of new discursive contexts and opening up spaces for new voices that have not been heard yet. These eccentric speakers, these defecting and subterranean voices, are still fully situated; there is nothing otherwordly about them. Those who abandon (or are forced to abandon) the so-called insider's standpoint in a given practice may not even be outside the practice in question, let alone outside all possible linguistic practices and outside language itself. This is why Crary's analogy between the radical critic of our linguistic practices and the radical skeptic is flawed. Unlike the radical skeptic, the radical critic has no need (or use) for a practice-transcendent perspective. Let me briefly comment on this analogy before I go on to criticize the other horn of the therapeutic dilemma.

Unlike the radical skeptic, radical feminist theorists, queer theorists, and critical race theorists do not target *all possible* linguistic practices and do not need to occupy a practice-independent standpoint. However, Crary contends that both the radical skeptic and the radical theorist argue for a "wholesale rejection" of our practices and conceptual resources and, therefore, "they put themselves [. . .] in a traditional philosophical position of speechlessness in the face of what they want to say, while at the same time insisting that their silence is pregnant with meaning" (2001, p. 387). But there is a crucial ambiguity in the expression "wholesale rejection of practices." This can be construed in a weak sense as meaning the rejection of a whole practice or set of practices (even all current practices) in their entirety, or in a strong sense as meaning the rejection of *all* practices that are *humanly possible*. The radical theorist is after the former (she targets clusters of language games); the radical skeptic after the latter (she targets all possible language games). What Wittgenstein criticizes and deems futile is the idea of radical detachment from our practices, that is, the attempt to step outside *all* language games. But he has nothing against the critique and rejection of particular language games (or clusters of them): entire discursive practices can be questioned and repudiated when they enter into conflict with other practices or with certain aspects of our "form of life," getting in the way of human flourishing.[3] Therefore, Wittgenstein should be thought of as an enemy of radical skepticism but as a friend of radical critique.[4]

Radical critique is certainly after something more extreme than the internal changes proposed by reformist and meliorist approaches; and yet it does not require the rejection of all practices from a practice-transcendent perspective. When radical theorists call our attention to the impossibility to speak, they relativize this radical silence to particular practices, typically explaining their genesis in terms of radical but contingent exclusions. At least in principle, these radical exclusions can be undone and the silences they produce can be overcome. This is why there is nothing mysterious about the radical theorist's claim that there are voices that cannot yet speak and meanings that cannot yet be expressed. For these silenced voices are in principle audible and these presently unspeakable meanings are in principle expressible. It is important that, unlike the skeptic, the radical theorist develops her view with an eye to new language games in which new voices can be heard and new meanings expressed. This makes all the difference in the world; and Crary actually recognizes this "difference between the sceptic and this theorist" (2001, p. 387). In feminism, she remarks, the radical theorist differs from the skeptic in holding "that as we gradually develop a 'feminist language' we will better understand what (currently nonsensical) 'female thoughts' attempt to express" (p. 387). But Crary minimizes this difference. She contends that "despite this difference, there is a deep similarity" between the radical skeptic and the radical theorist in that they share a "position of speechlessness" (p. 387). However, the speechlessness of the skeptic and that of the radical theorist could not be more different. The latter is not the result of adopting a practice-transcendent perspective, of placing oneself outside language. Unlike the skeptic, the radical theorist is not forced to take up an illusory standpoint outside all practices, an impossible view from nowhere. There is nothing illusory about the perspective of the radical theorist or about the radical silences and exclusions she denounces and fights against.

The real illusion, the real philosophical myth, if there is one, is that of the *insider's perspective* to which the therapeutic view appeals. The apparently innocent invitation "Please stand over *here* if you want to speak" forces us to buy into the illusion of the participant's perspective, the "here" of our practices. This is the other horn of the therapeutic dilemma. When we are told "either here or nowhere" we are bullied into occupying an illusory discursive perspective, into taking up a position that doesn't exist. This is because there is not *one* "here," because the standpoint of our practices is always unavoidably fractured. And this is for two reasons. First, there is no such thing as the *inside* of language because the irreducible multiplicity of discursive practices or language games does not amount to a unified symbolic space. Another way to put this point is to say that there is no such thing as *language*,[5] that the very concept of a language is an empty philosophical abstraction. There are only particular discursive practices. Wittgenstein warns us against the philosophical temptation of talking about *all* language games and thinking of them as constituting a *totality* (see esp. PI §65). There is a dangerous totalizing tendency in philosophy that entices us to adopt an impossible bird's-eye view of all our language games. This omniscient view makes us "unconscious of the prodigious diversity" of linguistic practices to which we are exposed in our daily lives (PI II p. 224). Many of these practices overlap or intersect in multifarious ways; others do not. This complex and heterogeneous multiplicity of language games does not amount to a closed linguistic system: "this multiplicity is not something fixed, given once for all; but new types of language, new language games, as we may say, come into existence, and others become obsolete and get forgotten" (PI §23). We should be suspicious of any appeal to *the* perspective of the language user, *the* standpoint of those who are inside language; for what is typically referred to as *language* comprises a wild variety of discursive contexts, perspectives, and voices.

In the second place, language games are not only multiple and diverse, but also *radically heterogeneous* in their internal functioning. Even if we restrict ourselves to a single language game in all its social and historical specificity, we still do not find such thing as *the* participant's perspective. For no matter how rigidly constrained by rules it is, a language game always admits different ways of interpreting and applying its rules and, therefore, different ways of playing. A language game always allows for different voices, inflections, stances, and perspectives. There is no unique viewpoint that we can call "the participant's perspective." The participants in a language game lack a single unified perspective. And this is not just because there are typically different participants playing the game. Even if we allow for the possibility of a language game with a single player,[6] even if we narrow down our search for the insider's perspective to a newly invented language game with its creator as the only player, we still don't have a single, wholly unified viewpoint that excludes all differences, for the player's perspective is shattered in a chain of performances that redefine the game at every step and are always open to reinterpretation. In our discursive practices, heterogeneity and difference really do go *all the way down*, down to the perspective of each individual speaker, leaving nothing unquestionably one and the same. The individual players of a language game adopt different perspectives and speak in different voices as they perform different speech acts; and there is no reason why these voices and perspectives have to be, should be, or even can be, unified. This is something that Wittgenstein emphasizes in his critique of the notion of a *self* or of a unified center of consciousness that plagues philosophical conceptions of subjectivity. I discussed this critique in the previous chapter and used it to motivate and develop my contextualist alternative: a *polyphonic view* of speaking subjectivities. I will now use this view to explain the apparently contradictory notion of "intelligible nonsense" and the radical exclusions and silences associated with it.

4.2. Making Sense of Radical Silences and Exclusions: A Polyphonic Perspective

Wittgenstein's critique of the subject has been further elaborated by contemporary feminists such as Wendy Lee-Lampshire (1992), Naomi Scheman (1993), and Janet F. Smith (2002). What this critique denounces is that the philosophical notion of a unitary self or a transcendental ego brings with it an implicit attempt to explain the unity of all our experiences and actions by appealing to an internal proprietary subject. On this proprietary model of subjectivity, experiences and actions are thought of as *objects* that can be claimed as one's *property* and are thus unified by being *owned* by the *same* subject, that is, by belonging to the *same* estate. As Smith (2002) puts it, this metaphorical concept of proprietorship is the "philosopher's myth that leads us into positing an abstract center of consciousness—a self, subject, or soul as owner" (p. 350). Smith as well as other Wittgensteinian feminists have shown that the proprietary model of subjectivity has a fundamental sociopolitical dimension in that it facilitates and justifies the internalization of relations of domination. The problem with this model is not simply that it promulgates an illusory unity, but that this illusory unity makes certain forms of subordination inescapable, building reification and subjugation into the very structure of subjectivity.[7] As we saw in the previous chapter, Wittgenstein's critique of the proprietary subject calls into question the assumption that a speaker must have a unified perspective from which to speak and to which everything must be subordinated. On Wittgenstein's view, the speaker's perspective typically is (and, at any rate, always can be) divided or fractured. For, in our speech performance, as we navigate our way through discursive contexts, we are constantly given the opportunity to take up different perspectives; and the different perspectives that we in fact adopt may or may not be harmonized and fused together (we may find ourselves incapable of, or uninterested in, this unification). In a similar vein (but drawing on a different hermeneutical tradition), María Lugones (1989, 1991, and 2003) has argued for a pluralistic conception of speaking subjects which appreciates the inevitable heterogeneity of their voices and enables them to recognize that they are not one but many.[8] For Wittgenstein too, the normal predicament of the speaking subject is to be divided or fractured, or (at the very least) on the verge of being divided or fractured.

Borrowing Bakhtin's term, I have subsumed these points about the unavoidable multiplicity and heterogeneity of symbolic perspectives that our discursive practices exhibit under the heading of the uncontrollable *polyphony* of language games. A language game is a polyphonic activity,[9] a dialogue of multiple voices. In a language game new voices can always crop up, even if the voices that are allowed to speak are heavily constrained by the normative structure of the game. Sometimes these unexpected voices can arise from unlikely and obscure places within the game; sometimes new voices can come from other discursive practices and surprise us by unpredictably "intruding" in "our" practice. And it is important to note that these different voices and the discursive perspectives they embody and performatively express can enter into *radical conflicts*. There can be a clash of perspectives that brings the dialogue to a halt. This clash sheds light on the oxymoronic notion of "intelligible nonsense" or "'meaning' in spite of senselessness" that Crary and others criticize from a therapeutic perspective. We can make sense of these paradoxical expressions as descriptions of a clash between divergent perspectives on intelligibility: one that deems an utterance or silence nonsensical and another one that deems it intelligible. It is important to note that these conflicting perspectives rarely compete as equals in our actual practices. And given the likely inequalities between them, it is crucial that we raise questions about the distribution of power among discursive perspectives in conflict. We have to be wary of those perspectives that present themselves as "mainstream" and marginalize all others, and even more watchful of those perspectives that claim exclusivity and deny all others; for the imbalance of power can be such that it gives hegemonic status to a single perspective at the expense of all possible alternatives.

When we consider the perspectival nature of our assessments of intelligibility in the light of the intrinsic polyphonic nature of language games, we can understand those cases in which speakers claim to envision meanings that are unintelligible in the contexts and practices available to them. Given the indomitable and unpredictable polyphony of language games and the multiple ways of assessing the intelligibility of speech acts, there is nothing mysterious or illusory about these cases; and there is no reason why we must always try to undo the contradiction involved in a claim of "'meaning' in spite of senselessness." A case of "intelligible nonsense" can involve a recalcitrant contradiction that cannot be dissolved. Why should these cases be dismissed offhand? It is simply not true that either the alleged intelligibility or the alleged nonsensicality of an utterance or a silence has to be rejected as illusory, for they can both be fully real if the discursive contexts and practices from which these judgments of intelligibility are made prove to be rich enough. In this sense, "either intelligible or nonsensical," like "either inside or outside language," is a false dichotomy that is forced on us in a vain attempt to tame—to discipline and constrain—the constitutive polyphony of our discursive practices. But the indomitable polyphony of language games makes intelligible nonsense a ubiquitous possibility. There is nothing self-defeating about claiming meaning for my experiences, thoughts, and actions, even if there are no (at least not yet) established discursive contexts and fully developed practices that can render them intelligible. I can meaningfully assert the intelligibility of my attempts to speak even if my inchoate utterances do not contain linguistic articulations that can enjoy the recognition of a consolidated community of speakers. To deny this is to overlook two central features of meaning claims: our assessments of intelligibility have a crucial *normative* and *projective* dimension; that is, they involve an 'ought' and they are future oriented.

When we claim that something has meaning, we are *not simply describing* linguistic behavior, we are judging how things *should* be done in our linguistic interactions, that is, how people *should* respond to one another when certain things are said or when certain silences are maintained. A meaning claim is not *just* a factual statement about linguistic usage; it is never purely descriptive (not even in so-called descriptive linguistics). For it involves a judgment about the things that are and are not allowed in our discursive practices, which always projects usage into the future and sanctions discursive norms in a particular way. In these claims and assessments the appearance of neutrality hides a complacent attitude toward accepted norms that helps maintain the status quo. Although they may appear to be factual and retrospective judgments, meaning claims are normative statements that look into the future.[10]

What kind of speech act is a meaning claim such as "This makes sense"? The illocutionary force of a meaning claim is more akin to that of a command than it is to that of a report or description. Asserting that something is intelligible or unintelligible is prescribing a direction for linguistic performance. It is not reporting on a preexisting reality. Therefore, why should it be warranted for speakers to claim that their utterances and silences have meaning *only after* the conditions have been met for such meaning to be recognized in a language game? To contend (or simply to assume, as it is typically done) that meaning claims have to be post facto judgments is tantamount to an arbitrary decree that we won't accept radical departures from current discursive norms or radical additions to current discursive practices. But it is simply unreasonable to exclude from our negotiations of meaning claims those judgments that assert intelligibility where no one yet sees it. Why can't a speaker claim that her silences are pregnant with meaning even when this alleged meaning cannot be linguistically articulated in the language games available to her? Since meaning claims are prescriptive and forward looking, there is nothing illicit about asserting the existence of a meaning whose intelligibility cannot be recognized in our discursive practices. In fact, these radical meaning claims are not only legitimate but the most interesting and productive ones: they constitute a form of *critical intervention* in our practices. These perplexing and even paradoxical assessments of intelligibility call for the restructuration of our practices in order to make room for new voices; and they are, in this sense, a source of linguistic creativity and change. But it is important to note, though, that meaning claims do not have magical powers: they do not have any intrinsic transformative potential. Saying that this or that "has meaning," by itself, will change nothing. The proclamation alone does not revolutionize existing practices or inaugurate a brand-new practice. When Wittgenstein talks about radical innovations in our language games he emphasizes that they involve deep social changes. These deep changes involve practical and structural transformations, which include changes in the material conditions of life and in what Wittgenstein calls our "consensus of action" (our shared ways of doing things, with and without linguistic aids), in short, changes in our "forms of life" (*Lebensformen*).[11] But with this proviso, disruptive meaning claims that run contrary to available perspectives on intelligibility can be understood as calls for mobilization and concerted action toward deep social changes.

It makes sense to claim that in the linguistic practices currently available to us there are things that cannot be said and voices that cannot be heard. We can intelligibly and legitimately make this claim in two very different ways. In some cases we may find that, as Crary insists, it is simply the *present configuration* of our practices that produces those exclusions and silences, and the internal transformation of the available practices suffices to change the situation: it may happen that other possible configurations of the *same* practices will make new voices heard and will allow for the articulation of new meanings. But there is no reason why we should assume this will always be the case. In other cases we may find that for the silenced voices to be heard and for the repressed meanings to become recognizable and communicable we have to move to *different* practices, better and more inclusive language games, whose development requires the dismantling and eventual abandonment of current practices. With my polyphonic view of language games, I hope to have shown that radical claims about silenced voices and repressed meanings (such as those of radical feminists, race theorists, and queer theorists) are perfectly intelligible, legitimate, and even fruitful if and when they are properly contextualized. Those radical critiques of our linguistic practices that are motivated by radical exclusions and silences do not fall into incoherence and metaphysical delusion. They operate in a concretely situated way as calls for linguistic transformations that require substantial social and political changes—that is, they require a significant restructuration of our practices. These critical claims are not only intelligible and legitimate but also potentially fruitful, for they alert us to the presence of deep social problems afflicting our discursive practices and show that in order to address these problems successfully we need *more than mere linguistic reform*: we need radical political *action*, that is, *critical and subversive agency* directed at radical transformations of the material and normative conditions underlying our practices.

We are not always full participants or equal players in the language games in which we find ourselves. A hermeneutics of silence needs to address critical questions concerning discursive agency: how it can be curtailed and denied; how it can be acquired and exercised, and at what expense; how normative structures are sedimented and become perpetuated through the agency of speakers; how power is transmitted and distributed through speech acts, and so on. Philosophical issues concerning the complex relations between intelligibility, power, and oppression have been taken up by an emerging school of thought that reads Wittgenstein's philosophy alongside queer, feminist, and race theory. This sort of reading can be found in the pioneer work of Scheman (1996, 1997) and more recently in papers contained in Scheman and O'Connor (2002). My argument here is in line with this emerging school of thought. The polyphonic contextualism that I derive from Wittgenstein has a marked critical dimension: it calls upon our ethical and political responsibility as speakers and agents for resisting and fighting (or otherwise complying with) the silencing of certain voices and the marginalization and oppression of certain groups and individuals. On my polyphonic analysis, claims about the radical exclusion and silencing of certain voices and the inability to articulate certain meanings should be read in the following way: they demand that practices be dismantled and restructured so as to allow for voices that *now* cannot express themselves and for meanings that *now* cannot be articulated. When there are radical exclusions and silences, linguistic reform is not enough: the piecemeal transformation and improvement of language games will not do; deeper changes are needed: we need a profound transformation of our *forms of life*, which requires sustained social and political changes that can alter the material conditions and normative structures of our practices.

4.3. Spaces of Intelligibility and Marginality

It is a *social reality* that discursive contexts are delimited by borders or boundaries that create marginal spaces. The sociology and anthropology of language games teach us that discursive practices involve relations of inclusion and exclusion, bringing certain voices to the very *center* of these practices and relegating others to the *periphery* or the margins. My polyphonic contextualism provides the theoretical resources appropriate not only to analyze this reality but also to *subvert* it, for it makes possible the critical questioning and the destabilization of the normative relations between what is at the *center* and what is at the *periphery* of a discursive practice. In this section and the next I will try to show that the view from *elsewhere* I have developed in this book has in fact this critical and subversive potential. I will start by making explicit the role that spatial categories play in my contextualist perspective.

   In talking about differently *situated* voices my contextualism draws heavily on spatial conceptualizations. It is a spatial conceptualization of our discursive practices that enabled me to argue that voices can be marginalized and even completely silenced by being *excluded*. Only by relying on such conceptualization can we talk about the *margins* of our practices and about dissenting or eccentric voices being condemned to *exile* or to a *subterranean* existence when there are forces in the language game that fight and contain its polyphonic nature. But can we make sense of different *spaces* of intelligibility without relying on spatial dichotomies such as being inside or outside language, holding an insider's or an outsider's perspective, and so forth? Isn't my view implicitly invoking the very dichotomies I want to reject by recognizing *distances* between voices? I'm not prepared to accept this. But let me first make a concession by way of a clarification. There are two different questions that we should distinguish here. One question is whether spatial metaphors and analogies are unavoidable in a contextualist view given that the very notion of a context is a spatial category. I think the answer to this question is clearly yes; and I see no problem whatsoever in accepting that my polyphonic contextualism is articulated through spatial metaphors and analogies. However, a different question is whether the spatial conceptualization and analysis of intelligibility makes it unavoidable to appeal (explicitly or implicitly) to the inside/outside dichotomy, or to one of its variants and associated dilemmas. My answer here is no. I will try to show this through one last elucidation of the Wittgenstenian notion of language game. Wittgenstein certainly uses spatial metaphors and analogies to describe language games. But far from relying on a sharp distinction between the inner and the outer, his metaphorical and analogical conceptualizations call into question the very notions of inside and outside and problematize any boundary between sense and nonsense that philosophers or other theorists may draw, showing that these boundaries are always open to being challenged and blurred.

Through spatial metaphors and analogies Wittgenstein builds polyphony into the very notion of a discursive context in such a way that there is no longer room for posing the "in or out?" question with respect to utterances, silences, or voices (whether these are actual or imagined). It is because of its indomitable polyphonic character that, on Wittgenstein's view, a discursive context does not admit fixed limits or rigid boundaries that can ground the distinction between inside and outside; for having polyphony built into it means always having differences, multiplicity, heterogeneity, and instability. Insofar as the contexts in which language games are played are intrinsically polyphonic, they are intrinsically open, since their uncontrollable polyphony can destabilize and subvert any boundary between the inner and the outer that we may want to draw. I will try to show this through an analysis of the most celebrated spatial conceptualization that Wittgenstein offers, namely, the analogy between language and an ancient city—although there are others that support my interpretation equally well if not better.[12] He writes:

> Our language can be seen as an ancient city: a maze of little streets and squares, of old and new houses, and of houses with additions from various periods; and this surrounded by a multitude of new boroughs with straight regular streets and uniform houses. (PI §18)

While the spatial metaphors and analogies we find in philosophy of language are typically atemporal, Wittgenstein's analogy, by contrast, shows how a discursive context, like a city, has *historicity* built into it: it is formed by residues from the past (often incongruent and even contradictory), which constitute archeological strata that interact in complex ways and prefigure certain directions for the future, without determining the future shape that the context will take. As often pointed out in the literature, this analogy emphasizes the *indeterminacy* of a discursive context, which, like an urban space, always contains plenty of room for unpredictable changes, for developing new forms of edification and remodeling that cannot be anticipated. Nothing in an urban or a discursive context is fixed once and for all; the boundaries drawn in language are, like city limits, contingent and arbitrary. Wittgenstein's analogy underscores that there is always some amount of indeterminacy in deciding when we have a new language game, or when a subset of activities within a language game becomes a different practice: "And how many houses or streets does it take before a town begins to be a town?" (PI §18). But besides these points about temporality and indeterminacy, there are also other aspects and implications of the city analogy that have only recently been recognized by commentators. Following Jane Braaten, Scheman (2002) argues that the city analogy identifies different ways in which linguistic innovations can result from our agency. As she puts it, "it is not only in the newly constructed outlying boroughs that change can occur; rather, moving around in the inner city in different ways can subtly reshape its face, even as we acknowledge the importance of the ancient and nondeliberate history embedded in the old walls and lanes" (p. 10). This point about the different kinds of discursive agency that can lead to innovation can be further elaborated through a polyphonic interpretation of the city analogy. My contention is that this analogy can be understood as a figurative explanation of the polyphonic character of discursive practices.

How is the polyphony of language games captured by the city analogy? It is captured in the suggestion that the vast multiplicity and heterogeneity of voices in our language games are analogous to the enormous diversity of city dwellers. This diversity can never be fixed unless the very activities involved in language use and city life are terminated. For in language use, as in city life, there are always new possibilities for interaction cropping up. Hence the unavoidable openness and unpredictability of speaking and city dwelling. The identity of a speaker (or a city dweller) is never fixed because one's location in the game (or in the city) and one's relation to others are constantly changing. Like the people who inhabit a city, the voices that populate a language game are differently situated; and their localizations both constrain and enable their agency, affecting their interactions: depending on where you are, you can do certain things and not others. But these constraining and enabling conditions are always open to change. Just as the streets and roads of a city channel the traffic of city dwellers in particular ways while allowing for changes of all kinds, the paths created by previous speakers constrain our discursive freedom of movement within the language game without annulling the spontaneity of the players. In this way the city analogy highlights an important feature of discursive agency: its hybridity, its mixture of freedom and constraint, of spontaneity and control, of action and reaction. As voices move discursively through the maze of pathways inherited from previous voices, they unknowingly modify with their movements the discursive structures sedimented in linguistic practices. Like the activities of city dwellers, our discursive activities acquire shape in and through the way they are conducted in our day-to-day interactions. On this view, there is a constant rearticulation of discursive practices and restructuration of discursive contexts through an agency that is always, at some level, unconscious and nondeliberate. For our speech acts and the changes they produce in our practices are not driven by our conscious desires and intentions, but by life itself. My Wittgensteinian contextualism maintains that no matter how much planning we put into the changes we want to produce or prevent, these changes are effected or thwarted only by means of *situated performative chains*, that is, by means of sequences of actions performed by embodied agents in very specific socioeconomic and historical contexts that are gendered, sexualized, racialized, and ethnicized in particular ways. The situatedness of voices (as that of city dwellers) is not (at least not entirely) of their own choosing; and neither is the efficacy of their agency. This is not, of course, to deny that changes can be quite deliberate and calculated: there is such a thing as urban planning; and Wittgenstein does mention "new boroughs with straight regular streets and uniform houses." But even the most careful and meticulous planning cannot fully control its genesis and performative deployment and eliminate all unknowingness; that is, it cannot bring discursive agency under full control, managing how the impetus for change is formed, developed, and carried out in actions. There is always a level of unknowingness in our discursive agency (see chapter 3). There are always interests and needs that go unrecognized. There are always implications and ramifications that cannot be predicted.

What follows from this contextualist view is the crucial importance of keeping discursive spaces as open as possible and of empowering speakers and their voices in order to allow for their creative agency to be expressed. The critical task that derives from my contextualism is to make it possible for all speakers to have access and full participation in the cultural practices in which they lead their lives. This involves creating opportunities for critical interventions and transformations that come from the margins, that is, from the agency of those whose voices have been silenced or disproportionately constrained.

Using the city analogy, I would like to distinguish between different kinds of silence in terms of different kinds of *exclusion*, which correspond to different silenced voices that can haunt an actual city. These different silences can be grouped in the following categories: (1) the silence of those absent, those killed or exiled, those banned from the city, which thereby defines itself as a space where certain voices cannot enter; (2) the silence (or diminished voices) of those impoverished and oppressed groups (often racial and ethnic minorities) that live in the outskirts or margins of the city and cannot be full participants in city life; (3) the silence of those who are "homeless,"[13] those who live fully exposed and are nonetheless treated as invisible, those who have to conduct their lives in the open, in other people's pathways, without having a place that they can call their own; and, finally, (4) the silence of those who have to become truly invisible, those who have to subsist underground, in hiding places where they live a subterranean existence invisible to the city above. Take as a historical example the post Civil War Madrid of the 1940s and 1950s during the Franco dictatorship, whose public discourses and public language games marginalized and silenced these different groups: those exiled and those murdered by the regime for political reasons; those who lived in huts outside the city limits ("los chabolistas," who were mainly gypsies); the homeless, who had been left without jobs and homes; and the dissidents in hiding called *los topos* (the moles), who lived underground—literally underground—in tunnels expressly built as hiding places. The silences of these different groups are beautifully illustrated in Luis Martín-Santos's novel *Time of Silence*, which portrays Madrid as a suffocating space haunted by voices that are rarely heard. In this historical example the silencing of voices is the result of an overtly repressive political system with explicit censorship, but of course silences are produced more subtly in nondictatorial regimes as well. Imposed silences are typically produced by different forms of exclusions that overlap and intersect in complex ways: the exclusion of a political class, of an economic class, of a racial and ethnic class, and of a class of gender and sexual nonconformists. This is of course not an exhaustive list of exclusions and silences, but only a sample list that indicates where we can start directing our attention in our critical task of empowering marginalized voices.

4.4. Speaking from the Margins

A contextualist analysis of imposed silences can show how voices that were previously speaking and making sense can fall out of the bounds of sense after being silenced, but also how these voices can survive their nonsensicality and become intelligible again. While the study of language in philosophy and the social sciences tends to focus on what is involved in making sense, I contend that it is equally important to examine what is involved in losing sense and in recuperating sense. Part of losing sense is losing one's voice; and, consequently, regaining sense involves getting back one's voice or acquiring a new one. This is the challenge that my contextualism offers to any study of language games or discursive practices that wants to have relevance for and critical impact on the social and political problems of our time. My argument in this chapter has called attention to the important task of developing contextualized critical elucidations of our linguistic practices through situated accounts of the processes of gaining, losing, and regaining sense as they appear in sociohistorical discursive contexts. This task involves the critical examination of the normative structures that regulate discursive contexts, as well as the study of how these structures can silence certain voices and of how we can fight the silences so produced, that is, how we can provide means and opportunities for critical interventions and radical transformations that can change an unequal distribution of powers and resources across speakers. In short, the critical task proposed by my contextualism consists, fundamentally, in the task of *empowering marginal voices*.

As we saw, we are not always players in the language games in which we find ourselves. Imposed silences are performatively produced in particular contexts by the normative structure of discursive practices. In local discursive contexts speakers can be silenced in many ways: they can be literally excluded from the practice altogether, or they can be variously disempowered and silenced while remaining speaking subjects, that is, participants in the discursive practice in question. So even when speakers have a voice in discursive practices, their voice is often constrained in important ways; that is, although they are players in the language game, their discursive moves are very limited. And the important point is that it is often the case that some voices are more constrained than others, some players have more freedom of movement while the moves of other players are more limited. This discursive disempowerment or silencing often takes place through informal and unnoticeable ways of constraining speech in situated interactions, that is, through normative expectations constantly reinforced in daily practices (for example, expectations about what is proper or improper for a woman to say in particular contexts). But it is not uncommon to find this silencing process produced both by informal and implicit discursive constraints and by explicit forms of censorship.

For example, in the discursive practices associated with the expression of one's sexuality, it is clear that gay and lesbian voices are more heavily constrained (and silenced) than the voices of heterosexual speakers. And this silencing of gay and lesbian voices takes place not only through normative expectations informally reinforced in everyday interactions, but also through public policies that explicitly deny these voices the opportunity and sometimes even the right to speak freely about their sexuality, prohibiting all kinds of expressions of their sexual identity (from public displays of affection such as kisses or holding hands to alluding to someone of the same sex as one's partner). One such policy is the "Don't Ask, Don't Tell" in the U.S. military, a policy designed and sanctioned by the government which violates the First Amendment rights of a group of citizens by curtailing their freedom of expression in all aspects of their lives including those that happen outside military premises and are unrelated to their activities as soldiers (such as their leisure activities or their political activities).[14] It is crucial to notice the reverberating effects of this kind of silencing for all the gay and lesbian voices in the community, whether they are directly affected by the policy or not (that is, whether military or not). The "Don't Ask, Don't Tell" policy disempowers directly those participants in military practices whose voices are silenced, but it also disempowers indirectly all the gay and lesbian voices that live in a society that considers it appropriate (and constitutionally valid) to constrain their freedom of expression and to silence their voices in particular activities and contexts, or under particular circumstances. This is just one example of how silences can help us to comparatively determine the lack of discursive agency of certain speakers, the lack of power of certain voices, in specific contexts and specific practices. As my example illustrates, certain silences (those that are imposed through implicit or explicit forms of censorship) constitute a sign of being discursively disempowered and call for the empowerment of voices through critical interventions in current practices and through critical discourses that open up new spaces and sometimes even new practices.

In order to fight against the marginalization and silencing of voices, we have to constantly bring to light the *diversity* of symbolic perspectives inherent in discursive practices; we have to *recognize and empower marginal voices* that have become disadvantaged. We can achieve this goal by creating discursive spaces (i.e., public venues and forums) in which all voices can be expressed in a positive way and can gain recognition and social acceptance. We must do everything we can to provide every speaker with the opportunity and the power to participate fully in cultural practices and to critically intervene in them and call into question their normative structure. In short, we need to fight discursive disempowerment with discursive empowerment, silence with speech. This is precisely what radical theorists (in feminist theory, queer theory, and race theory) have tried to do with their paradoxical claims about "intelligible nonsense" and "'meaning' in spite of senselessness." Scheman, for example, talks about "the intelligibility of the normatively unintelligible" (1997, p. 132). This paradoxical formulation contains an important insight: it expresses a crucial *critical attitude*—an attitude that places ethical and political demands on us. Such critical insight and attitude are conveyed by reminding us of the following: namely, that certain possibilities, experiences, and actions are rendered unintelligible by the discursive norms of our linguistic practices, but that nevertheless it is conceivable and in principle *possible* that we will be able to find or create new discursive contexts or new practices in which those possibilities, experiences, and actions become intelligible.[15] We have to take *responsibility* for these critical and transformative possibilities. As Scheman explains, "placement at the intelligible center is always a matter of history, of the playing out of privilege and power, and is always contestable" (1997, p. 132).

How can we take up this critical challenge? What are the critical discourses that can open up new discursive spaces and can inaugurate new discursive practices? Both nonacademic and academic discourses can contribute to the arduous process of contesting the normative structure and power dynamics of discursive practices, and of breaking the silences they produce. In everyday practices as well as in artistic activities, silences are sometimes broken in unexpected ways by the uncontrollable creativity of speakers, which produces, often unconsciously, new forms of expression that signify in new ways. Sometimes unthinkingly and even unnoticeably, our agency as speakers can shake the discursive processes of oppression and marginalization at their very foundations, calling into question the power dynamics that regulate current discursive practices and undermining discursive authorities. More explicitly and self-consciously, academic discourses can continue this process of contestation implicit in many ordinary practices and artistic activities. In order to do so, the academic discourses of the Humanities have to become *critical discourses*, that is, discourses that critically question the normative structures of our discursive practices and challenge any unequal distribution of competences, powers, resources, and opportunities that can lead to the silencing of voices. In this way critical discourses are committed to contribute to the transformation of discursive practices, that is, to rearranging and reshaping our practices in order to empower silenced speakers. These discourses take upon themselves the critical task of opening new discursive spaces for oppressed and marginal voices. It is in this sense that the polyphonic contextualism I have defended in this book offers a new critical direction for the Humanities, a direction that I summarize under the descriptive rubric of *speaking from elsewhere*.

This critical new direction of study that my contextualism proposes connects with the critical trends and counterdiscourses recently developed in the Humanities, especially in postcolonial theory, critical race theory, feminist theory, and queer theory. The upshot of my argument is that the Humanities must not only make room for these marginal voices to be expressed in academia, but must also empower them, exploit their critical potential, and give center stage to their critical discourses. In short, my contextualism submits that Cultural Studies should become Critical Studies of cultural practices that pay attention to their *situatedness* and to their intrinsic *polyphony*, that is, to the diversity of voices within them. I would like to conclude by offering some examples of these local critical studies in the recent literature. In Communication and Film Theory, for example, José Muñoz (1999) has developed situated analyses that empower the voices of sexual, racial, and ethnic minorities, of "queers of color" as he puts it. In particular, through his analyses of processes of identification in performance art, Muñoz critically examines ways in which gay Latinos disidentify with cultural images of Hispanic masculinity and how their subversive rearticulations of these images can contribute to the transformation of cultural paradigms of identity. Drawing on Muñoz as well as on other critical theorists as different as Alain Locke and Judith Butler, I have also developed situated analyses intended to empower marginalized voices in theories of identity and in Ethnic Studies (see Medina 2003c and 2004a; see also the papers contained in Medina 2004c). My contextualist theoretical framework has been applied in Latin American Studies by Laura Redruello in her critical studies of subversive cultural movements in Cuba. Through situated analyses of discursive mechanisms in literature, music, and film, Redruello's research studies the power of marginal discourses for the critique and transformation of institutions. Redruello (2005) offers a contextualized account of discursive transgressions from the cultural margins in Caribbean countries such as Cuba. This is a good example of the situated critical discourses in the Humanities that can contribute to empowering marginalized voices.

I have provided a theoretical framework for the kind of situated critical studies of language and cultural practices that are needed in the Humanities and the Social Sciences. These studies are critical discourses that should be continuous with the critical and transformative activities contained in everyday and artistic practices. They face the critical challenge of empowering marginal voices and maintaining discursive spaces open to diversity. As argued above, we have to fight discursive disempowerment with discursive empowerment, silence with speech. In order to do so, the different disciplines in academia have an obligation to bring to light the diversity of symbolic perspectives in our cultural practices and to empower those marginal voices that have been disproportionately disadvantaged, constrained, and silenced. But I hope that the new kind of contextualism I have articulated in this book makes more than a purely academic point. I hope the critical and political contribution of this new approach can go beyond the (often narrow) bounds of academia. My eccentric polyphonic contextualism brings to the fore our normative commitments in and outside academia, our echoing responsibility not only as critics and intellectuals, but also—more importantly and more generally—as speakers and agents. What my view from *elsewhere* underscores is the commitment to critical innovation, that is, to exploit the openness of discursive contexts and practices in creative and liberating ways. For there are always indefinitely many *elsewheres* from which to speak and act, from which to articulate criticisms, and from which to enrich our communities and practices. Let me use Butler's words about subversive resignification to describe the critical task of *eccentric echoing* that my polyphonic contextualism proposes:

> Indeed, as we think about worlds that might one day become thinkable, sayable, legible, the opening up of the foreclosed and the saying of the unspeakable become part of the very "offense" that must be committed in order to expand the domain of linguistic survival. *The resignification of speech requires opening new contexts, speaking in ways that have never yet been legitimated, and hence producing legitimation in new and future forms.* (1997, p. 41; my emphasis)

Notes

Chapter 1. Contextualizing Meaning

1. One version of the determinacy requirement is the Fregean requirement that concepts have "sharp boundaries." For a discussion of the *sharp boundaries* requirement and the criticisms that Wittgenstein develops against it, see Medina (2002), chapter 4.

2. Strictly speaking, this label is a misnomer, for it is used to cover both skeptical challenges concerning the lack of semantic determinacy and skeptical challenges concerning the lack of semantic fixity. It would be more appropriate to talk about *indeterminacy* problems and *instability* problems in order to classify skeptical problems according to the semantic requirements they challenge.

3. See G. P. Baker and P. M. S. Hacker (1984), esp. pp. 57–97; P. Horwich (1990); C. Diamond (1991), pp. 39ff; Me. Williams (1991), esp. pp. 98–101; and Read (2000). See also my (2002) and (2003a).

4. See esp. Cavell (1979), pp. 329ff.

5. Strictly speaking, my interpretation of Wittgenstein as a theoretical diagnostician of meaning skepticism is compatible with therapeutic interpretations, such as Williams's, which focus exclusively on the skeptical problems of other minds and the external world. However, I do have reservations about the adequacy of the therapeutic interpretation even with respect to those skeptical problems. See my (2003a) for a discussion of these reservations and of the problems facing any interpretation that assimilates Wittgenstein's view to a traditional position in epistemology.

6. This regress of definitions can be stopped only if (and when) we reach words that the learner can already understand. But how was that mastery of these first words attained? This question is precisely what the appeal to ostensive definitions was supposed to answer, but it can't; for an ostensive definition that does not rely on previously acquired linguistic competence remains wholly indeterminate. What this argument shows is that ostensive definitions cannot explain the acquisition of linguistic competence, that they are not at all what gives us primitive access to language; they are in fact quite sophisticated linguistic acts.

7. See Quine's *Word and Object* (1960), chapter 2, pp. 26–79, and *The Pursuit of Truth* (1992), chapter 1, pp. 1–21.

8. The most famous example is the predicate "grue" that Nelson Goodman (1979) used to illustrate his New Riddle of Induction. Kripke's "quus function" or "quaddition" has a similar structure and rationale behind it. Kripke notes that his Skeptical Paradox about meaning and rule following is inspired by Goodman's Riddle. Moreover, he underscores the similarities between Goodman's, Quine's, and Wittgenstein's indeterminacy arguments and claims that they support a similar semantic skepticism. See Kripke (1982), pp. 58ff.

9. One important point I am overlooking for now (hiding it really, keeping it in my sleeve as a secret weapon) is the distinction between underdetermination and indeterminacy. I will use this distinction in the next section to develop the idea of "contextual determinacy," which is compatible with underdetermination but not with radical indeterminacy.

10. See Putnam's critique of the Myth of Self-Identifying Objects in *Reason, Truth, and History* (1981).

11. See Medina (2002), chapter 6.

12. In philosophy of science Helen Longino's *contextualism* offers an account of this point through her examination of the role that contextual values play in the development of scientific knowledge and in the comparative evaluation and choice between scientific theories. See especially her (1990).

13. As Thomas Kuhn's arguments (1970, 1977) have emphasized, there are also nonepistemic factors that contribute to narrow down the set of hypotheses that are considered reasonable or plausible in science at any particular time given the socio-historical conditions that affect the development of the discipline in question. It is important to note that the issue of plausibility and rational acceptability goes beyond epistemic warrant.

14. Quine, Davidson, Lewis, Dennett, Block, and Churchland, just to name a few.

15. Although most philosophers of language accept some version of semantic holism, this view still has its critics. For a thorough critique of semantic holism in many of its versions, see Fodor and Lepore (1992).

16. Williams uses the distinction between homogeneous and heterogeneous holism to underscore the differences between Quine's idea of a network of interconnected propositions and Wittgenstein's concept of background. See Me. Williams (1999), chapter 8, "The Etiology of the Obvious: Wittgenstein and the Elimination of Indeterminacy," esp. pp. 227–28.

17. Although I have echoed Quine in this paragraph by using his celebrated example, I want to bracket the issue of whether Quine is truly a skeptic in the standard sense. Some have argued that Quine's thesis of the indeterminacy of translation is not a skeptical thesis in the sense of making the claim that there is some *thing* we cannot know, but rather as an attempt to dereify or deontologize meaning. According to this interpretation, Quine is simply advancing the claim that there is *nothing* to be known, *nothing* in which the meaning of words consists. It may be possible to interpret Quine's arguments as being diagnostic and therapeutic and to understand his semantic view as being quite close to the one I have ascribed to Wittgenstein in this chapter. This convergence obtains if we read Quine's indeterminacy arguments (as I have read

Wittgenstein's) as simply denying the *thing-ness* of meaning. For a reading of Quine along these lines see Dreben (1994) and (2004).

18. In particular, it is a mistake to think that the pragmatic perspective of Wittgenstein's and Dewey's contextualism involves a refusal to consider certain interpretative hypotheses *just in order to get things done*. There is no reason why pragmatic contextualism must be tied to utilitarian considerations of this kind. This interpretation is a mere caricature of the pragmatist perspective.

19. Of course, this convergence is no accident but the result of the long interaction between Dewey and Mead at the University of Michigan and the University of Chicago. Some central aspects of Mead's social account of mind and identity will be discussed in the next chapter.

20. I have offered a critique of this interpretation in my (2002) and in my (2003a and 2003b).

21. See esp. Diamond (1991) and Crary and Read (2000).

22. However, here too I want to take exception to one part of Sleeper's analysis of the contrast between Dewey and Peirce. He contends that "what Dewey is arguing is that we get our semiotic from our semantics, not our semantics from our semiotic" (p. 139). But this is (at best) misleading because the most fundamental level of Dewey's view of language is pragmatics, not semantics. Although Sleeper recognizes that social action is at the core of Dewey's account of language and communication, his realist interpretation gives to semantics a conceptual priority that it should not have.

23. There are also unlearned elements that constitute preconditions for the participation in linguistic activities. The very possibility of training requires certain unlearned spontaneous reactions on the part of the trainee which support the learning process. In this respect Wittgenstein calls our attention to the "natural reactions" that are prerequisite for the pupil being trainable in the practice (cf. esp. *Brown Book*, 1958b, pp. 89–90, p. 93, and p. 105). In a similar vein, in the passage quoted above Dewey talks about innate reactions to the movement of the pointing gesture as the requisite starting point of the learning process. (It must be pointed out, however, that whether these reactions are in fact innate has been called into question by recent research in developmental psychology. See, for instance, Tomasello, 1999.)

24. This account of intersubjective mediation through language has been made popular by Davidson's idea of *triangulation* (cf. 2001, pp. 86–88, pp. 117–21, and pp. 128–29). This idea of triangulation was already present in Vygotsky's genetic account of linguistic competence: "The path from object to child and from child to object passes through another person" (1978, p. 30). It is also present in Mead's account of pointing (cf. 1934, chapter 2), which is very similar to Dewey's.

25. "Meaning [. . .] is primarily a property of behavior [. . .]. But the behavior of which it is a quality is a distinctive behavior; cooperative, in that response to another's act involves contemporaneous response to a thing as entering into the other's behavior, and this upon both sides" (EN p. 141). "Intelligence and meaning are natural consequences of the peculiar form which interaction sometimes assumes in the case of human beings" (EN p. 142).

26. This claim will be clarified in the next section. It is also intimately related to my contextualist claims in later chapters.

27. Butler's view of discursive agency and her performative account of meaning and identity will be further discussed in later chapters.

28. Lance and O'Leary-Hawthorne (1997) have developed an excellent pragmatic account of the normativity of meaning that sheds light on this example, for their account brings to the fore the normative presuppositions of our semantic attitudes and the normative implications of maintaining the fixity or promoting the semantic change of a term such as "marriage."

29. We can find such an explanation in the material-inferentialist account recently developed and defended by Brandom (1994). As I have argued elsewhere, Wittgenstein also offers a pragmatic account of the special semantic stability of certain terms in his discussions of logic, mathematics, and "grammar." See my (2002) and (2003a).

30. It would be a mistake to assimilate Dewey's distinction to the traditional distinction in philosophy of language between *speaker's meaning* and *semantic meaning*. See Strawson (1950), Donnellan (1966), Putnam (1973), and Searle (1985). Although there may be some surface similarities between this distinction and Dewey's, there are crucial differences. One of these differences is that for Dewey both proximate and ultimate meanings are social through and through, whereas in the traditional distinction there is a divide between social (semantic) meanings and individualistic (speaker's) meanings.

31. This, however, is not to deny the social phenomenon of the division of linguistic labor recognized by Putnam (1975). There are indeed terms for whose meanings we defer to those in the community who are taken to be experts in that semantic domain. For certain terms (especially technical terms such as, for example, terms for diseases used in medical diagnostics), there are special semantic authorities recognized by the community and not all speakers have equal status. But note that even in these cases the special semantic authority of experts is not final and irrevocable and their judgments should not be taken as fixing or determining the meaning of terms once and for all, but rather, as special (but nonetheless defeasible) moves in the semantic negotiations that go into the domestication or stabilization of meaning—negotiations that remain always open and ongoing and can criticize and in principle reject the judgment of experts.

32. In fact, from our standpoint, it is surprising how much Dewey's discussion reads as a critical response to Kripke's and Putnam's semantic realism written fifty years earlier. Interestingly, Dewey even mentions the expression "the meaning of 'meaning'" (cf. his reference to Ogden and Richards's book in a footnote on p. 160), which Putnam will make famous in his (1975) paper.

33. See esp. Dewey's *Logic: A Theory of Inquiry* and Wittgenstein's *Remarks on the Foundations of Mathematics*.

34. This convergence between Dewey's and Wittgenstein's philosophy of mathematics is recognized by Sleeper. He points out that both Dewey and Wittgenstein view *action* as fundamental for the study of the logical foundations of mathematics, which should provide an account of the emergence of mathematical systems from ordinary practices and activities such as counting and measuring. See esp. Sleeper (2001), pp. 156–57.

35. Kripke's (1982) community view of meaning and rule following seems to come close to this semantic view; and it has been read in this way by many. For instance, in his critique of Kripke, Blackburn (1984) attributes this kind of social conventionalism to him.

36. A full discussion of this point can be found in section 6.4 of my (2002), pp. 185–94.

37. This point about the dependence of disagreement on a prior agreement may be reminiscent of Davidson's principle of charity. However, as I have argued elsewhere (2003b), there is a strong disanalogy between Wittgenstein's point and Davidson's principle. Part of this disanalogy consists in the difference between heterogeneous and homogeneous holism discussed above. While the holism of Wittgenstein's pragmatic contextualism is heterogeneous, Davidson's holism is homogeneous.

38. See my (2004b).

39. This notion is discussed in detail in my (2004b).

40. For an analysis of the Wittgensteinian notion of "alternative blindness," see Me. Williams (1991) and (1999), chapter 6, pp. 157–87.

41. That is, the learner's activity is circularly defined by her own actions: how things must be done is defined by how things have actually been done according to the learned procedure. For a full discussion of this point, see Me. Williams (1999), chapter 7, pp. 188–215.

42. For an analysis of the kind of *necessity* that results from initiate training processes, see chapter 6 of my (2002), esp. pp. 156–69. See also Me. Williams (1999), chapter 8, pp. 216–39.

43. In *Profiles in Injustice* (2003), Harris discusses all these cases that set limits and constraints on the application of the presumption of innocence, thus compromising the rights and liberties of certain classes of subjects. As noted by Harris, a political effect of the so-called "war on terrorism" has been the proliferation of widespread suspicion against those cultural Others who exhibit racial, ethnic, and religious differences.

44. The recent literature in feminism and queer theory contains many wonderful analyses and critical discussions of the construal of transgendered subjectivities as *impossible* or intrinsically *unintelligible* identities. See esp. Scheman (1997) and Butler (2004).

45. See especially my discussion of "silence" in chapter 4. This discussion supplements the contextualist view of nonsense and "logical madness" that I have articulated elsewhere (see 6.1 of my 2002 and my 2003b).

46. As I have argued elsewhere, "what characterizes this process is a gradual shift of responsibility and authority, a developmental progression *from other-regulation to self-regulation*" (2002, p. 165).

47. It is of course problematic how these linguistic formations are stigmatized in some contexts. But it is also problematic how they are celebrated in other contexts as being particularly "authentic," "creative," or simply "cool."

48. This point will be elaborated in my discussion of Mead in the next chapter.

49. In fact, some have argued that this pragmatist appeal to contexts and practices faces exactly the *same* problems and is open to the *same* skeptical challenges. See esp. Hurley (2002).

Chapter 2. Contextualizing Identity

1. See, for example, Searle (1986).

2. So, for example, I can map Archie Bunker's idiolect on to mine in such a way that his utterance "we need a few laughs to break up the monogamy" becomes equivalent to "we need a few laughs to break up the monotony" in my language or idiolect. According to Davidson (1984b), meaning is captured in the specification of the truth conditions of utterances. On his view, a theory of interpretation for a particular speaker at a particular time takes the form of an account of truth-in-L (where L is the language used by the speaker to be interpreted) according to the disquotational device specified in Tarski's Convention T "'p' is true if and only if p." Thus the correspondence between idiolects is provided by T-sentences, which are logical equivalences, one-to-one mappings, between the language to be interpreted ("object language") and the language of the interpreter ("metalanguage"), such as "'Es Regnet' is true if and only if it rains."

3. Although Davidson gives priority to individuals' subjectivities over "shared meanings" (which he considers unacceptable reifications), it is important to note that Davidson's account of language is not radically individualistic. He has argued repeatedly that in order to mean anything in her speech, it is necessary for a speaker to understand, and to be understood by, "a second person" (cf. his 1992 and 2001). But his account of language is not social either. On his view, communication requires intersubjectivity, but not sociality; that is, it presupposes the presence of another speaker, but not of a community of speakers.

4. The precarious and unstable nature of the agreement underlying our communicative practices was discussed in 1.5 and 1.6 and will be further clarified below.

5. Mead doubts that dogs exhibit this kind of reflexivity. If their responses to each other's gestures were purely automatic, as Mead seems to think, we would have to conclude that the meanings that we read into their gestures are meanings projected by the human observer which are not explicitly there for the dogs. This part of Mead's account may need emendation, but this does not affect the essential points of his argument.

6. In psychology Vygotsky (1986) offered a very similar genetic account of the development of thought as inner speech. Like Mead, Vygotsky (1978, 1986) and his disciple Luria (1976) also studied the development of personal identity through the internalization of the others' perception of oneself as revealed in linguistic interaction. (For more recent developmental research along Vygotskian lines, see Tomasello 1999; and Gentner and Medina 1997, 1998.) This developmental progression from others to self in the constitution of personal identity contrasts sharply with Piaget's developmental stages, which start with a form of egocentrism that presupposes a fully formed ego that will later acquire sophistication in interaction with others. See Piaget (1954) and (1962).

7. There are powerful contemporary accounts of the social formation of the self that emphasize the importance of the second-person perspective. Baier (1997), among others, has argued that becoming an 'I' requires first being a 'Thou.'

8. Many have noted that the problem of diversity and the problem of individuality are intimately connected. Friedman (2004), for example, has argued that individuality becomes possible thanks to the multiplicity of social groups in any one person's life.

9. For Dewey also, individuality is interactionally achieved through transactions with the natural and social environment (see esp. chapter 6 of *Experience and Nature*, pp. 162–190). Dewey emphasizes that the achievement of individuality requires creative agency: one makes oneself, not in an unconstrained way, but through the enabling conditions as well as the resistances encountered in one's environment. As Dewey puts it in *Art as Experience*: "Individuality itself is originally a potentiality and is realized only in interaction with surrounding conditions. In this process of intercourse, native capacities, which contain an element of uniqueness, are transformed and become a self. Moreover, through resistances encountered, the nature of the self is discovered. The self is both formed and brought to consciousness through interaction with environment" (p. 286). For an excellent discussion of Dewey's view of the self in relation to other pragmatist views, see chapter 12 of Stuhr (1997), pp. 219–230.

10. One might think that a difference between Mead and Borges is that the constituents of the 'me' for Borges are not distinctively communal and clearly related to a 'We'; they seem to be more like Sartrean *facticity*—that is, lived activities and feelings ossified into attributes. However, in an important sense, the preferences of the 'me' that are enumerated in Borge's story constitute social attributes with corresponding 'We's or possible communities: those who like hourglasses, those who like the taste of coffee, those who like the prose of Stevenson, etc. (These remarks summarize a conversation with Naomi Scheman on the possible differences between Mead and Borges.)

11. The lack of communication and common memory among the selves coexisting in one person has been one of the central diagnostic criteria of Multiple Personality Disorder. For a philosophical discussion of the history of this mental disorder and of its different diagnostic criteria, see Hacking (1991) and (1995).

12. A classic statement of the memory model can be found in Locke (1975, pp. 331–348). This model of identity has been highly influential in modern and contemporary philosophy of mind, but it has come under attack in recent decades. The most celebrated and exhaustive critique of the memory model was developed by Derek Parfit (1971) in a series of thought experiments. For other critical perspectives, see also Nagel (1971) and Hacking (1991, 1995).

13. For a good illustration, see Hacking's (1991, 1995) analysis and discussion of the medical account of Multiple Personality Disorder developed in the 1980's, which explains this pathology as a result of sexual abuse during infancy.

14. He does mention that a pathological lack of unity, "the dissociation of a person's self," results in the compartmentalization of behavior (through "a process of setting up two sorts of communication which separate the behavior of the individual"; MSS, p. 143). But he offers no argument as to why the compartmentalization of behavior is something to be avoided.

15. This is fully elaborated in part IV of *Mind, Self, and Society* (pp. 227–336). I will discuss here only the aspects of Mead's cosmopolitanism that are crucial to understand his account of the *enlarged* self. For a full discussion of Mead's cosmopolitan vision and its impact on his view of identity, see Aboulafia (2001).

16. It is worth noting that the unification of the self does not have to take a cognitive and transcendental shape, as in Mead. It can be cast in moral, emotional, and existential terms and in ways that are immanent and contextdependent. For example, one can motivate unification by appealing not to transcendental rationality, but to responsible agency and the ability to plan a life, for these too seem to require unified subjectivities, that is, that one's diverse selves communicate, share memories, and act cooperatively.

17. Note the gender exclusion performed by this generic language of universal inclusion. The exclusionary nature of purportedly inclusive terms such as "brotherhood" is informative because it reveals how people (or certain aspects of their identity) can be excluded while being included. Relations of *inclusion* and *exclusion*, far from being pure opposites, are often (if not typically) entangled in complex dialectical relations.

18. For an interesting discussion of the distinction between individuality and individualism, see Scheman (1993). Scheman argues that individuality (but not individualism) involves levels of idiosyncracy, is necessarily social, and requires diversity. She offers a social account of individuality that is very congenial with Mead's and my own.

19. This relates to the earlier discussion of unity and diversity of the self above. There is a rich body of literature on this issue in feminist theory. See esp. Card (1991), Friedman (2004), Lugones (1989 and 2003), and Scheman (1993).

20. See esp. Butler (1990, 1993) and Sedgwick (1990).

21. See esp. Anzaldúa (1990) and Moraga and Anzaldúa (1981).

22. This famous Wittgensteinian notion has often been read very narrowly as referring to purely physical similarities. It is unlikely that this is what Wittgenstein had in mind since he introduces the notion to clarify the meaning of terms such as "game" and "number" whose application does not seem to rely on a set of physical characteristics. See PI §§66–67. In order to avoid the narrow interpretation of the notion of "family resemblance," I will use instead the broader and more abstract notion of *similarity* to cover all kinds of commonalities that can be indicative of group membership.

23. It is important to note that these networks of similarities and differences that become indicative of familial identity have a history: they result from the continued use of certain associations, that is, from treating things in a particular way in our shared linguistic practices. Therefore, these networks of similarities and differences should *not* be thought of as *unexplained explainers*; they acquire diagnostic value simply because of the (criterial) significance they have been given in our practices, because they have come to be seen as symptoms of membership in a group. On my view, the networks of similarities and differences that sustain familial identity call for a *genealogical* account, that is, a genealogy of their formation through the shared ways of speaking and acting enforced by our practices.

24. I have taken from Gracia's familial-historical account those points that support the Wittgensteinian approach sketched above. But there are features of this

account (concerning an externalist approach to the historical constitution of ethnicity) that are inconsistent with the view of identity I develop in this chapter. For a critical assessment of Gracia's view, see my (2003d).

25. See, for instance, Armstrong and Tennenhouse (1992).

26. See, for instance, Butler (1993) pp. 124ff, for interesting remarks on the critical rearticulation of kinship in the film *Paris Is Burning*. This 1991 documentary (produced and directed by Jennie Livingston) is about drag balls in Harlem, which take place in (African-American and Latina) "houses" that are organized as "families" with parental figures and role models of different kinds.

27. There is more to Frye's critique of my view than I can address here. In particular, her critical commentary also highlights the danger of a *cognitivist* bias that can operate in the application of the familial metaphor to identity categories. See her (2005) and my reply (2005a).

28. This is not to deny that disidentification can be used for oppression. One can be led to assume a submissive position through disidentifications that accentuate one's differences with those in a position of power and one's similarities with disempowered subjects. Nor do I want to imply that identification and counteridentification are always oppressive, for there are certainly contexts in which they can function as subversive mechanisms.

29. It is worth noting that free-standing or primary accounts of gender have become quite rare in the feminist literature and there is currently a widespread effort to develop intersectional accounts.

30. Lugones (1989) recommends "playfulness" and "world-travelling" as ways of overcoming the obstacles that block cross-cultural and cross-racial identification. On Lugones's view, "world-travelling" involves the exploration of phenomenal domains in which different identities can flourish; and being "playful" involves having an experimentalist attitude with respect to one's self and the "worlds" one inhabits. Through playful explorations we can develop a loving empathy toward those who are significantly different from ourselves, thus transforming our relationship with them; and at the same time we can transform and enlarge our own selves.

31. Given this diversity of contexts in which identity categories are negotiated and get articulated, there are different levels of abstraction at which these categories can operate depending on how narrow or broad the range of contexts considered happens to be. In some cases the articulation of an identity category can be rich in detail and specificity, being tied to very concrete and full-blooded contexts. In other cases, though, identity categories such as "woman" or "Hispanic" may become quite abstract and schematic, covering a wide range of different contexts with very tenuous commonalities.

32. Among other things, this logic is to blame for the systematic exclusion of transgendered people in the queer movement.

33. For example, within the queer community, same-sex couples who are interested in attaining marital status and in adopting children or raising their own certainly seem to resemble traditional families more closely than queer subjects who are not interested in maintaining monogamous relations or in raising children; and, as

O'Connor notes, it is the former who have been put at the center of the GLBT political agenda today while the others have been relegated to the margins as if their social, political, and legal demands for recognition, equal opportunities, and equal rights, did not matter as much or did not deserve as much attention.

34. Spivak (1987) has argued for "a *strategic* use of positivist essentialism in a scrupulously visible political agenda." (p. 205) According to Spivak, essentialism can be a useful political strategy that dispossessed subjects can use to align themselves with privileged subjects.

35. See Butler (1997b) for a discussion of this point (in her critical exchange with Nancy Frazer).

36. See, for example, Alarcón (1990) and Lugones (2003).

37. This dialogical perspective underscores the crucial importance of creating and maintaining interconnected networks and efficient paths of communication among the members of a group, so that they can share their problems and experiences and articulate their needs and interests. It is of course not always easy (not even always possible) to bring together the different voices that make up a group. Oppressed minorities typically face obstacles that make it difficult (if not impossible) for them to be in conversation and to engage in community-building (think, for example, of closeted homosexual in homophobic societies that punish severely any expression of gay identity). On the other hand, there are also identity categories or groups that are so broad, abstract, or diffused across contexts that connecting the different voices within the group becomes quite challenging (even in the absence of social resistance and oppression). The formation of these networks of communication and interaction is the challenging task of political activism.

38. This point echoes Scheman's (1993) argument that individuality differs from individualism in being fundamentally relational.

39. See, for example, Young (1997).

40. Bourdieu frequently uses the term "disposition" in connection with the habitus. But although this term has unquestionable psychologistic connotations, Bourdieu does not want to explain the habitus in terms of psychological mechanisms and he carefully avoids any psychologistic reduction. His account puts the emphasis on the *normative* structuration and generation of dispositions. This is why when he describes the habitus in terms of dispositions he refers to them as "structuring dispositions" (cf. 1990, p. 52). In the same way Bourdieu describes the habitus as containing "structuring structures" (cf. 1990, p. 53), but he clearly does not identify it with a set of static structures, for the postulation of such structures is one of the targets of his critique. So although Bourdieu uses dispositionalist and structuralist language, it is clear that he does not want to endorse dispositionalism or structuralism. But this is not to deny that there may be tensions and incongruities in Bourdieu's analysis. For an interesting discussion of paradoxes in Bourdieu's theory, see Schatzki (1987).

41. See my comparative analysis of Wittgenstein's and Bourdieu's views of consensus in my (2003a).

42. There is a strong convergence on this point between Bourdieu's and Wittgenstein's thought. As we saw in chapter 1, Wittgenstein too emphasizes that the acquisition

of mastery in a practice involves a practical form of identification: it involves becoming a member of a community of practitioners, becoming "one of us." For Wittgenstein too, this process of acculturation involves the internalization of the tacit norms that govern our practices. In Wittgenstein's discussions the process of initiate learning is also described as a matter of establishing a *second nature*, as a process through which new patterns of behavior become natural to the learner and certain normative assumptions are incorporated in her sense of the obvious. For an analysis of the idea of *second nature* in Wittgenstein's later philosophy, see my (2004b). For an analysis of the convergence between Bourdieu's and Wittgenstein's views, see my (2003a).

43. Lynn Enterline uses this expression in her stimulating account of the mimetic formation of identity in *Imitating School Boys* (book manuscript). Enterline studies how the mechanism of imitation was used in the rhetorical training of grammar schools in the 16th Century. She shows how even rigid mimetic training produces internal divisions, contradictions, or lack of agreement in the identities of pupils or trainees. Enterline's analysis is also sensitive to the fact that even the most rigid mimetic training cannot prevent differences and deviations, but will simply pathologize them, creating obsessive attitudes toward certain failures of imitation. This study shows that the rhetorical training of grammar schools through imitation did not succeed in imposing rigid gender and sexual categories and often invited their problematization. As Enterline puts it: "the school's institutionalized habit of imitation didn't fix the cultural distinctions defining gender or identity so much as it subjected them to constant negotiation." (p. 22)

44. As Tomasello puts it, the evolution of culture "requires not only creative invention but also, and just as importantly, faithful social transmission" (1999, p. 5). Cultural transmission takes place through processes of imitation that hide their dynamism and make cultures appear stationary; but in fact, through these processes, "cultural traditions accumulate the modifications made by different individuals over time" (Tomasello, 1999, p. 37).

Chapter 3. Contextualizing Agency

1. This model typically relies on a pragmatic theory of mental representations. See Marcelo Dascal, esp. (1984) but also (2003).

2. Bourdieu has also been read by his critics as proposing a thoroughgoing sociological account of linguistic performance. See Shusterman (1999). My interpretation of Bourdieu challenges this reading (see previous chapter and my 2003a).

3. See Skinner (1957).

4. See Quine (1960).

5. Of course, there are also hybrids of all sorts. Sometimes the same things or phenomena have both subjective and objective elements or internal and external aspects; and sometimes the inner/outer distinction does not coincide (or run parallel to) the subjective/objective distinction: arguably, there are external subjective phenomena (e.g. acts of love or hate) and internal objective phenomena (e.g. brain processes).

6. And of course the processes of internalization/externalization and the processes of subjectification/objectification can cross paths in different ways. See the previous footnote for some remarks about these intersections and their hybrid products.

7. See Vygotsky (1978) and (1986).

8. See Tomasello (1999), esp. pp. 5–6 and pp. 37–43.

9. An illustration of this contradictory tension between discursive processes of objectification and subjectification can be found in Shakespearean studies. For example, in her analysis of sexual meanings in Shakespearean texts Enterline (1999) has argued that while on the one hand women are objectified and denied discursive agency as sexual subjects, on the other hand their voices and speech acts are obsessively sexualized, and sexual meanings are read into everything they say precisely because they cannot talk about sexuality explicitly. Enterline's analysis suggests that in Shakespearean texts women are at the same time subjects and objects of discourse, and that it is precisely this tension (rather than an absolute objectification that deprives them of a voice, or an umproblematic discursive subjectification) that defines their contradictory position in speech.

10. For an analysis of this rhetoric in the feminist literature, see Haraway (1997).

11. "The internal master, one's internal proprietary subject modeled on the external one, does not overcome, but simply replicates, the subordination one attempts to overcome. So, the question arises: How can such overcoming be accomplished by an internal master that represents, or simply is, the legacy of the external political master itself?" (Smith 2002, pp. 354–5)

12. In her introduction to Scheman and O'Connor (2002), p. 17.

13. See Habermas (1984, 1992) and Peirce (1991).

14. A full discussion of indeterminacy and underdetermination was developed in chapter 1. In that discussion I examined and criticized various indeterminacy problems and alleged solutions, arguing for a *dissolution* of indeterminacy problems that still retains a semantic level of underdetermination while rejecting radical indeterminacy and meaning skepticism.

15. As Austin already noted in "Performative Utternaces," the contrast between constatives and performatices ultimately collapses, for even assertions are clearly illocutionary acts which involve commitments and entitlements that are performatively produced in their enunciation.

16. See Cavell (1976).

17. I have examined these arguments in chapter 1 and at greater length in my (2002), chapter 6.

18. For Butler's own account of the relation between performative instability and subversion, see her discussion of being *critically queer* in chapter 8 of her (1993), pp. 223–42.

19. See the analysis and discussion of this Bourdieuan notion in my (2003a).

20. *Singularity* here should be understood as the unique perspective of a particular individual vis-à-vis the perspectives of others. As stated above, my polyphonic

contextualism rejects radical singularity in the sense of a private linguist or of an isolated voice that can be understood independently of any other.

21. See my (2004).

22. See Mouffe (2000) and (1996). See also Laclau and Mouffe (2001). Another political framework very congenial to my radical pluralism can be found in Iris Marion Young (1990, 1997, 2000).

23. I am here echoing the label of "the new Wittgenstein"—see esp. Crary and Read (2000). With this I am trying to establish a parallel between the impact that Diamond et alia's reading had for a new understanding of Wittgenstein's philosophy, and the impact that Cavell et alia's eccentric reading should have for a new understanding of Austin's view of performativity and contextuality.

24. This relates directly to what I described above as the praxiological (and not merely epistemic) uncontrollability and unownability of speech acts.

25. But of course the legal and political battle is still ongoing and this decision could be reversed by the Supreme Court.

26. The normative distinctions between felicity, infelicity, and radical performative failures appear to be fixed, absolute, and incontestable only when there is a background agreement about the norms of conduct which is taken for granted by (or simply forced upon) most—if not all—the members of the linguistic practice. This apparently unquestionable normative order can always become unstable and sometimes even break down when the background consensus is called into question.

27. As Butler notes, "the question of mechanical breakdown or 'misfire' and of the unpredictability of speech is precisely what Austin repeatedly emphasizes when he focuses on the various ways in which a speech act can go wrong" (1997, p. 19).

28. Thus, by not calling into question the received reading of Austin, Derrida also misses the critical potential of Austin's view. It is because of his reliance on the received reading that Derrida contends: "That the value of *risk* or of being *open to failure*, although it might, as Austin recognizes, affect the totality of conventional acts, is not examined as an essential predicate or *law*. Austin does not ask himself what consequences derive from the fact that something possible—a possible risk—is *always* possible, is somehow a necessary possibility. And if, such a necessary possibility of failure being granted, it still constitutes an accident. *What is a success when the possibility of failure continues to constitute its structure?*" (1982, p. 324; emphasis preserved and added). My alternative interpretation of Austin—the *New* Austin—should make clear that these observations should be considered as critical elaborations of Austinian ideas, not as critical challenges to them.

29. See Garfinkel (1967) and Garfinkel and Sacks (1970). See also Boden and Zimmerman (1991).

30. Although in general my interpretation of Austin agrees with Felman's, I think she goes too far in assimilating Austin to Nietsche and Lacan as thinkers who "do not believe in the promising aninal" (p. 111). Austin does believe in the promising animal—every linguistic agent is one! But, on his view, this belief has to be properly qualified: a speaker is as much a promise maker as a promise breaker, an animal with a very fragile capacity for making and maintaining promises.

31. As Butler puts it, "no text can be fully freed from the shackles of censorship because every text or expression is in part structured through a process of selection" (p. 253).

32. See Muñoz (1999) and Somerville (2000). See also Butler (1997) as well as my (2003c) and (2004c).

33. For an examination of this topic, see also chapter 6 of my (2005b).

34. I am here echoing Anzaldúa's (1987/1999) terminology. For an analysis and discussion of her view, see chapter 6 of my (2005b).

35. A clear example of infelicitous subjectivity that is produced as a result of processes of oppression and marginalization can be found in transgendered subjects. These subjects have been used as negative exemplars of the violation of gender norms; and, when they have not been silenced completely, their expression of gender meanings have been considered intrinsically unintelligible. See Scheman (1997) and Butler (2004). (See also my discussion above on page 42 and in note 44.)

Chapter 4. *Speaking from Elsewhere*

1. See Diamond (1991), Crary (2001, 2002), and Crary and Read (2000).

2. See especially Sedgwick (1990); but also Dollimore (1991) and Halperin (1990).

3. For a full discussion of this point as it emerges in Wittgenstein's thought experiments, see Medina (2002), pp. 144–52.

4. Let's not forget that one of Wittgenstein's main objections against skepticism is that it leads to *inaction* (see *On Certainty*, esp. §§409–11), which is something that does not apply to radical feminist theorists, queer theorists, and critical race theorists.

5. This is, of course, the provocative claim made famous by Davidson's (1986) "A Nice Derangement of Epitaphs." It has also been made in a very different way by the sociologist Pierrre Bourdieu (1991) who argues that what circulates in the "linguistic market" are the "stylistically marked" discourses or speeches of speaking subjects and groups, but not French, English, Italian, etc., which are ideological abstractions (see esp. pp. 38–39 and 44–49).

6. This possibility may seem to be in conflict with Wittgenstein's Private Language Argument, but it isn't, for Wittgenstein certainly allowed for solitary players and for language games which, contingently, happen to have only one player (see PI §243). These uses of language do not qualify as *radically private* because their intelligibility depends on the possibility of being shared as well as on the existence of other language games that are actually shared.

7. As Scheman (1993) puts it, "the unity of the self is an illusion of privilege" (p. 98).

8. Lugones calls our attention to the fact that it is everywhere demanded of us that we be *one*, that all the different aspects of our personality be integrated in a unified center. This general anxiety about being one induces in us the fear of duplicity or plurality, which are depicted as a loss of self or as fractures of the self. Lugones proposes

ambiguity as "a creative strategy of resistance" against this unified picture of the self (1991, p. 43).

9. Wittgenstein's language games can be considered as performative counterparts of the polyphonic dialogues that Bakhtin's semiotics analyzes (cf. 1981, 1984).

10. For a full analysis of the normativity of meaning claims see Lance and O'Leary-Hawthorne (1997).

11. "The sickness of a time is cured by an alteration in the mode of life of human beings, and it was possible for the sickness of philosophical problems to get cured only through a changed mode of thought and of life, not through a medicine invented by an individual" (RFM II.23).

12. Another important spatial conceptualization that deserves attention is the metaphor of "feeling at home in language." One might argue that Wittgenstein's references to language games as "homes" entail a clear-cut inside/outside dichotomy, for don't we know where our home is and who is part of it and who isn't? Actually, we don't. In Wittgenstein's metaphorical sense, a "home" is not something given, but something in the making, an elusive something that we strive for and is never fully achieved, so that in a sense we are always "homeless," for the task of finding ourselves "at home in language" is infinite, it involves a neverending process. Wittgenstein describes our philosophical journeys as a search for "homeliness" that starts with a linguistic estrangement, with a feeling of being alienated in one's discursive practices. But since, as speakers, we are all to some extent estranged or alienated and therefore "homeless," we all need to undertake a critical journey in order to achieve some degree of "homeliness" in the language games in which we find ourselves. This spatial metaphor stresses the importance of emotional attachments to words and their uses in our agency and in the discursive contexts we inhabit, bringing to the fore a rich emotional dimension that is implicit in the analogy of the city. This *elusive homeliness* relates to the *unownability* of discursive agency discussed in the previous chapter.

13. In an important sense we all fall into this category since, as speakers, we are all "homeless," that is, we are always engaged in the endless task of trying to feel "at home in language" (see previous note for an explanation of this point).

14. It is important to keep in mind that the way in which the policy has been implemented has constantly extended the limits of the discursive disempowerment or silencing of homosexual members of the military. As some critics of the policy warned from the beginning, the separation of the public and the private has been constantly challenged by the enormous diversity of discharges that the "Don't Ask, Don't Tell" policy has produced. Any of the following expressions of homosexual identity or homosexual behavior seems to be considered an appropriate basis for discharge: engaging in GLBT activities such as a gay parade; becoming involved in political organizations, advocacy groups or movements with a gay agenda (such as the so-called gay rights movement); expressing one's homosexual identity in any communication that goes through military channels (even if it is personal correspondence or personal phone calls); bringing partners of the same sex to military events (whether official or unofficial); relating to people of the same sex as partners in any respect or in any activity (even if it is part of an apparently personal and private activity such as the registration

in a hotel during a vacation); speaking freely about one's homo-social life, including relationships and lifestyle; openly leading a homosexual life and the public expressions typically associated with it (public displays of affections, frequenting certain associations, bars, etc). And this is of course only a sample of an apparently always growing multitude of cases.

15. As many feminist, queer, and race theorists have emphasized, it is often the case that what the normative structure of our practices renders unintelligible is not simply particular experiences and actions, but entire identities and the lives they lead. Scheman (1997), for example, shows how the identity and life of the transsexual are rendered unintelligible by heteronormativity, and how the identity and life of the secular Jew are rendered unintelligible by Christianormativity. As a result, she contends, transsexuals and secular Jews are forced to "live as impossible beings" (p. 152).

References

Aboulafia, M. (2001). *The Cosmopolitan Self: George Herbert Mead and Continental Philosophy* (Urbana and Chicago: University of Illinois Press).

Alarcón, N. (1990). "The Theoretical Subject(s) of *This Bridge Called My Back* and Anglo-American Feminism," in G. Anzaldúa (ed.), pp. 356–69.

Alonso, A. M., and M. T. Koreck (1989). "Silences: 'Hispanics,' AIDS, and Sexual Practices," in *Differences: A Journal of Feminist Cultural Studies* Vol. 1, No. 1, pp. 101–24.

Althusser, L. (2001). *Lenin and Philosophy and Other Essays* (New York: Monthly Review Press).

Anzaldúa, G. (1987/1999). *Borderlands/La Frontera: The New Mestiza* (San Franscisco: Aunt Lute).

———, ed. (1990). *Making Face, Making Soul/Haciendo caras: Creative and Critical Perspectives by Feminists of Color* (San Franscisco: Aunt Lute).

Armstrong, N., and L. Tennenhouse (1992). *The Imaginary Puritan: Literature, Intellectual Labor, and the Origins of Personal Life* (Berkeley: University of California Press).

Austin, J. L. (1975). *How to Do Things with Words* (Cambridge: Harvard University Press).

——— (1979). *Philosophical Papers.* Third edition (Oxford and New York: Oxford University Press).

Baier, A. (1997). *The Commons of the Mind* (Chicago: Open Court)

Baker, G. P., and P. M.S. Hacker (1984). *Scepticism, Rules and Language* (Oxford: Blackwell).

Bakhtin, M. M. (1981). *The Dialogic Imagination*, edited by M. Holquist (Austin: University of Texas Press)

——— (1984). *Problems in Dostoevsky's Poetics*, edited and translated by C. Emerson (Minneapolis: University of Minnesota Press).

Benhabib, S., ed. (1996). *Democracy and Difference* (Princeton and Oxford: Princeton University Press).

——— (2002). *The Claims of Culture* (Princeton and Oxford: Princeton University Press).

Blackburn, S. (1984). "The Individual Strikes Back," *Synthese* 58, 281–301.

Boden, D., and D. H. Zimmerman (1991). *Talk and Social Structure: Studies in Ethnomethodology and Conversation Analysis* (Berkeley and Los Angeles: University of California Press).

Borges, J. L. (1981). "Borges and I," in D. R. Hofstadter and D. C. Dennett (eds.), *The Mind's I: Fantasies and Reflections on Self and Soul* (New York: Basic).

Bourdieu, P. (1977). *Outline of a Theory of Practice* (Cambridge: Cambridge University Press).

——— (1984). *Distinction* (Cambridge: Harvard University Press).

——— (1990). *The Logic of Practice* (Stanford: Stanford University Press).

——— (1991). *Language and Symbolic Power* (Cambridge: Harvard University Press).

Braaten, J. (2002). "The Short Life of Meaning: Feminism and Nonliteralism," in Scheman and O'Connor, pp. 176–92.

Brandom, R. (1994). *Making It Explicit* (Cambridge: Harvard University Press).

Bushan, N. (2002). "Eleanor Rosch and the Development of Successive Wittgensteinian Paradigms for Cognitive Science," in Scheman and O'Connor (eds.), pp. 259–83.

Butler, J. (1990). *Gender Trouble: Feminism and the Subversion of Identity* (New York: Routledge).

——— (1993). *Bodies That Matter: On the Discursive Limits of "Sex"* (New York and London, Routledge).

——— (1997). *Excitable Speech: A Politics of the Performative* (New York and London: Routledge).

——— (1997b). "Merely Cultural," *Social Text* 52/53, pp. 265–77.

——— (1998). "Ruled Out," in R. Post (ed.), *Censorship and Silencing* (Indianapolis: Getty Research Institute), pp. 247–59.

Butler, J. (2004). *Undoing Gender* (New York and London, Routledge).

Card, C., ed. (1991). *Feminist Ethics* (Bloomington: Indiana University Press).

Cavarero, A. (2000). "Shadow Writing," unpublished manuscript presented at the International Association for Philosophy and Literature, January meeting in Italy [text quoted by Perpich (2003)].

Cavell, S. (1976). *Must We Mean What We Say?* (Cambridge: Cambridge University Press).

——— (1979). *The Claim of Reason* (Oxford: Oxford University Press).

——— (2002). "Foreword to *The Scandal of the Speaking Body*," in Felman (1983, 2002), pp. xi–xxi.

Crary, A. (2001). "A Question of Silence: Feminist Theory and Women's Voices," *Philosophy* 76, pp. 371–95.

———— (2002). "What Do Feminist Want in Epistemology?" in Scheman and O'Connor, pp. 97–118.

Crary, A., and R. Read, eds. (2000). *The New Wittgenstein* (London and New York: Routledge).

Dascal, M. (1984). *Pragmatics and the Philosophy of Mind* (London: John Benjamins).

———— (2003). *Interpretation and Understanting* (London: John Benjamins).

Davidson, D. (1984a). "Communication and Convention," *Synthese* 59, pp. 3–18.

———— (1984b). *Inquiries into Truth and Interpretation* (Oxford: Clarendon).

———— (1986). "A Nice Derangement of Epitaphs," in R. E. Grandy and R. Warner (eds.), pp. 157–74.

———— (1992). "The Second Person," *Midwest Studies in Philosophy 17*, pp. 255–67.

———— (1994). "The Social Aspect of Language," in B. McGuinness (ed.), *The Philosophy of Michael Dummett* (Dordrecht: Kluwer)

———— (2001). *Subjective, Intersubjective, Objective* (Oxford: Clarendon Press)

de Lauretis, T. (1986). "Feminist Studies/Critical Studies: Issues, Terms, and Contexts," in T. de Lauretis (ed.), *Feminist Studies/Critical Studies* (Bloomington: Indiana University Press).

Derrida, J. (1982). *Margins of Philosophy* (Chicago: University of Chicago Press).

Dewey, J. (1987). *Art As Experience. John Dewey. The Later Works, 1925–1953. Volume 10: 1934* (Carbondale and Edwardsville: Southern Illinois University Press).

———— (1988a). *Experience and Nature*, in *John Dewey. The Later Works, 1925–1953, Vol. 1: 1925* (Carbondale: Southern Illinois University Press).

———— (1988b). *Logic*, in *John Dewey: The Later Works, 1925–1953, Vol. 12: 1938* (Carbondale: Southern Illinois University Press).

Diamond, C. (1991). *The Realistic Spirit: Wittgenstein, Philosophy, and the Mind* (Cambridge: MIT Press).

Dollimore, J. (1991). . *Sexual Dissidence: Augustine to Wilde, Freud to Foucault* (Oxford: Oxford University Press).

Donnellan, K. (1966). "Reference and Definite Descriptions," *Philosophical Review*, pp. 281–304.

Dreben, B. (1994). "In Mediis Rebus," *Inquiry* 37 (4), pp. 441–47.

———— (2004). "Quine on Quine," in R. Gibson (ed.), *The Cambridge Companion to Quine* (Cambridge: Cambridge University Press), pp. 287–93.

Dummett, M. (1994). "Reply to Davidson," in B. McGuinness (ed.), *The Philosophy of Michael Dummett* (Dordrecht: Kluwer).

Ebbs, G. (1997). *Rule Following and Realism* (Cambridge: Harvard University Press).

Enterline, L. (1999). "What 'Womanhood Denies' the Power of 'Tongues to Tell,'" *Shakespeare Studies*, pp. 25–36.

Felman, S. (2002). *The Literary Speech Act: Don Juan with J. L. Austin, or Seduction in Two Languages*. New edition (Ithaca: Cornell University Press).

Fodor, J., and E. Lepore (1992). *Holism* (Oxford: Blackwell).

Foucault, M. (1978). *The History of Sexuality Vol. 1* (New York: Random House).

Friedman, M. (2004). "Diversity, Trust, and Moral Understanding," in C. Calhoun (ed), *Setting the Moral Compass: Essays by Women Philosophers* (Oxford: Oxford University Press), pp. 217–32.

Frye, M. (2005). "Category Skepticism and Its Cure: A Comment on José Medina's 'Identity Trouble: Disidentification and the Problem of Difference,'" *Symposia on Gender, Race, and Philosophy II*. http://web.mit.edu/sgrp/

Garfinkel, H. (1967). *Studies in Ethnomethodology* (Englewood Cliffs: Prentice Hall).

Garfinkel, H., and H. Sacks (1970). "On Formal Structures of Practical Actions," in C. McKinney and E. A. Tiryakian (eds.), *Theoretical Sociology* (New York: Appleton-Century-Crofts), pp. 338–66.

Gentner, D., and J. Medina (1997). "Comparison and the Development of Cognition and Language," *Japanese Journal of Cognitive Science* 4, pp. 112–49.

—— (1998). "Similarity and the Development of Rules," *Cognition* 65, pp. 263–97.

Goodman, N. (1979). *Fact, Fiction, and Forecast* (Cambridge: Harvard University Press).

Gracia, J. (2000). *Hispanic/Latino Identity* (Oxford: Blackwell).

Grandy, R. E., and R. Warner (1986). *Philosophical Grounds of Rationality* (Oxford: Oxford University Press).

Habermas, J. (1984). *The Theory of Communicative Action, Volume 1* (Boston: Beacon).

—— (1987). *The Theory of Communicative Action, Volume 2. Lifeworld and System: A Critique of Functionalist Reason* (Boston: Beacon).

—— (1990). *Moral Consciousness and Communicative Action* (Cambridge: MIT Press).

—— (1992). *Postmetaphysical Thinking: Philosophical Essays* (Cambridge: MIT Press).

Hacking, I. (1991). "Two Souls in One Body," *Critical Inquiry* 17, pp. 838–67.

—— (1995). *Rewriting the Soul: Multiple Personality and the Sciences of Memory* (Princeton: Princeton University Press).

Hall, J. D. (1983). "The Mind That Burns in Each Body: Women, Rape, and Racial Violence," in A. Snitow, C. Stansell, and S. Thompson (eds.), *Powers of Desire: The Politics of Sexuality* (New York: Monthly Review Press), pp. 302–16.

Halperin, D. (1990). *One Hundred Years of Homosexuality* (New York and London: Routledge).

Haraway, D. (1997). "Women and Geography Study Group: 'Why Study Feminist Geography?'" in L. McDowell and J. P. Sharp (eds.), *Space, Gender, Knowledge: Feminist Readings* (London, New York: Arnold).

Harris, D. (2003). *Profiles in Injustice: Why Racial Profiling Cannot Work* (New York: New Press, Norton).

Hegel, G. W. F. (1969). *Hegel's Science of Logic*, translated by A. V. Miller (New York: Humanity Books).

———— (1977). *Phenomenology of Spirit*, translated by A. V. Miller (Oxford: Oxford University Press).

Horwich, P. (1990). "Wittgenstein and Kripke on the Nature of Meaning," in *Mind and Language* 5(2), 105–21.

Hurley, S. (2002). *Consciousness in Action* (Cambridge: Harvard University Press).

Kripke, S. (1972). *Naming and Necessity* (Cambridge: Harvard University Press).

———— (1982). *Wittgenstein on Rules and Private Language* (Cambridge: Harvard University Press).

Kuhn, T. (1970). *The Structure of Scientific Revolutions*. Second edition (Chicago: University of Chicago Press).

———— (1977). "Objectivity, Value Judgment, and Theory Choice," in T. Kuhn, *The Essential Tension: Selected Studies in Scientific Tradition and Scientific Change* (Chicago: University of Chicago Press), pp. 320–39.

Laclau, E., and C. Mouffe (2001). *Hegemony and Socialist Strategy: Toward a Radical Democratic Politics* (New York: Verso).

Lance, M. N., and J. O'Leary-Hawthorne (1997). *The Grammar of Meaning: Normativity and Semantic Discourse* (Cambridge: Cambridge University Press).

Laudan, L. (1990). "Demystifying Underdetermination," *Minnesota Studies in the Philosophy of Science* 14, pp. 267–97.

Lee-Lampshire, Wendy (1992). "Moral 'I': The Feminist Subject and the Grammar of Self-Reference," *Hypatia* Vol. 7, No. 1, pp. 34–51.

Lévi-Strauss, C. (1985). *The View from Afar* (New York: Basic).

Locke, J. (1975). *An Essay Concerning Human Understanding* (Oxford: Oxford University Press).

Longino, H. (1990). *Science as Social Knowledge: Values and Objectivity in Scientific Inquiry* (Princeton: Princeton University Press).

Lugones, María (1989). "Playfulness, 'World-Travelling,' and Loving Perception," *Hypatia* Vol. 2, No. 2, pp. 3–19.

———— (1991). "On the Logic of Pluralist Feminism," in C. Card (ed.), *Feminist Ethics* (Bloomington: Indiana University Press).

———— (2003). *Pilgrimages/Peregrinajes: Theorizing Coalition against Multiple Oppression* (New York: Rowan and Littlefield).

Luria, A. R. (1976). *Cognitive Development: Its Cultural and Social Foundations* (Cambridge: Harvard University Press).

Margolis, J. (1996). "The Politics of Predication," *Philosophical Forum* 27, pp. 195–219.

———— (1999). *What, After All, Is a Work of Art?* (University Park: Pennsylvania State University Press).

Martín-Santos, Luis (1961). *Tiempo de Silencio* (Barcelona: Seix Barral).

Mead, G. H. (1913). "The Social Self," *Journal of Philosophy* 10 (1913), pp. 374–80.

———— (1932). *The Philosophy of the Present* (Chicago, Open Court).

————— (1934). *Mind, Self, and Society* (Chicago: University of Chicago Press).

Medina, J. (2002). *The Unity of Wittgenstein's Philosophy* (Albany: State Univeristy of New York Press).

————— (2003a). "Wittgenstein and Nonsense: Psychologism, Kantianism, and the *Habitus*," *International Journal of Philosophical Studies* 11 (3), 293–318.

————— (2003b). "On Being 'Other-Minded': Wittgenstein, Davidson, and Logical Aliens," *International Philosophical Quarterly* 43 (4), 463–75.

————— (2003c). "Identity Trouble: Disidentification and the Problem of Difference," *Philosophy and Social Criticism* 29 (6), 657–82.

————— (2003d). "Hispanic/Latino Identity: A Philosophical Perspective," *Journal of Speculative Philosophy* 17, 139–41.

————— (2004a). "Pragmatism and Ethnicity: Critique, Reconstruction, and the New Hispanic," *Metaphilosophy* 35 (1/2), 115–46.

————— (2004b). "Wittgenstein's Social Naturalism: The Idea of Second Nature after the Philosophical Investigations," in Danièle Moyal-Sharrock (ed.), *The Third Wittgenstein* (London: Ashgate), pp. 79–92.

—————, ed. (2004 c). *Identity and Ethnicity, Special Issue of The Journal of Speculative Philosophy* 18, 93–167.

————— (2005a). "Being Critical about Identity: A Response to My Critics," *Symposia on Gender, Race, and Philosophy II*. http://web.mit.edu/sgrp.

————— (2005b). *Language* (London: Continuum).

Mouffe, C. (2000). *The Democratic Paradox* (New York: Verso).

————— (1996). *The Return of the Political* (New York: Verso).

Moraga, C., and G. Anzaldúa, eds. (1981). *This Bridge Called My Back: Writings by Radical Women of Color* (New York: Kitchen Table).

Muñoz, J. E. (1999). *Disidentifications: Queers of Color and the Performance of Politics* (Minneapolis: University of Minnesota Press).

Nagel, T. (1971). "Brain Bisection and the Unity of Consciousness," *Synthese* 22.

————— (1986). *The View from Nowhere* (Oxford: Oxford University Press).

Narayan, U. (1997). *Dislocating Cultures: Identities, Traditions, and Third-World Feminism* (New York and London: Routledge).

O'Connor, P. (2002). "Moving to New Boroughs: Transforming the World by Inventing Language Games," in Scheman and O'Connor, pp. 432–49.

————— (2005). "Identity Trouble and the Politics of Privilege," *Symposia on Gender, Race, and Philosophy II*. http://web.mit.edu/sgrp.

Parfit, D. (1971). "Personal Identity," *Philosophical Review*, pp. 3–27.

Peirce, C. S. (1991). *Peirce on Signs: Writings on Semiotics* (Chapel Hill: University of North Carolina Press).

Perpich, D. (2003). "Subjectivity and Sexual Difference: New Figures of the Feminine in Irigaray and Cavarero," *Continental Philosophical Review* 36, 391–413.

Piaget, J. (1954). *The Construction of Reality in the Child* (New York: Basic).

——— (1962). *Play, Dreams and Imitation in Childhood* (New York & London: Norton).

Putnam, H. (1973). "Meaning and Reference," *Journal of Philosophy*, pp. 699–711.

Putnam, H. (1975). "The Meaning of 'Meaning,'" in his *Mind, Language and Reality: Philosophical Papers, Vol. 2* (Cambridge: Cambridge University Press), pp. 215–71.

——— (1981). *Reason, Truth, and History* (Cambridge: Cambridge University Press).

Quine, W. v. (1960). *Word and Object* (Cambridge: MIT Press).

——— (1990). *Pursuit of Truth* (Cambridge: Harvard University Press).

Read, R. (2000). "What 'There Can Be No Such Thing as Meaning Anything by Any Word' Could Possibly, Mean," in A. Crary and R. Read (eds.), pp. 74–82.

——— (2002), "Culture, Nature, Ecosystem (or Why Nature Can't Be Naturalized)," in Scheman and O'Connor (eds.), pp. 408–31.

Redruello, L. (2005). "Discursive Transgressions from the Cultural Margins during Cuba's *Special Period*," Doctoral Dissertation in the Department of Spanish and Portuguese at Vanderbilt University.

Rosch, E. H., and C. B. Mervis (1975). "Family Resemblances: Studies in the Internal Structure of Categories," *Cognitive Psychology* 7, 573–605.

Schatzki, T. R. (1987). "Overdue Analysis of Bourdieu's Theory of Practice," *Inquiry* 30, 113–35.

Scheman, N. (1993). *Engenderings: Constructions of Knowledge, Authority, and Privilege* (New York: Routledge).

——— (1996). "Forms of Life: Mapping the Rough Ground," in H. Sluga and D. G. Stern (eds.), *The Cambridge Companion to Wittgenstein* (Cambridge: Cambridge University Press), pp. 383–410.

——— (1997). "Queering the Center by Centering the Queer," in D. T. Meyers (ed.), *Feminists Rethink the Self* (Boulder: Westview), pp. 124–62.

Scheman, N., and P. O'Connor, eds. (2002). *Feminist Interpretations of Ludwig Wittgenstein* (University Park: Pennsylvannia State University Press).

Searle, J. (1985). *Expression and Meaning: Studies in the Theory of Speech Acts* (Cambridge: Cambridge University Press).

——— (1986). "Meaning, Communication, and Representation," in R. E. Grandy and R. Warner (eds.), pp. 209–26.

Sedgwick, E. K. (1990). *Epistemology of the Closet* (Berkeley and Los Angeles: University of California Press).

Shusterman, R., ed. (1999). *Bourdieu: A Critical Reader* (Oxford: Blackwell).

——— (1995). "Bourdieu et la philosophie anglo-américaine," *Critique* 579/580, 595–609.

Skinner, B. F. (1957). *Verbal Behavior* (New York: Appleton-Century-Crofts).

Sleeper, R. W. (2001). *The Necessity of Pragmatism: John Dewey's Conception of Philosophy* (Urbana and Chicago: University of Illinois Press).

Smith, J. F. (2002). "'No Master, Outside or In': Wittgenstein's Critique of the Propri-etary Subject," in Scheman and O'Connor, pp. 344–64.

Somerville, S. B. (2000). *Queering the Color Line: Race and the Invention of Homosexual-ity in American Culture* (Durham: Duke University Press).

Spivak, G. (1987). *In Other Worlds: Essays in Cultural Politics* (New York and London: Methuan).

Strawson, P. (1950). "On Referring," *Mind*, pp. 320–44.

Stryker, S. (1994). "My Words to Victor Frankenstein above the Village of Chamounix: Performing Transgender Rage," *GLQ: A Journal of Lesbian and Gay Studies 1*.

Stuhr, J. (1997). *Genealogical Pragmatism: Philosophy, Experience, and Community* (Albany: State University of New York Press).

Tomasello, M. (1999), *The Cutural Origins of Human Cognition* (Cambridge: Harvard University Press).

Tomasello, M., A.C. Kruger, and H.H. Ratner (1993). "Cultural Learning," *Behavioral and Brain Sciences* 16, pp. 495–552.

Vygotsky, L. (1978). *Mind in Society* (Cambridge: Harvard University Press).

——— (1986). *Thought and Language* (Cambridge: MIT Press).

Williams, Me. (1991). "Blind Obedience: Rules, Community, and the Individual," in K. Puhl (ed.), *Meaning Scepticism* (Berlin and New York: Walter de Gruyter, pp. 93–125.

——— (1999). *Wittgenstein, Mind and Meaning: Toward a Social Conception of Mind* (London and New York: Routledge).

Williams, Mi. (1991). *Unnatural Doubts* (Oxford: Blackwell).

Wittgenstein, L. (1958a). *Philosophical Investigations* (Oxford: Blackwell).

——— (1958b). *The Blue and Brown Books* (Oxford: Blackwell).

——— (1969). *On Certainty* (Oxford: Blackwell).

——— (1975). *Wittgenstein's Lectures on the Foundations of Mathematics* (Chicago and London: University of Chicago Press).

——— (1978). *Remarks on the Foundations of Mathematics* (Oxford: Blackwell).

——— (1980a). *Culture and Value* (Chicago: University of Chicago Press).

——— (1980b). *Remarks on the Philosophy of Psychology, Vols. I and II* (Chicago: Univer-sity of Chicago Press).

Young, I. M. (1990). *Justice and the Politics of Difference* (Princeton: Princeton University Press).

——— (1997). *Intersecting Voices: Dilemmas of Gender, Political Philosophy, and Policy* (Princeton: Princeton University Press).

——— (2000). *Inclusion and Democracy* (Oxford: Oxford University Press).

Index